THE DIALOGUES OF PLATO

VOLUME 3

PLATO

ION · HIPPIAS MINOR · LACHES · PROTAGORAS

Translated with Comment by
R. E. ALLEN

Yale University Press
New Haven and London

Designed by Sally Harris
and set in Baskerville type by
The Composing Room of Michigan, Inc., Grand Rapids, Michigan
Printed in the United States of America by
BookCrafters, Inc., Chelsea, Michigan

Plato.
The dialogues of Plato.
Includes index.
Contents: v. 3. Ion; Hippias
minor; Laches;
Protagoras
1. Philosophy—Collected works. I. Allen, Reginald
E., 1931– . II. Title.
B358.A44 1984 184 84–17349
ISBN 0–300–06343–1 (v. 3: alk. paper)

A catalogue record for this book is available
from the British Library.

The paper in this book meets the guidelines for
permanence and durability of the Committee on
Production Guidelines for Book Longevity
of the Council on Library Resources.

10 9 8 7 6 5 4 3 2 1

From the dawn of philosophy, the question concerning the summum bonum, *or, what is the same thing, concerning the foundation of morality, has been accounted the main problem of speculative thought, has occupied the most gifted intellects, and divided them into sects and schools, carrying on a vigorous warfare against one another. And after more than two thousand years the same discussions continue, philosophers are still ranged under the same contending banners, and neither thinkers nor mankind at large seem nearer to being unanimous on the subject, than when the youth Socrates listened to the Old Protagoras, and asserted (if Plato's dialogue be grounded on a real conversation) the theory of utilitarianism against the popular morality of the so-called sophist.*

John Stuart Mill, Utilitarianism, *chapter I*

CONTENTS

PREFACE

Herewith four dialogues, the *Ion, Hippias Minor, Laches,* and *Protagoras.* The first three are commonly regarded as early, though they are not for that reason immature: Plato was in his thirties when he wrote them, and a philosophical and artistic genius. The *Protagoras* is closely connected with the *Meno.* It is a boundary dialogue: it goes beyond the earlier dialogues of search both in content and complexity of dramatic form, and leads on to such great middle dialogues as the *Phaedo* and *Symposium, Republic,* and *Phaedrus.*

The relation of the four dialogues here presented in paratactic; yet there are inward connections which all stretch, finally, to the *Protagoras.* The *Ion* treats actors and the poets they depend on as connected by a kind of inspired magnetism, and we are reminded that poetry is said to be a form of divine madness in the *Phaedrus.* But then, poets and dramatists, and by derivation actors, are said to be rhetoricians in the *Gorgias;* if this is so, Ion and Protagoras, despite apparent difference in their outward and visible callings, are inwardly engaged in like enterprise. The argument of the *Hippias Major* is in important part matched by a similar pattern in the *Ion,* and issues in an aporetic conclusion which, thought through, shows that virtue is not and cannot be an art—a conclusion by which the hedonism analyzed in the *Protagoras* must be judged. The *Laches,* a dialogue too much neglected, shows by its account of βουλή, counsel, the inner connection between Socrates' search for definitions, which may seem merely and dryly logical, and his concern for the moral improvement of his respondents; it also places in sharpest contrast two concepts of courage: the raw animal spirits raised in battle, which may yet be accompanied by dishonesty, and that courage which, because it is allied to wisdom, is allied to justice. This is to anticipate the question of the unity of the virtues in the *Protagoras.*

xi

Two aspects of the comment on the *Protagoras* perhaps themselves deserve comment.

First, the argument at 349e–351b, which proves that wisdom and courage are coimplicatory, logically equivalent, has often been rejected as invalid. In fact, it is valid, logically demonstrable, and though it does not by itself prove that the virtues are not detachable, it proves by use of *reductio ad absurdum*, on the basis of premises it is reasonable to grant, that courage and wisdom are not detachable; this goes a long way toward establishing the more general conclusion. The result is of substantial importance to moral theory: the argument must be considered in any informed discussion of the virtues and their unity.

Second, the comment denies a proposition which most people, if they think they know anything about Socrates, think they know: that virtue is knowledge, that to know the good is to do it, that incontinence or ἀκρασία is impossible. The claim that virtue is knowledge is, as *Republic* VI points out, circular and empty, for if one asks what kind of knowledge virtue is, what it is knowledge *of,* the answer must be that it is knowledge of virtue. Nothing in this result outstrips the logical resources of the early dialogues, whose analysis of art makes it obvious.

The assumption that to know the good is to do it and that ἀκρασία is impossible has a variety of roots. First, Aristotle claims it is true; but this is on the basis of the *Protagoras*, relying on a text we have before us, and one which does not in context mean what he says it means. Second, the *Protagoras* (352a–c) affirms it on the basis of hedonism, a theory Socrates assumes but does not assert, since he concludes the dialogue with an implied confession of ignorance, still inquiring what virtue is. Third, critics who have adduced other texts to show that it is true have confused two different claims: that virtue is knowledge, and that no one voluntarily does injustice or wrong. Confusion over these claims derives from a failure of analysis to which Plato himself was not subject. The claim that no one voluntarily does injustice or wrong is connected in the *Symposium* and *Gorgias* with an analysis of βούλησις, rational wish, directed toward happiness conceived as righteousness and the basis of human freedom; it is the foundation of the argument of the *Crito* which led Socrates to his death. That argument casts its light backwards over the Socratic dialogues which in dramatic date have gone before, and it destroys the possibility of a hedonistic or utilitarian account of Socratic moral theory. The Socratic theory is in fact very like Kant's concept of a Good Will, unburdened by the analytic/synthetic distinction: it is as though the two great moralists, working from different premises, had touched a common reality.

I have undertaken to connect the argument of the *Protagoras* with the

Benthamite tradition of hedonism and utilitarianism, and certain of its consequences for nineteenth- and twentieth-century ethical theory in Mill, Sidgwick, and Moore, as well as Freud.

The *Protagoras*, like its companion dialogue, the *Meno*, ends in a dialectical tangle. In the *Meno*, Socrates undertakes to inquire whether virtue can be taught by using a method of hypothesis borrowed from the geometers. He assumes that if virtue is knowledge, it can be taught; argues that it is knowledge; that it cannot be taught because there are no teachers of it; and concludes that it is present in men "by divine apportionment, without intelligence." That is, he assumes an implication, affirms the antecedent, denies the consequent, and having pitted *modus ponens* against *modus tollens*, ends in skepticism. Socrates and Meno have tried to determine whether virtue can be taught without first saying what it is. They end in perplexity, and the new method of hypothesis borrowed from the geometers cannot save them. The *Meno* emphasizes the priority of the search for essence, for what a thing is in and of itself, the account of which is a definition.

This is also the conclusion of the *Protagoras*. Socrates and Protagoras become so tangled that the argument itself intervenes to mock them. Socrates, who began by asserting that virtue cannot be taught, ends by assuming that virtue is knowledge, which suggests that it therefore can be taught; Protagoras, having maintained that virtue can be taught and that he is a teacher of it, ends by denying that it is knowledge, which suggests it cannot be taught. The moral is explicitly drawn: Socrates and Protagoras must first find out what virtue is, and then go back to inquire whether or not it is teachable. The "What is it?" question, the question of essence, is prior to all other questions about virtue.

The *Protagoras* by its structure makes clear that the search for essence bears directly on the good of the soul. The connection is not far to seek. The aim of each of us, the primary and fundamental aim, is to live well. We can live well only if we care for our own souls, we can care for our own souls only by living virtuously, and we can live virtuously only if we know what virtue is.

This is a simple claim, but it constitutes what may be described, without apology to either Copernicus or Kant, as the Socratic Revolution: a turning from outer to inner, from such goods as wealth and political power to justice and virtue, which involve self-knowledge. In the *Protagoras*, the Socratic Revolution is brought into contrast with a group of professional teachers of rhetoric who expounded their wisdom by telling their audience what their audience wanted to hear—with the sophists and the chief of the sophists, Protagoras, with Hippias and Prodicus in his

train. The *Protagoras* offers a contrast between two cultures: the sophistical culture of *paideia* which was the dominant element in the intellectual
climate of Athens, and directly or indirectly swayed by speech the history
of a great people; and the Socratic concern for virtue, offered by a man
whom the Athenians would eventually kill.

In both the *Crito* and the *Protagoras*, Socrates assumes that life has a
goal: the meaning of life is to live, and not only to live but to live well, εὖ
ζῆν. But the *Protagoras* suggests that to live well is to live pleasantly, the
Crito that it is to live justly. The difference is marked. To a hedonist, justice
or any virtue has only instrumental value, as a means to attaining pleasure; it may therefore, sometimes or often, be better to do injustice than
to suffer it. But if justice is not a means to living well but constitutive of
living well, it must always be better to suffer injustice than to do it. Socrates' analysis of living well in terms of hedonism implies a contrast between
appearance and reality.

THE ION

COMMENT

Introduction (530a–d)

Socrates in the *Apology* tells how after examining the politicians he went to the poets and questioned them, and found that though they had the reputation of being wise, they were not: almost anyone present could give a better account than they of what they had themselves produced. From this Socrates inferred that they composed their works not by wisdom but by a kind of natural disposition and divine inspiration, like seers and prophets who also say many fine things and do not know what they mean. The *Ion* expands on this theme. Ion is not a poet but a rhapsode or "song-stitcher," a professional reciter of poetry, especially of Homer. Homer and Hesiod themselves are elsewhere described by Plato as wandering rhapsodes (*Republic* X 600d). By the fifth century B.C., rhapsodes had become professional performers, journeying from city to city to perform and compete in public contests; they were to epic poetry as actors were to drama. Ion performs before large audiences on a small stage, a βῆμα, sumptuously clothed in many colors and crowned with a golden crown (535d–e). He sings his recital (532d, 535a) without instrument, as recitative; since ancient Greek was pitched rather than stressed, such a performance must have been extraordinarily musical. The performance also involved acting, and Ion is caught up in the emotions he represents to the audience (535c), though those emotions combine with the very different emotions of a paid entertainer carefully estimating his audience's reaction (535e).

But Ion thinks that the most important ἔργον of his art—its work, product, function, object—is interpreting the thought of Homer (530c). He not only interprets Homer as an actor interprets a part but also explains his meaning, both actor and commentator. It may be, as Méridier

3

thought,[1] that rhapsodic commentary reduced to eulogistic paraphrase; Ion is an ἐπαινέτης, a "praiser" of Homer (536d, 542b). Yet Socrates treats him as a putative teacher, and Ion himself believes that as a rhapsode he possesses a τέχνη, an art (530c). The *Ion* is a useful introduction to what such a claim involves. The term is not primarily limited, as in English, to the fine arts: the art of the rhapsode, like the art of the poet, was associated in the Greek mind with such disparate arts as medicine, angling, backgammon, horseracing, and prophecy.

Art Implies Knowledge of Who Speaks Well and Badly about the Same Subjects: Ion Does Not Possess an Art (530d–533c)

Though Ion claims as a rhapsode to possess an art, his art is limited to Homer; of other epic poets or poets generally, he has nothing to say. Socrates uses this admission to suggest that Ion does not in fact possess an art.

The first step of the argument consists in ἐπαγωγή, induction. The arithmetician knows who speaks well or badly about number, the doctor about diet; in general, the man clever or skilled in a given field knows who speaks well or badly about it (531e–532a; cf. 540a ff.) Socrates elsewhere insists that art involves knowledge of opposites (e.g., *Republic* I 332d ff.; *Hippias Minor* 367c–368a; *Phaedrus* 261c–262c, 273d–274a); but speech about an art, unlike the practice of it, admits that trick of persuasion which is the essence of base rhetoric, namely, the ability to seem to the ignorant to have knowledge without in fact having it (cf. *Gorgias* 459a–c; *Phaedrus* 259e ff.).

Ion can deal only with Homer, not with Hesiod or Archilochus or other poets, though they discuss the same subjects, because he lacks art and knowledge (cf. 537c–538a). For to get or receive an art is to get it as a whole, a point established by a further induction involving painters, sculptors, and musicians (532d–533c). Since possession of an art implies ability to discern who speaks well and badly about its subject matter, Ion, if he had an art, would be as skilled in interpreting other poets as he is Homer. By his own admission, he is not. This poses a problem which Ion himself puts. Given that he cannot speak about other poets and lacks knowledge and does not have an art, how is it that he can speak so beautifully about Homer?

1. *Ion* (Budé edition), p. 11.

Poetry and Divine Possession: Rhapsodes as Messengers of Messengers (533c–536d)

Socrates explains Ion's ability to interpret Homer without art or knowledge by a striking metaphor: the Magnesian or Heraclean stone, the magnet. The poet is inspired by the magnetic power of his Muse, whose messenger or interpreter he is. The rhapsode in turn is inspired by the magnetic power of his poet: he becomes a messenger of the messenger. Finally, the audience is inspired by the magnetic power of the rhapsode, a power of enchantment similar to the power of rhetoric. (Compare *Ion* 539c–d and *Menexenus* 235a–c.) This inspiration is a kind of divine possession, the result not of art and mind but of 'divine apportionment,' without intelligence. This account of poetry and rhapsody as the result of divine possession is implied by Socrates' examination of the poets in the *Apology* (22b–c; cf. *Meno* 99c) and stated in the *Phaedrus* (244a–245a), where Socrates claims that the greatest blessings come through madness, μανία, sent as a gift of gods to men. The possession and madness of the Muses, if we may trust Socrates' metaphor of the magnet in the *Ion*, stirs the rhapsode by derivation from the poet.

An eighteenth-century English poet, invoking his Muse, meant little more than his own powers of invention. But Milton in the seventeenth century invoked the Holy Spirit in *Paradise Lost* as a source of truth, a divine power not his own which taught him. Homer invoked his Goddess at the beginning of the *Iliad* and asked the Muse to teach him at the beginning of the *Odyssey*. Hesiod on Mount Helicon knew that the Muse could speak the truth and some things which are not the truth. Divine inspiration is not alien to truth, not even to demonstration: Parmenides tells how his vision of the unshaken heart of well-rounded truth was revealed to him by a Goddess beyond the Gates of Night and Day, and couches his deductive revelation in dactylic hexameter, the meter of epic, as an odyssey of the intellect.

Just as the rhapsode says what he says about Homer not by art but by divine apportionment, without intelligence (*Ion* 534b–c, 536c, 542a), so in the *Meno* (99e–100a) politicians get their virtue by divine apportionment, without intelligence; they have no more wisdom than seers and soothsayers, who say many fine things but know nothing of what they say; politicians are divine and inspired like poets, and possessed by the god (*Meno* 99b–e). The irrational effects of poetry and rhapsody are directly comparable to the irrational effect of vulgar politics, whose servant is vulgar rhetoric (cf. *Gorgias* 502c).

Arts Defined by Their Objects: Ion Does
Not Possess an Art (536d–542b)

Nowhere in the *Ion* is it supposed that poetry possesses an autonomous value. Homer was the greatest of poets because he was the greatest of teachers; on issues of education and conduct, he was studied as a guide to regulate the whole of life (cf. *Republic* X 606e), quoted and misquoted as we quote and misquote Scripture. In this didactic claim lay incoherence, since Homer and other poets imitate or represent many men in many moods (cf. *Laws* IV 719c).

Our present text of Homer derives from Alexandrian editors of the third century B.C. There is reason to believe that Plato, writing in the fourth century, knew a different text.[2] That there was a settled text reduced to writing is suggested by the *Ion* itself, for the competition of rhapsodes at Epidaurus and Athens (530a–b) would seem to require it; it is also suggested by the *Hipparchus* (228b), which, if not Plato's, is almost certainly the work of a student in the early Academy, and implies that there was a textual tradition in Athens believed to derive from the Pisistratid Hipparchus, in the late sixth century. That Plato used a text of Homer different from our own is strongly suggested by manifold variants in the quotation from Homer in *Republic* II and III. It is less clear, however, what that text was; for though Plato may often be quoting a different text, he also may often be quoting from sometimes fallible memory, and he may also sometimes intentionally and ironically misquote to make a point. When Ion assures us that he remembers the lines in which Nestor advises his son Antilochus in chariot racing (537a–b) and offers five lines, of which the last four coincide exactly with the modern text while the first considerably differs, a contemporary reader may have inferred that Ion's memory was not as good as he claims. When Nestor's concubine gives the wounded Machaon a potion of wine and goat cheese sprinkled with white onion (438b–c), and our own text says white barley, a contemporary reader may have inferred that Ion's descriptions of medicine are somewhat deficient in medical art—or meant for heroes indeed. Such irony would be very like Plato, but we cannot know he intended it, because we do not know what text of Homer he knew.

If rhapsody and poetry were arts, then on the analogy of other arts, they would have an object, a subject matter. Homer has things to say about many different arts: for example, those of the charioteer, the doctor, the fisherman, the seer. But what is the object of the rhapsode's art? Ion is

2. See J. A. Davison, "The Transmission of the Text," in A. J. B. Wace and F. H. Stubbings, *A Companion to Homer*, New York, 1962, pp. 219–21.

unable to answer, but takes refuge in the claim that due to his study of Homer he knows the art of generalship (cf. *Laches* 182c).

What is said in the *Ion* of rhapsody applies to poetry, the first of the rings on which the rhapsode hangs as the audience hangs on the rhapsode. If Ion lacks the universality implied by knowledge and knows only Homer, poets know how to compose only in dithyrambs, or odes, or epics, or lyrics, each poet worthless with respect to any other form (534c). Nor does the poet as poet, any more than the rhapsode, understand the product of the arts of which he tells: Homer was neither charioteer nor doctor. This point is analogous to the criticism of rhetoric in the *Gorgias* (449d–453a).

The *Ion* does not present a theory of poetry, or of rhapsody, and to describe rhapsody or poetry as a matter of divine apportionment without intelligence is not to praise it but to dismiss it. The Socratic heritage, distinguished by its respect for argument, the ability to render an account, is also distinguished by its recognition of the power of the irrational forces which move the human soul. Ion is "divine" (542a–b) because he would be a wrongdoer filled with false pretense if he were human. He is divine, that is to say, by default or disjunctive syllogism.

TRANSLATION

SOCRATES / ION

Introduction (530a–d)

530a SOC. Greetings, Ion. Where from on this present visit? Your home in Ephesus?

ION No, Socrates, from Epidaurus and the festival of Asclepius.

SOC. You don't mean the Epidaurians also offer the god a contest of rhapsodes?

ION They do indeed, and the other branches of music and poetry too.

SOC. Really? You competed for us? How did you do?

b ION I took first prize, Socrates.

SOC. Excellent. See to it that we win the Panathenaea too.

ION Why, so we shall, god willing.

SOC. Really, Ion, I've often envied the art of you rhapsodes. It's always part of our art to adorn your body and look as beautiful as

c possible, and again, you necessarily spend your time with many other good poets, but most especially Homer, the best and most divine of poets, and learn not only his lines but his thought. This is to be envied. For one could never become a good rhapsode without understanding what the poet says: the rhapsode must interpret the poet's thought to his audience, and it's impossible to do that well without knowing what the poet means. This then is worthy of all envy.

ION True, Socrates. For me, at any rate, it has provided the most important product of my art. I think I speak most beautifully

9

d   about Homer, because neither Metrodorus of Lampsacus nor
Stesimbrotus of Thasos nor Glaucon nor anyone else ever born
has so many and such beautiful thoughts to tell about Homer as
I do.

soc. Excellent, Ion. Clearly you won't begrudge me an exhibition.

ion Why really, Socrates, it's worth hearing how well I've embel-
lished Homer: I think I should be crowned with gold by the
Homerids.[1]

Art Implies Knowledge of Who Speaks Well and Badly about the Same Subjects: Ion Does Not Possess an Art (530d–533c)

531a soc. Yes, and eventually I'll find time to hear you, but right now
answer me this: are you skilled only in Homer, or in Hesiod and
Archilochus too?

ion No, only in Homer. I think he's quite enough.

soc. Is there any subject about which Homer and Hesiod say the
same things?

ion Yes, I suppose, many.

soc. Then could you explain what Homer says about them better
than what Hesiod says?

b   ion Equally, Socrates, where they say the same things.

soc. What about where they don't? For example, Homer and Hesiod both have something to say about prophecy?

ion Of course.

soc. Then where the two poets agree or disagree about prophecy,
would you offer a better explanation than one of our good
prophets?

ion No.

soc. But if you were a prophet, then since you'd be able to explain
the things in which they agree, you'd also know how to explain the
things in which they differ?

ion Clearly.

c   soc. Then what subject are you clever about in Homer but not in
Hesiod or the other poets? Does Homer tell of other things than
all other poets do? Doesn't he explain many things about war, and

1. A family or guild of poets in Chios whose members claimed descent from Homer and
who handed on from father to son the tradition of reciting and interpreting his poems. Cf.
Phaedrus 252b; *Republic* X 599e.

the familiar intercourse of good men and bad with one another, and craftsmen and laymen, and about how gods interact with one another and with men in their intercourse with them, and things that occur in the heavens and in the underworld, and the births of gods and heroes? Aren't those the things about which Homer has composed poetry?

d ION Yes, Socrates.

SOC. Then what about other poets? Not about these same subjects?

ION Yes—but Socrates, surely not equal to Homer.

SOC. Really? Worse?

ION Much worse.

SOC. Homer is better?

ION Emphatically better.

SOC. Well now, my dear Ion, when many people speak about number and one given person speaks best, surely someone will recognize who speaks well?

e ION I agree.

SOC. The same person also recognizes those who speak badly, or someone else?

ION The same, surely.

SOC. He having the art of arithmetic?

ION Yes.

SOC. Again, when many people speak about what foods are healthy, and one given person speaks best, will the same person or different people recognize that the best speaks best and the worse speaks worse?

ION Clearly the same.

SOC. Who is he? What name does he have?

ION A doctor.

532a SOC. Then to sum up, we're saying that the same person will always know who speaks well and who speaks badly when many people speak about the same subjects. If he doesn't know who speaks badly, then clearly he won't know who speaks well about the same subject.

ION That's so.

SOC. So the same person is skilled in both?

ION Yes.

SOC. Now, you claim that Homer and the other poets, Hesiod and Archilochus among them, speak about the same things, but not equally—the one well, the others worse?

ION And I'm right.

b soc. Then since you know who speaks well, you'd also know that those who speak worse do speak worse.

ION Yes, it seems so.

soc. Then, my friend, we won't err in saying that Ion is equally skilled in speaking about Homer and about the rest of the poets too, since he himself agrees that the same person will be a sufficient judge of everyone who speaks about the same subjects, and that all poets, pretty nearly, deal with the same things.

c ION Then why is it, Socrates, that when anyone discusses any other poet, I'm unable to pay attention or contribute anything worth mentioning, but simply go to sleep, whereas when somebody calls Homer to mind, I'm immediately wide awake and attentive and not at a loss for what to say?

soc. It's not hard to guess, my friend. It's clear to everyone that you're unable to speak about Homer with art and knowledge. For if you could, you'd be able to speak about all the other poets too. The art of poetry is surely one whole, is it not?

ION Yes.

d soc. Well, when anyone grasps any other art as a whole, the same kind of inquiry will exist concerning every art. Do you need to hear what I mean by this, Ion?

ION Yes, please, Socrates. For I enjoy listening to you wise men.

e soc. I might wish you were right, Ion. But surely it's you rhapsodes and actors who are wise, and those whose poems you recite; I only speak the plain truth natural to an ordinary man. So too for the question I just asked: look how worthless and ordinary it is. Anybody can tell what I meant in saying it's the same inquiry when one understands an art as a whole. Let's understand it by this: there's an art of painting as a whole?

ION Yes.

soc. And there are and have been many painters, good and worthless?

ION Of course.

533a soc. Then did you ever see anybody skilled in declaring what kinds of things Polygnotus, son of Aglaophon, paints well and what he doesn't, who couldn't do this with other painters? And who goes to sleep and is at a loss and has nothing to contribute when someone shows the works of other painters, but when he must offer judgment about Polygnotus or whatever other painter you please, and that one only, is wide awake and attentive and not at a loss for what to say?

ION No, certainly not.

b SOC. What about sculpture? Did you ever see anybody who is skilled in explaining what Daedalus, son of Metion, or Epeius, son of Panopeus, or Theodorus of Samos, or any other sculptor has executed well, but who is at a loss and asleep among the works of other sculptors, with nothing to say?

ION No, I certainly haven't seen that either.

c SOC. Nor I think in flute playing or lyre playing or singing lyrics or reciting did you ever yet see a man skilled in explaining Olympus or Thamyras or Orpheus, or Phemius, the rhapsode of Ithaca, but at a loss about Ion, the rhapsode of Ephesus, with nothing to contribute about which poems he performs well and which he does not.

ION I can't contradict you in this, Socrates. But I'm conscious that I speak most beautifully of all men about Homer, and I'm not at a loss and everybody else says I speak well; but not about other poets. And yet, please see what this means.

Poetry and Divine Possession: Rhapsodes as Messengers of Messengers (533c–536d)

d SOC. I do see, Ion, and I'm going show you what I think it is. For your speaking well about Homer is not an art, as I was just saying, but a divine power which moves you like the stone which Euripides called Magnet, but most people call Heraclean. In fact, this stone not only attracts iron rings but also puts power in the rings so that they also have power to do the same thing the stone does and attract other rings. Sometimes quite a long chain of iron rings hangs suspended one from another; but they're all suspended by

e the power derived from that stone. So too the Muse herself causes men to be inspired, and through these inspired men a chain of others are possessed and suspended. For all our good epic poets speak all their beautiful poems, not through art, but because

534a they're inspired and possessed, and so similarly our good lyric poets too. Just as the Corybants do not dance in their right minds, so lyric poets do not compose these beautiful songs in their right minds, but when they step to the mode and the rhythm they are filled with Bacchic frenzy and possessed, as Bacchants are possessed when they draw honey and milk from the rivers, be-

b cause they're not in their right minds; and the soul of lyric poets

does this too, as they themselves say. For the poets tell us that they carry honey to us from every quarter like bees, and they fly as bees do, sipping from honey-flowing fountains in glens and gardens of the Muses. And they tell the truth. For a poet is a delicate thing, winged and sacred, and unable to create until he becomes inspired and frenzied, his mind no longer in him; as long as he keeps his hold on that, no man can compose or chant prophecy. Since, then, it is not by art that poets compose and say many beautiful things
c about their subjects, as you do about Homer, but by divine apportionment, they each can do well only that to which the Muse directs them—this one dithyrambs, that one odes, or encomia, or dances, or epics, or iambics—each of them worthless in respect to the others. For they speak these things not by art but by divine power, since if they knew how to speak well by art about one thing, they could do it about all the rest. This is why the god takes the
d mind out of them and uses them as his servants, as he uses oracles and divine prophets: so that we their hearers may know it is not they, in whom mind is not present, who tell things of such great value, but the god himself who speaks, making utterance to us through them.

A great proof of this is Tynnichus of Chalcis, who never produced another poem anyone would think worth remarking, but
e then produced the paean everyone keeps singing, very nearly the most beautiful of songs—completely, as he himself says, "a discovery of the Muses." In this especially, I think the god shows us in order that we may not doubt it that these beautiful poems are not human things nor of men, but divine things and of gods, and that poets are nothing other than messengers of the gods, each possessed by some one of the gods. To show this, the god purposely sang the most beautiful song through the most worthless poet. Don't you think I'm right, Ion?

535a ION Yes, emphatically. For you somehow touch my soul with your words, Socrates, and our good poets seem to me to bring these poems to us by divine apportionment as messages from the gods.

SOC. Again, you rhapsodes interpret the poets?

ION That's true too.

SOC. Then you're messengers of messengers?

ION Exactly so.

b SOC. Hold it right there. Tell me this, Ion—answer what I ask without concealment. When you recite lines well and quite astonish the spectators, when you sing of Odysseus leaping onto the threshold

and revealing himself to the suitors and pouring out the arrows at his feet, or of Achilles rushing at Hector, or something pitiful
c about Andromache or Hecuba or Priam—are you then in your right mind, or outside yourself? Does your soul, inspired, suppose you're in the midst of the doings you describe in Ithaca or Troy, or wherever the lines have it?

ION How clear to me is this proof you give, Socrates—for I'll tell you without concealment. When I say something pitiable, my eyes brim with tears, and when I say something fearful or terrible, my hair stands straight on end from fear and my heart pounds.

d SOC. Are we then to say, Ion, that a man decked out in many-colored clothing and crowned with gold is in his right mind when he weeps in the midst of festivals and sacrifices, though deprived of none of his finery? Or when he's afraid while standing among more than twenty thousand friendly people, not one of whom is stripping or wronging him?

ION Surely not, Socrates, if truth be told.

SOC. Do you know that you rhapsodes also affect the majority of your spectators the same way?

e ION I know it very well. I look down from time to time from the stage and see them weeping and gazing up at me fearfully, sharing the astonishment of what is being said. I have to pay close attention to them: because if I make them cry, I'll later laugh myself for the money I make, but if they laugh, I'll myself cry for money lost.

536a SOC. Do you also know then that the spectator is the last of those rings I spoke of as receiving power by the Heraclean stone? You, the rhapsode and actor, are the middle ring; the first ring is the poet himself. But it's the god who draws the soul of men through all of them in whatever direction he may wish, making the power of one depend upon the other. As though from that stone there is suspended a great chain of choral dancers and directors and assis-
b tants; they're suspended sideways from the rings hanging down from the Muses. This poet hangs from one Muse, that from another—we call it possession, and indeed it is close to it, for he is had and held. From the first of these rings, that of the poets, others again hang one from another and are inspired, some by Orpheus, some by Musaeus, but the majority possessed and held by Homer. Of whom you're one, Ion. You're possessed and held by Homer; when some other poet sings, you go to sleep and are at
c a loss for what to say, but when someone utters a song from this poet, you immediately wake up and your soul dances and you're

not at a loss for what to say. It's not by art or knowledge that you say what you say about Homer, but by divine apportionment and possession, even as the Corybantes are only aware of that shrill song which belongs to the god by whom they're possessed, and in respect to that song they're not at a loss for figures and words, but

d   they pay no heed to the rest. So too with you, Ion. When someone reminds you of Homer, you're not at a loss, but you're perplexed about the rest. You ask me why you're not at a loss about Homer as opposed to the rest. It's because you're skilled in praising Homer by divine apportionment, not by art.

Arts Defined by Their Objects: Ion Does Not Possess an Art (536d–542b)

ION   You speak well, Socrates. I'd be surprised, though, if you could speak so well as to convince me that I'm possessed and mad when I praise Homer. I don't think I'd seem that way to you if you heard me speak about Homer.

e   SOC. And I'm quite willing to hear, though not before you first answer me this: about which things Homer tells do you speak well? Surely not all of them.

ION   Rest assured, Socrates, there are none about which I do not.

SOC. Not, surely, about things you don't know, but Homer tells.

ION   And just what does Homer tell that I don't know?

537a SOC. Doesn't Homer tell many things in many places about arts? Chariot driving, for example—if I can remember the lines, I'll recite them for you.

ION   Why, I'll recite them, for of course I remember.

SOC. Then tell me what Nestor says to his son Antilochus when he warns him to be careful at the turn in the horse race in honor of Patroclus.

b   ION   "And yourself," he says, "in the well-polished chariot, lean over a little to the left of the course, and as for your right horse, whip him and urge him along, slackening your hands to give him his full rein, but make your left-hand horse keep hard against the turning post so that the hub's edge of your fashioned wheel will seem to be touching it, yet take care not really to brush against it."[2]

---

2. *Iliad* xxiii 335–40, after Lattimore; the *Ion*'s text in the first line reads "well polished" for the Homeric vulgate's "strong fabricated."

c SOC. Enough. Now then, Ion, who'd know better whether Homer
    spoke these lines correctly or not, a doctor or a charioteer?

ION A charioteer, surely.

SOC. Because he has this art, or for some other reason?

ION No, because of art.

SOC. Now, it's given by the god to each of the arts to be able to know
    some particular work? For surely what we know by piloting we
    won't also know by medicine.

ION Of course not.

SOC. Nor what we know by medicine also by building.

d ION Of course not.

SOC. So too then with all the arts: what we know by one art we don't
    know by another? But first answer me this: you claim one art is
    different from another?

ION Yes.

SOC. Do you judge as I do? When one art is knowledge of one kind of
    thing, another of another, I call one art different from the other.
    Do you?

e ION Yes.

SOC. For surely, if it were a knowledge of the same things, how could
    we claim one different from another when it would be possible to
    know the same things from both? For example, I know that these
    are five fingers, and you, like me, know the same thing about
    them; if I asked you whether you and I know the same things by
    the same art, arithmetic, or by a different art, you'd doubtless say,
    by the same.

ION Yes.

538a SOC. Then please now answer what I was just about to ask: whether
    you think it's so of all arts generally that the same things are
    necessarily known by the same art, and different things by a dif-
    ferent art; if in fact it differs, it necessarily also knows different
    things.

ION I think so, Socrates.

SOC. Now, anyone who doesn't possess a given art won't be able to
    know properly what is said or done in that art?

b ION True.

SOC. Now about those lines you recited: will you know better than a
    charioteer whether Homer speaks well or not?

ION No.

SOC. Because of course you're a rhapsode, but not a charioteer.

ION Yes.

soc. And the art of the rhapsode is different from the charioteer's?

ION Yes.

soc. If different, knowledge of different things?

ION Yes.

c soc. What about when Homer tells how Hecamede, Nestor's concubine, gives the wounded Machaon a potion to drink? He says
something like this: "With Pramnian wine," he says, "she grated
goat's-milk cheese into it with a bronze grater, with onion on the
side as an appetizer for the drink."[3] Does it belong to the medical
art or the rhapsode's to properly diagnose whether Homer says
this correctly or not?

ION The medical art.

d soc. What about when Homer says, "She plummeted to the sea
floor like a lead weight which, mounted along the horn of an ox
who ranges the fields, goes downward and takes death with it to
the raw-ravening fish"?[4] Should we say it belongs to the fisherman's art or the rhapsode's to judge what he means, and whether
or not he speaks well?

ION Clearly, Socrates, the fisherman's.

e soc. Consider then whether, if you were questioning, you'd ask me,
"Since then, Socrates, you find in Homer what it belongs to each of
these arts to judge, come and discover for me also what belongs to
the seer and his art, about which he's able to discern whether
Homer has composed well or badly." Consider how easily and
truly I'll answer you. There are many places where he talks about
it in the *Odyssey*, for example, where the seer Theoclymenus, de-
scendent of Melampus, says to the suitors, "Fortunate fellows,
539a what evil has come upon you? Your heads and faces and limbs are
shrouded in night and darkness; a sound of wailing has broken

---

3. *Iliad* xi 639–40 (cf. 630), after Lattimore. The vulgate text of Homer gives barley for
Plato's onion—with considerable difference, one may suppose, in medicinal effect; perhaps
then Socrates intentionally misquotes to make a point, that Ion, a rhapsode, doesn't understand the subject matter of medicine. But onion was in any case served (xi 630), not as
medicine but as an appetizer (ὄψον).

4. *Iliad* xxiv 80–82, trans. Lattimore. This passage has been much discussed in histories of
angling. Is there perhaps reference to an artificial lure made of horn and weighted with
lead—in effect, a jig? (Cf. *Odyssey* XII 251–54, and Haskins in *Journal of Philology* 19 238 ff.)
Or is the horn used, as Aristotle and Theophrastus thought, to shield the line? The simplest
solution, perhaps, is that the oxhorn was used as a bobber, the lead as a sinker. There is
another possibility: oxhorn is easily worked even with stone tools when first cut, but hardens
as tough as bone, especially at the tip, which may be shaped into well-formed fishhooks.

out, your cheeks are covered with tears. All the forecourt is hud-
dled with ghosts, the yard is full of them as they flock down to the
underworld and the darkness. The sun has perished out of the
sky, and a foul mist has come over."[5] There are many places in
the *Iliad* too, for example in the Battle at the Walls,[6] where he says,
"As they were urgent to cross, a bird sign had appeared to them,
an eagle, flying high and holding to the left of the people and
carrying in its talons a gigantic snake, blood-colored, alive still and
breathing, it had not forgotten its warcraft yet, for writhing back it
struck the eagle that held it by chest and neck, so that the eagle let
it drop groundward in pain of the bite, and dashed it down in the
midst of the battle and itself, screaming high, winged away down

d   the wind's blast."[7] I'll say it belongs to the seer to examine and
judge such passages as these.

   ION Yes, and you're right, Socrates.

   soc. Yes, and you're right to say so, Ion. But come and do as I did. I
picked out from the *Odyssey* and the *Iliad* what sorts of things
concern the seer, and the doctor, and the fisherman. Since you're
so much more experienced than I am about Homer, Ion, will you
in this way also pick out for me what sorts of things belong to the
rhapsode and the rhapsode's art? What does the rhapsode consider and judge beyond the rest of men?

   ION Everything, Socrates, I claim.

   soc. Surely not everything, Ion—or are you so forgetful? And yet, it
would hardly suit a rhapsode to be forgetful.

540a ION What am I forgetting?

   soc. Don't you recall that you were saying the rhapsode's art is
different from the charioteer's?

   ION I do.

   soc. Then as different, you agreed it will know different things?

   ION Yes.

   soc. So by your account, the rhapsode's art will not know everything, nor will the rhapsode.

   ION Except perhaps such things as these, Socrates.

b soc. By "these sorts of things" you pretty nearly mean "except what

---

5. *Odyssey* XX 351–57, after Lattimore. Plato's text shows omissions and several changes.
   6. The Greeks located passages in Homer by referring not to books, a convention deriv-
ing from a written text, but to famous scenes.
   7. *Iliad* xii 200–207, trans. Lattimore. Plato's text here coincides with the Homeric vulgate.

belongs to the other arts." But what sorts of things will it know, since not everything?

ION What it befits a man to say, I suppose, and what sorts of things befit a woman, a slave and a free man, ruled and ruler.

SOC. The rhapsode will know better than the pilot, you mean, what a ruler should say on a storm-stricken ship at sea?

ION No, the pilot knows that.

c SOC. Or better than the doctor what a ruler of the sick should say?

ION Not that either.

SOC. But what a slave should say, you mean?

ION Yes.

SOC. For example, you mean the rhapsode but not the cowherd will know what a cowherd should say if he's a slave calming cattle when they get wild?

ION Of course not.

SOC. But he'll know what a woman should say if she's a spinning woman talking about working wool?

d ION No.

SOC. Or what a man should say if he's a general exhorting his troops?

ION Yes, the rhapsode knows that sort of thing.

SOC. Then the rhapsode's art is generalship?

ION At any rate I'd know what a general should say.

SOC. Perhaps because you're also a skilled general, Ion. Certainly if you happened to be at once a skilled horseman and a skilled lyre
e player, you'd know whether horses are well or badly handled. But suppose I asked you, "By what art, Ion, do you know that horses are well handled? As a horseman or a lyre player?" How would you answer me?

ION I'd answer, as a horseman.

SOC. Then again, if you recognized good lyre playing, you'd agree you do so as a lyre player, not as a horseman.

ION Yes.

SOC. But since you know what has to do with generalship, do you know it by being a general or a good rhapsode?

ION I don't think there's any difference.

541a SOC. What? No difference, you say? Do you mean that the art of the rhapsode and the general is one art or two?

ION One, I think.

SOC. So whoever is a good rhapsode is also a good general?

ION Quite so, Socrates.

soc. Then whoever is a good general is also a good rhapsode?

ION No, I don't think that.

soc. But you do think whoever is a good rhapsode is a good general?

b ION Of course.

soc. Now, you're the best rhapsode in Greece?

ION Yes, by a great deal, Socrates.

soc. And you're also the best general in Greece, Ion?

ION Rest assured of it, Socrates. And I learnt it from Homer.

c soc. Then how is it, in heaven's name, Ion, that since you're both the best general and the best rhapsode in Greece, you go about Greece performing as a rhapsode but not as a general? Do you think there's great need among the Greeks for a golden-crowned rhapsode but none for a general?

ION It's because my city is ruled by yours, Socrates, and commanded by a general and doesn't need a general, but your city and the Spartans wouldn't choose me to be a general because they think they suffice themselves.

soc. My dear Ion, don't you know Apollodorus of Cyzicus?

ION Who's he?

soc. A foreigner the Athenians have many times chosen general.

d And Phanosthenes of Andros and Heracleides of Clazomenae, whom this city invests with generalships and its other offices even though they're foreigners, because they've shown themselves worthy. Won't then Ion of Ephesus be chosen general and honored if he seems worthy? Really? Are you Ephesians not anciently Athenians, and Ephesus a city inferior to none? Actually, Ion, if you are telling the truth about how you're able to praise Homer by art and

e knowledge, you're doing a wrong. You promised me you knew many fine things about Homer and said you'd display them, but you deceived me and are far from showing them. You refuse even to say what things you're clever about, though I keep begging you.

542a You're exactly like Proteus, twisting back and forth, assuming every shape until at last you escape me by appearing as a general, in order not to display how skilled you are in wisdom about Homer. So if you have the skill of an artist and you deceive me in promising a display of Homer, then, as I just said, you're doing a wrong. If you don't have the skill of an artist, but by divine apportionment are possessed by Homer and know nothing of the many fine things you say about the poet, you're not in the wrong. Choose then how you wish us to consider you: as a wrongdoer or as divine.

b ION It makes a big difference, Socrates. For the divine is considered much more beautiful.

soc. Then for our part, Ion, the greater beauty belongs to you. You're divine, and you don't praise Homer with the skill of an artist.

THE HIPPIAS MINOR

COMMENT

Introduction

The *Hippias Minor* is an informal *reductio ad absurdum*, brilliantly conceived, of the assumption that virtue is a τέχνη, an art. In the *Protagoras* (318e–319a), Protagoras is represented as claiming that there is an art of politics and that he can make good citizens; this is equivalent to the claim that virtue is teachable (320b–c), and Hippias and Prodicus are in this associated with Protagoras (357e). The *Hippias Minor*, assuming an analogy with other arts, concludes that only the good man can voluntarily do wrong, and that it is better to do wrong voluntarily and intentionally, willingly and wittingly, ἑκών, than involuntarily and unintentionally, ἄκων. This result is not an apology for sin but an invitation to identify the premises which produce the absurdity. The *Hippias Minor,* in short, is aporetic.

There are three characters: Eudicus, Socrates, and Hippias. Their discussion takes place in Athens, and out of doors. Eudicus, son of Apemantus, is mentioned at *Hippias Major* 286b as a patron of Hippias; he is otherwise unknown. Hippias of Elis was alive at the time of Socrates' execution in 399 B.C. (*Apology* 19e), and Protagoras was old enough to be Hippias's father (*Protagoras* 317c; cf. *Hippias Major* 282e). Hippias, as we will see, is appropriately chosen to fit the dialogue which bears his name: he is a polymath, a professor who in his omniscience is unable to follow a Socratic argument.

Hippias's abilities were considerable. He was a mathematician of distinction who made important contributions to the problem of the trisection of any angle and the discussion of quadrature, the construction of a square equal in area to a given circle.[1] Protagoras accuses him of maltreat-

1. See T. L. Heath, *History of Greek Mathematics*, vol. 1, Oxford, 1921, pp. 23, 225–26.

ing the young by leading them back into the arts they are trying to escape: calculation, astronomy, geometry, and music (*Protagoras* 318d–e). The opening scene of the *Protagoras* (315c) has him lecturing on astronomy to Phaedrus, Eryximachus, and Andron; he is also a literary expert, with a set speech ready on Simonides (347b), and a legal theorist who contrasted φύσις and νόμος, nature and law or convention; like Antiphon, he described law as a tyrant which compells men contrary to nature (*Protagoras* 337d).

The *Hippias Minor* portrays the range of his learning as still broader. He once went to the Olympic festival having made everything he wore— ring and engraved seal, oil bottle and scraper, shoes, tunic, and a fancy Persian belt. He took with him epics, tragedies, and dithyrambs, as well as all kinds of prose. And he had a system of mnemonics, an art of recollection.

The interpretation of the *Hippias Minor* is aided by Aristotle's sole reference to it (*Meta.* IV 1025a 2–13, trans. Ross):

> [A] false man is one who is ready at and fond of such accounts, not for any other reason but for their own sake, and one who is good at impressing such accounts on other people, just as we say things are false, which produce a false appearance. This is why the proof in the Hippias that the same man is false and true is misleading. For it assumes that he is false who can deceive (i.e. the man who knows and is better); and further that he who is willingly bad is better. This is a false result of induction—for a man who limps willingly is better than one who does so unwillingly—by "limping" Plato means "mimicking a limp," for if the man were lame willingly, he would presumably be worse in this case as in the corresponding case of moral character.

This states some of the conceptual problems which arise in the interpretation of the *Hippias Minor,* and provides an admirable account of its structure: the main divisions of the argument are that the same man is true and false (365d–369b), and that he who is willingly bad is better," that is, that only the good man voluntarily errs (373c–376c). There is an interlude (369b–373c) in which Socrates provides (tendentious) evidence from Homer for the first claim, and introduces the second. The *Hippias Minor* is tightly constructed.

When Aristotle refers to "the *Hippias,*" he means the *Hippias Minor.* This may perhaps be thought to raise a presumption that he does not know the *Hippias Major.* But the Greek definite article used with a proper name does not imply uniqueness, and it appears that Aristotle indirectly refers to the *Hippias Major* (297e, 299c) at *Topics* VI 146a 21. The *Hippias Major*, of course, is major to minor only in that it is longer.

The Same Man Is Both True and False (365d–369b)

Hippias takes from Homer the lesson that Achilles is true and simple, Odysseus wily and false (365b). Socrates proceeds to use Hippias's own admissions to stand that bit of literary piety on its head. The argument is a variant of *Ion* 530d–533c: art implies knowledge of who speaks well and badly about the same subject. If one substitutes "falsely" for "badly" and "truly" for "well," it is the same person who knows how to speak falsely and truly about the same subject, and he is the artist, the man who knows. So Achilles and Odysseus, if they have knowledge, must be the same in precisely the respect in which Hippias claimed they differ.

Put otherwise, the ability to lie is an epistemic achievement. For to lie is not merely to say what is false—though the Greek verb ψεύδομαι, here sometimes translated "to lie," also has the weaker meaning "to speak falsely"—nor even to intend to say what is false, but to know it is false when you say it. So the false man insofar as he is able to lie must have knowledge of what he is lying about, and an ignorant man, who lacks ability to speak falsely except by accident, is not a false man. Precisely because Hippias is a polymath and possessed of many arts, he is the more able to lie because he is more able to tell the truth. If then ability to tell the truth defines a true man, and ability to lie defines a false man, the true man and the false man are not opposite but the same, and since knowledge is an excellence, and the possessor of an art is in that respect good, Socrates infers, and Hippias agrees, that the false man, like the true man, is a good man. This is a lovely piece of reasoning, but much decried by those who balk at the result. The *Hippias Minor*, because it is an informal *reductio ad absurdum*, requires a taste for validity as distinct from truth.

Interlude: Dialectic and Literature (369b–373c)

Socrates here proves that he can interpret Homer, as in the *Protagoras* (342a–347a) he interprets Simonides. Hippias, like Gorgias (*Gorgias* 447e–448a), offers himself for questioning by anyone who wishes, and he has just been giving an exhibition on Homer; since Homer is not present, he is asked to answer Socrates' questions himself, and he can scarcely in the circumstances refuse. But in the *Protagoras* (337c–338e; cf. *Gorgias* 461e–462a, 471e–472d, 474a–b), Hippias shows himself unfamiliar with the distinction between speeches and Socratic dialectic or conversation, which finds a point and sticks to it, following the argument wherever it leads; he now begins to chafe at Socrates' peculiar questions, as their precision and logic drive him to conclusions he can neither forsee nor accept.

Clinging to common sense, Hippias tries to refute the claim that the same man is true and false by repeating his comparison of Odysseus and Achilles. Socrates replies with a retort courteous, verging on a counter-check quarrelsome: Achelles, whom Hippias praises as the better man, contradicts himself in what he says to Odysseus and Ajax, and is therefore a liar. Socrates' interpretation is no doubt tendentious, in that Achilles has been persuaded by Phoenix and Ajax himself to change his mind, and does so, as Hippias says, out of εὔνοια, good will, kindly regard. Yet Hippias is dialectically helpless.

Socrates has offered an argument to show that the same man is true and false, that there is no relevant difference between Achilles and Odysseus. When Hippias claims that Achilles does not mean to lie even though he contradicts himself, but that Odysseus is wily and scheming, he is met with the previous result: those who lie willingly are better than those who lie unwillingly. Socrates, then, interprets Homer in such a way as to support a paradox; Hippias objects to his interpretation but leaves the paradox unsolved; and the paradox undermines his objection.

Socrates next proceeds to extend the paradox to the reach of its reason: only the good man is voluntarily or willingly bad.

Only the Good Man Errs Voluntarily (373c–376c)

Aristotle suggests that "he who is willingly bad is better" is a false induction: a man who limps voluntarily is better than one who limps involuntarily, but by limping Plato must mean pretending to limp, "for if the man were lame willingly, he would presumably be worse in this case as in the corresponding case of moral character." That is, the induction confuses voluntarily limping and voluntarily pretending to limp.

The objection proves too much, trading on an ambiguity in χωλαίνω between limping and being lame. It is not possible to be voluntarily lame, though it is possible voluntarily to cause oneself to become lame, as by chopping off one's big toe, and possible also to pretend to be lame. But it is surely possible willingly, voluntarily, intentionally, to limp—not to mimic a limp, or pretend to limp, but limp. And this is all Socrates' induction needs, for its point is that it is better to have a defect, for example of gait, willingly rather than unwillingly, ἑκών rather than ἄκων, and, more generally, that it is better to have the ability to do something or not do it, than otherwise. "If you want to see Criso and me running in the same place, ask him to keep even with me; for I can't run fast, and he can run slowly" (*Protagoras* 336a).

Like Hippias, the modern reader is shocked at the conclusion of the induction: "He who willingly errs and does disgraceful and unjust things, *if in fact there is such a man,* would be none other than a good man." (376b; cf. Xenophon, *Memorabilia* IV ii 8–23) The *if* is obviously important: that only good men willingly can err does not imply that there are good men who err willingly.[2] But if it is false that good men voluntarily err, then the argument implies that no man voluntarily errs; whence it follows that all wrong doing is involuntary. This is a conclusion Plato continued to accept to the end of his life, in the *Laws* (IX 860d; cf. V 731c, 734b; see also *Timaeus* 86e ff.).

Aristotle, analyzing voluntary action, offers as critiera that the act issue from the agent and that he be aware of the particular circumstances in which he acts (*E.N.* III 1111 22–23). Aristotle also supposes that what is done by reason of ignorance is *not* voluntary, though, introducing a useful distinction not found in the *Hippias Minor*, it is only what produces pain and repentance that is *in*voluntary (*E.N.* III 1110b 17–18; but see also 1110b 31 ff.). But to admit this much is to confirm the paradox of the *Hippias Minor.*[3]

The claim that virtue is an art was characteristic of sophistic culture, providing the basis for the further claim that virtue could be taught. The *Hippias Minor* makes clear the limits of an imperfect analogy. If virtue is an art, then the good man can voluntarily do wrong, and it is better to do wrong intentionally than unintentionally. If this is not true, then virtue is not an art.

---

2. Notice that here, as generally in Plato, there is no assumption of existential import, a fact relevant to discussing whether, and in what sense, he assumed a referential theory of meaning.

3. *Nicomachean Ethics* VI 1140b 20–25. See also Philippa Foot, *Virtues and Vices*, Berkeley, Calif., 1978, pp. 7–8.

TRANSLATION

EUDICUS / SOCRATES / HIPPIAS

Introduction (363a–365d)

363a EUD. Why then are you silent, Socrates, when Hippias has given so imposing a display? You don't join in praising what he said, or refute it if you think anything not well said—especially now that we who especially claim a share in philosophical pursuits have been left by ourselves.

b SOC. Why really, Eudicus, there's something I'd gladly learn from Hippias about what he was just saying of Homer. I used to hear from your father Apemantus that Homer's *Iliad* is a finer poem than the *Odyssey,* in the degree that Achilles is better than Odysseus. For he said the one poem is about Odysseus, the other about

c Achilles. If Hippias is willing, I'd gladly ask what he thinks of these two men, and which of them he says is better, since he's displayed so many other various things to us about other poets, and especially Homer.

EUD. Why, if you ask him something, Hippias clearly won't begrudge an answer. You'll answer, won't you, Hippias, if Socrates asks you something?

HIP. It would be strange in me indeed, Eudicus—since I always return from my home in Elis to the assembly of the Greeks at the

d sacred precinct when the festival is held at Olympus, and offer to speak about any subject one wishes among those I've prepared for display and answer whatever questions asked—if I now were to avoid the questioning of Socrates.

31

364a SOC. You're fortunate, Hippias, if at each Olympiad you come to the sacred precincts so hopeful of your soul and its wisdom. I'd be surprised if any of the athletes who compete there are as fearlessly confident of their bodies as you say you are of your mind.

HIP. And reasonably, Socrates. Ever since I began to compete at Olympia, I haven't met anyone better than me at anything.

b SOC. Excellent, Hippias. Your fame is a monument to your wisdom, for both the city of Elis and your parents. But what do you tell us about Achilles and Odysseus? Who do you claim is better, and why? There were a great many people in the room when you were making your display, and I didn't quite follow what you were saying, but I shrank from asking questions because there was a crowd, and I was afraid questioning would hinder your display.

c But now, since we're fewer and Eudicus here bids me ask, speak and teach us clearly what you meant to say about the two men. How did you distinguish them?

HIP. Why, Socrates, I'm prepared to explain to you what I say about them and others even more clearly than before. I claim Homer makes Achilles the best man among those who went to Troy, and Nestor wisest, and Odysseus the most wily.

SOC. Oh dear, Hippias. Would you be kind enough not to laugh at me if I scarcely understand what you've said, and repeat my question? Please try to answer gently and kindly.

d HIP. It would be shameful, Socrates, if I educated others in these very things and thought fit to charge money for it, but couldn't make allowances and answer gently when questioned by you.

e SOC. Very well. When you were saying the poet makes Achilles best and Nestor wisest, I thought I understood what you meant. But when you said he makes Odysseus the most wily, there, to tell the truth, I don't at all know what you mean. But tell me—perhaps here I may understand somewhat better. Doesn't Homer make Achilles wily?

HIP. Not at all, Socrates, but extremely simple and truthful. Because in *The Prayers*, when he makes them talk to each other, he has

365a Achilles say to Odysseus:[1] "Son of Laertes and seed of Zeus, resourceful Odysseus: I must make my answer plainly about how I shall act and what I think will be accomplished. . . . For as I detest the doorways of death, I detest that man who hides one thing in

---

1. *Iliad* xi 308–14, after Lattimore, considerably modified due to differences between Plato's text and the Homeric vulgate. In particular, line 311 of the vulgate, which describes what a false persuader would do, is missing entirely in all MSS of Plato.

the depths of his heart and speaks forth another. But I will tell
b   you the way it will be accomplished." In these lines Homer makes
clear the character of the two men: Achilles is true and simple,
Odysseus wily and false, because Homer makes Achilles say this to
Odysseus.

soc. Now I think I understand what you mean, Hippias: you mean
the wily man is false, it appears.

c HIP. Exactly, Socrates. Homer makes Odysseus speak that way in
many places, in both the *Iliad* and the *Odyssey.*

soc. So Homer, it seems, thought one man true, the other false, but
not the same man.

HIP. Exactly, Socrates.

soc. And you think so too, Hippias?

HIP. Certainly. In fact, it would be strange if I didn't.

d soc. Then let's dismiss Homer, since we can't ask him what he intended in composing those lines. But since you appear to have
taken up his cause and you concur in what you say Homer means,
answer jointly for Homer and yourself.

HIP. Of course. Ask briefly whatever you will.

The Same Man Is Both True and False (365d–369b)

soc. Do you mean that false men are like sick men in being without
power to do something? Or are they capable of doing something?

HIP. They're able to do quite a few things, especially deceive people.

e soc. So by your account, it seems, they have power, and they're wily.
Not so?

HIP. Yes.

soc. Are they wily and deceitful through simplemindedness and
folly, or through unscrupulousness and a kind of intelligence?

HIP. Through unscrupulousness most especially, and intelligence.

soc. So they're intelligent, it seems.

HIP. Yes. Too much so.

soc. Since they're intelligent, do they not know what they're doing,
or do they know?

HIP. Only too well. That's why they do ill.

soc. In knowing what they know, are they ignorant or wise?

HIP. They're wise at least in this very thing, deception.

366a soc. Hold it right there. Let's recall what it is you're saying. You
claim that the false are powerful and intelligent, knowing and
wise, in respect to the things in which they're false?

HIP. Yes, of course I do.

SOC. But true men and false are different and quite opposite from each other.

HIP. I'd say so.

SOC. Come then: false men, by your account it seems, are among the powerful and wise.

HIP. Definitely.

b SOC. When you say the false are powerful and wise in respect to their falsehoods, do you mean they specifically have power to speak falsely if they wish, or that they lack that power in respect to what they falsely say?

HIP. The former, I claim.

SOC. To sum up then, the false are wise and powerful in respect to speaking falsely.

HIP. Yes.

SOC. So an ignorant man without power to speak falsely would not be false?

HIP. That's so.

c SOC. But surely, that man has power who does what he wishes when he wishes. I don't mean someone hindered by disease or that sort of thing; I mean as you're able to write my name when you wish. Don't you say a man who can do that has power?

HIP. Yes.

SOC. Now tell me, Hippias, aren't you experienced in calculation and the art of calculating?[2]

HIP. More than anyone else, Socrates.

SOC. Then if someone asked you how much thrice seven hundred is, you could, if you wished, tell the truth about it much quicker and better than anyone else?

d HIP. Of course.

SOC. Because you're most powerful and wise in regard to it?

HIP. Yes.

SOC. Then are you only most wise and powerful, or are you also best at what you're most powerful and wise, namely, the business of calculation?

HIP. I'm surely also best, Socrates.

SOC. Then you're most able to state what's true in it. No so?

2. λογιστική. The Greeks calculated on base 10 but lacked a place-value notation, so calculation of large sums was an intricate business, often supplemented by skill in the use of an abacus, as in many parts of the world today.

e HIP. I think so.

SOC. And falsehood about the same things? Answer me as before, Hippias, nobly and imposingly: if someone asked you how much thrice seven hundred is, could you, much better than most people, lie and consistently tell falsehoods about it if you wished, and

367a never answer truly? Or would someone ignorant of calculation be better able to speak falsely than you, if you wished? Wouldn't the ignorant man, intending to speak falsely, often involuntarily tell the truth by accident, through lack of knowledge? Whereas you, the wise man, if you wished to speak falsely, could always do so with respect to the same things?

HIP. Yes, it's as you say.

SOC. Is the false man then false about other things but not about number? He wouldn't speak falsely about numbers?

HIP. Emphatically about number.

SOC. So we may also assume, Hippias, that there is someone who is false about calculation and number?

b HIP. Yes.

SOC. Who would he be? Since he's to be false, as you just now agreed, mustn't he have power to lie? For if you recall, you said that someone without power to speak falsely wouldn't be false.

HIP. I do remember, and it was so said.

SOC. Then you appeared just now to have most power to speak falsely about calculations.

HIP. Yes, that also was said.

c SOC. Then you also have most power to speak truly about calculations?

HIP. Of course

SOC. So the same person is most able to speak truly and falsely about calculations, namely, the person who is good at them, the expert calculator?

HIP. Yes.

SOC. Then who is false about calculations, Hippias, other than the good man? He in fact has power. And he is also true.

HIP. It appears so.

SOC. Do you see then that the same person is both false and true about calculation, and the true man no better than the false? Because he's surely the same person, and not utterly opposite, as you just now supposed.

d HIP. It appears not, at least here.

SOC. Do you wish us then to inquire elsewhere?

HIP. If you wish.

SOC. Now, you're also experienced in geometry?

HIP. I am.

SOC. Then isn't it also so in geometry? The same person is most able to speak falsely and tell the truth about constructions, namely, the expert geometer?

HIP. Yes.

SOC. Is anyone else good at this except him?

e HIP. No one.

SOC. Then the good and wise geometer is most powerful in respect to both? And if indeed anyone is false about constructions, it is he, the good geometer? For he is has power, but the bad man does not have power to lie; anyone without power to lie would not be false, as we agreed.

HIP. That's so.

SOC. Let's then inquire about still a third, the astronomer, whose art again you think you know even better than the previous ones. Not so, Hippias?

368a HIP. Yes.

SOC. Well, is it also the same in astronomy?

HIP. Yes, very likely, Socrates.

SOC. So in astronomy too, if indeed anyone is false, the good astronomer, who is capable of lying, will be false. Not someone incapable, surely; for he's ignorant.

HIP. It appears so.

SOC. So the same man in astronomy too will be both true and false.

HIP. It seems so.

b SOC. Come then, Hippias: consider whether this doesn't hold for all kinds of knowledge without more ado. You're the wisest of men in the largest number of arts by far, as I once heard you boast when you were describing your great and enviable wisdom in the marketplace at the money-changer's tables. You were telling how you once went to Olympia, and everything you wore was your own

c work: first, your ring—you started there—was your own work because you know how to engrave rings, and another seal was your work, and a bath-scraper, and an oil flask you'd made yourself. Next, the shoes you had on you said you'd cobbled yourself, and you'd woven your cloak and your tunic. And it seemed astonishing to everyone and proof of the greatest wisdom when you said the

d belt of the tunic you had on was of the costliest Persian kind, but you'd woven it yourself. In addition, you came with poems, epic

and tragic and dithyrambic, and a multitude of speeches of every
kind in prose; and your arrived there surpassing the rest in knowledge not only of the arts I just mentioned, but also of correctness
of rhythms, modes and letters, and many more things in addition,
as I seem to recall. And yet it seems I'd almost forgotten your art of
memory, a device in which you think you're at your most brilliant.
And I suppose I've forgotten a great many other things too. But as
I say, look to your own arts—they certainly suffice—and those of
others, and tell me if you anywhere find the true man and the false
separate and not the same, given what we've agreed. Examine this
in any sort of wisdom you please—or in any unscrupulousness or
369a whatever name you like. You won't find it, my friend, for it doesn't
exist—but you tell me.

HIP. Why, I can't, Socrates, at least not now.

SOC. Nor will you, I think. But if I'm right, remember what follows
from the argument, Hippias.

HIP. I don't at all understand what you mean, Socrates.

SOC. Maybe it's because you're not suing your art of memory right
now—clearly you don't think you need to—but I'll remind you.
You know you were saying that Achilles is true but Odysseus false
and wily?

b HIP. Yes.

SOC. Well, you're now aware that the same man has been revealed to
be both true and false, so that Odysseus if false becomes true and
Achilles if true becomes false. They don't differ from each other,
nor are they opposite, but alike.

Interlude: Dialectic and Literature (369b–373c)

HIP. Socrates, you're always weaving arguments of this sort. You
c take the most difficult thing in the argument and fasten on it in
petty detail, instead of contending with the subject of the argument as a whole. Although now, if you wish, I'll show you by
sufficient argument based on many proofs that Homer makes
Achilles better than Odysseus and without falseness, but Odysseus
a man of many treacherous falsehoods and worse than Achilles. If
you wish, you also may contend argument for argument that the
other man is better; and these people here will know which of the
two of us speaks better.

d SOC. I surely don't dispute that you're wiser than I am, Hippias. But

I've always been accustomed when someone says something to pay attention, especially when I think the speaker is wise. I want to learn what he means, and I thoroughly inquire and repeatedly examine and go over what is said, so I can learn. But if I think the speaker is worthless, I don't question him or care what he says. You'll always know by this who I think is wise, for you'll find me attentive to what he says, and I'll inquire of him in order to learn something and be benefited. Although now I've come to realize even as you speak that, in the lines you just recited to show that Achilles speaks to Odysseus as a deceitful man, it seems strange to me, if you're right, that Odysseus the wily nowhere appears to have lied, but Achilles appears by your account to be wily; at any rate, he speaks falsely. For he opens with the lines you just recited, "For as I detest the doorways of death, I detest that man who hides one thing in the depths of his heart and speaks forth another." A little later he says he would not be persuaded by Odysseus and Agamemnon, and wouldn't stay at Troy at all, but, "Tomorrow when I have sacrificed to Zeus and all the gods, and loaded well my ships and rowed out on the salt water, you will see, if you have a mind to it and if it concerns you, my ships in the dawn at sea on the Hellespont where the fish swarm and my men manning them with good will to row. If the glorious shaker of the earth should grant us a favoring passage on the third day thereafter we would go to fertile Phthia."[3] And even before that, upbraiding Agamemnon, he said: "Now I am returning to Phthia, since it is much better to go home again with my curved ships, and I am minded no longer to stay here dishonored and pile up your wealth and your luxury."[4] One time he says this in front of the whole army, another time to his own comrades, but nowhere does it appear that he undertook preparations to launch his ships to sail home; on the contrary, he had a quite noble disregard for telling the truth. Well, I questioned you at the beginning, Hippias, because I was at a loss as to which of the two men the poet portrays as better. I believe both are extremely good, and it's hard to decide which of the two is better, concerning truth and falsehood and the rest of virtue. For both men are in fact nearly equal in this.

HIP. No, you don't consider it properly, Socrates. For Achilles speaks

---

3. *Iliad* ix 357–63, after Lattimore. For the last line, compare *Crito* 44b.
4. *Iliad* x 169–71, after Lattimore.

falsely, it appears, not on purpose but involuntarily, compelled by
the misfortunes of the army to stay and help. But Odysseus speaks
falsely willingly and on purpose.

soc. You're deceiving me, dearest Hippias, and imitating Odysseus
yourself.

371a HIP. Not at all, Socrates! What do you mean? What are you referring to?

soc. You claim Achilles doesn't speak falsely on purpose, whereas
Homer makes him a cheat and plotter of deception: he appears so
much more intelligent than Odysseus that he easily gets away with
tricking him. He even had the effrontery to contradict himself
right in front of him, and Odysseus didn't even notice—at least, it
doesn't appear Odysseus said anything to him to indicate that he
was aware Achilles was speaking falsely.

b HIP. What's this you're saying, Socrates?

soc. Don't you know that after telling Odysseus that he'd sail at
dawn, he doesn't tell Ajax he's going to sail but says a different
thing?

HIP. Just where?

c soc. Where he says "that I shall not think again of the bloody fighting until such time as the son of wise Priam, Hector the brilliant,
comes all the way to the ships of the Myrmidons, and their shel-
ters, slaughtering the Argives, and shall darken with fire our ves-
sels. But around my own shelter, I think, and beside my black ship
Hecktor will be held, though he be very hungry for battle."[5] Now,

d   Hippias, do you suppose the son of Thetis, educated by most wise
Cheiron, so forgetful that, after abusing deceitful imposters a
little earlier with the extremity of abuse, he forthwith tells Odysseus he'll sail away and Ajax he'll remain—do you suppose he
wasn't scheming against Odysseus because he thought he was an
old fool, and that he could get around him by his own artfulness
and lying?

e HIP. I don't think so, Socrates. On the contrary, he was persuaded by
kindness of heart to tell Ajax something other than he told Odysseus. But even when Odysseus speaks truly, he always speaks with
a plan, and so too when he lies.

soc. Then Odysseus is better than Achilles, it seems.

HIP. Surely not, Socrates!

---

5. *Iliad* ix 650–55, trans. Lattimore.

soc. But didn't those who voluntarily speak falsely appear just now to be better than those who do so involuntarily?

372a HIP. And just how, Socrates, would those who willingly do wrong and willingly conspire to work evils be better than those who do them unwillingly? People think there is considerable excuse if someone unwillingly does wrong or speaks falsely or commits any other evil; the laws are surely much harder on those who voluntarily do evils and speak falsely than on those who do so involuntarily.

b soc. Do you see, Hippias, how true it is to say that I'm persistent in questioning the wise? Very likely it's the only good thing about me and everything else is quite worthless; for in practical affairs I get tripped up and don't know how to proceed. A sufficient indication of this is that when I meet any of you people who are famous for wisdom and to whose wisdom the Greeks all bear witness, I appear c to know nothing: because almost nothing seems the same to me as it does to you. And yet, what greater indication of ignorance than to disagree with wise men? But I have one wonderful good, which saves me: I'm not ashamed to learn. On the contrary, I inquire and ask questions and I'm very grateful to him who answers, and never deprive anyone of thanks. For I never deny having learned something, or pretend what I learned was my own discovery; on the contrary, I praise whomever taught me for being wise, and show d what I learned from him. And so now, I don't at all agree with what you're saying but differ quite emphatically; and I well know this, that it's my own fault, because I'm the sort of person I am—I claim no more. For it appears to me, Hippias, quite the opposite of what you say: those who harm people and do wrong and lie and mislead and err voluntarily rather than unwillingly are better than those who do so involuntarily. Sometimes indeed the opposite also seems true to me, and I wander in this, clearly for lack of knowl- e edge. But right now it's on me like a fit: I think those who err willingly about something are better than those who err unwillingly. I find the cause of my present condition in the previous arguments, so that it appears right now that those who do each of 373a these things involuntarily are worse than those who do them voluntarily. Gratify me, then, and don't begrudge me healing for my soul; for you'll surely render me a much greater good by putting a stop to ignorance of soul than disease of body. If you're going to make a long speech, I tell you in advance you won't heal me, because I can't follow it. But if you'll answer me as you did just now, you'll benefit me very much, nor do I think you'll be at all harmed yourself. But I would also justly call on you, son of Apemantus (*Socrates turns to Eudicus*); for you invited me to discuss with Hippias, and now if Hippias won't answer me, you must beg him on my behalf.

b EUD. Why, Socrates, I think Hippias will need no request from me: that's not the sort of thing he publicly proclaims, but rather that he avoids no man's questioning. Isn't that so, Hippias? Isn't that what you were saying?

HIP. Yes, I was. But Eudicus, Socrates is always making trouble in arguments and seems bent on harming them, as it were.

SOC. My dear Hippias, I certainly don't do so willingly—for then I'd be wise and clever, by your account—but unwillingly, so you must forgive me. For you claim that anyone who does wrong unwillingly must be forgiven.

c EUD. Please don't do anything else, Hippias. Both for our sake and for the sake of what you've publicly proclaimed, answer what Socrates asks you.

HIP. Why, I'll answer, since you request it. Ask what you wish.

Only the Good Man Errs Voluntarily (373c–376c)

SOC. Really, Hippias, I very much desire to consider what is now under discussion: whether those who err voluntarily or those who err involuntarily are better. I think then we might pursue the inquiry most correctly as follows. Please answer: might you call anyone a good runner?

d HIP. I do.

SOC. And bad?

HIP. Yes.

SOC. Then one who runs well is good, but one who runs badly is bad?

HIP. Yes.

SOC. Then one who runs slowly runs badly, one who runs fast runs well?

HIP. Yes.

SOC. So in a race, quickness in running is good but slowness is bad?

HIP. Of course.

SOC. Then who's the better runner: one who voluntarily or involuntarily runs slowly?

HIP. Voluntarily.

soc. Now, to run is in some way to act?

hip. It is.

soc. But if to act, also to do something?

e hip. Yes.

soc. So one who runs badly in a race does a bad and unseemly thing?

hip. He does. Of course.

soc. And whoever runs slowly runs badly?

hip. Yes.

soc. Then the good runner voluntarily does this bad and unseemly thing, the bad runner involuntarily?

hip. It does seem so, yes.

soc. So in a race, someone who involuntarily does bad things is worse than someone who does them voluntarily?

374a hip. In a race, yes.

soc. What about in wrestling? Who's the better wrestler, one who's thrown voluntarily or involuntarily?

hip. One thrown voluntarily, it seems.

soc. Is it worse and more disgraceful in wrestling to throw or be thrown?

hip. To be thrown.

soc. So in wrestling too, someone who voluntarily does what is bad and disgraceful is a better wrestler than someone who does it involuntarily?

hip. It seems so.

soc. What about every other function of the body? Isn't someone better in body able to do both what is strong and weak, unseemly

b   and beautiful? So that when bad things are done in respect to the body, one who is better in body does them voluntarily, one who is worse, involuntarily?

hip. It seems that's so in respect to strength.

soc. What about gracefulness, Hippias? Doesn't the better body voluntarily assume bad and ugly figures and postures, the worse body involuntarily? What do you think?

hip. Yes.

soc. And so, voluntary clumsiness is related to virtue of body, involuntary clumsiness to vice.

c hip. It appears so.

soc. What do you say about the voice? Which do you claim is better, to sing out of tune voluntarily or involuntarily?

hip. To do it voluntarily.

soc. To do it involuntarily is worse?

hip. Yes.

soc. Would you choose to possess good things or bad?

hip. Good things.

soc. Then would you choose to have feet which limp voluntarily or involuntarily?

d hip. Voluntarily.

soc. But isn't limping vice and clumsiness of foot?

hip. Yes.

soc. Again, dull sight is a vice of eyes?

hip. Yes.

soc. Then what kind of eyes would you wish to have and live with? Those with which one would see dully and mistakenly voluntarily, or involuntarily?

hip. Voluntarily.

soc. So you believe that those parts of yourself which do ill voluntarily are better than those which do so involuntarily?

hip. Yes, at least in cases like this.

soc. Then in general, for ears, nose, mouth, and all the senses, one
e   account applies. Those which involuntarily do ill are not worth having because they're bad, but those which voluntarily do ill are worth having because they're good?

hip. Yes, I think so.

soc. Again, which tools are better to work with, those which work badly voluntarily or involuntarily? For example, is a rudder with which one involuntarily steers badly better, or voluntarily?

hip. Voluntarily.

soc. And so similarly for bow and lyre and flute and everything else?

375a hip. True.

soc. Again, is it better to own a horse with a soul such that one may voluntarily ride it badly, or involuntarily?

hip. Voluntarily.

soc. So that soul is better?

hip. Yes.

soc. Then with a horse better in soul, one would do the bad works of this soul voluntarily, but with a horse of worse soul, involuntarily?

hip. Definitely.

soc. So too of a dog and all other animals?

hip. Yes.

soc. Again then: is it better for a man to have the soul of an archer which errs and misses the mark voluntarily or involuntarily?

b HIP. Voluntarily.

soc. This soul is better in respect to the art of archery?

HIP. Yes.

soc. And so a soul which errs and misses the mark unwillingly is worse than one which does so willingly?

HIP. In archery, yes.

soc. What about in medicine? Isn't the soul which voluntarily works ill on bodies more skilled in the medical art?

HIP. Yes.

soc. So this soul is better in this art than not?

HIP. It is.

soc. Again, the more musical soul in lyre playing and flute playing and everything else involving the various arts and kinds of

c knowledge—doesn't the better soul voluntarily work ill and do unbecoming things and miss the mark, but the worse soul involuntarily?

HIP. It appears so.

soc. Moreover, we'd surely choose to own slaves whose souls miss the mark and do ill willingly rather than unwillingly, because they're better in these matters.

HIP. Yes.

soc. Again, wouldn't we wish to have our own soul as good as possible?

d HIP. Yes.

soc. Then it will be better if our soul does evil and errs willingly rather than unwillingly?

HIP. But it would be a terrible thing, Socrates, if those who voluntarily do wrong are to be better than those who do wrong involuntarily.

soc. But they surely do appear to be, from what's been said.

HIP. Not to me.

soc. But I thought it also appeared so to you, Hippias. Answer again: isn't justice either a kind of power, or knowledge, or both? Isn't justice necessarily one of these?

e HIP. Yes.

soc. Now, if justice is power of the soul, the more powerful soul is more just? For surely that sort of soul appeared better to us, my friend.

HIP. Yes, it did.

soc. What if it's knowledge? Isn't the wider soul more just, the more foolish more unjust?

HIP. Yes.

soc. And what if both? Isn't the soul which has both knowledge and power more just, and the more foolish more unjust? Isn't that necessarily so?

HIP. It appears so.

soc. Then this wiser and more powerful soul, since it's better, appeared also more able to do both excellent and unbecoming things in all its works?

376a HIP. Yes.

soc. So when it does unbecoming things, it does them voluntarily, through power and art; but one or both of these appear to belong to justice?

HIP. It seems so.

soc. And to do injustice is to do evils, not to do injustice, goods?

HIP. Yes.

soc. Then the more powerful and better soul, if indeed it does injustice, will do injustice voluntarily, but the bad soul involuntarily?

HIP. It appears so.

b soc. Now, one who has a good soul is a good man, but one who has a bad soul is a bad man?

HIP. Yes.

soc. So it belongs to a good man to do injustice voluntarily, but to a bad man involuntarily, if indeed the good man has a good soul?

HIP. But surely he has.

soc. So one who errs and does disgraceful and unjust things voluntarily, Hippias, if indeed there is such a man, would be none other than the good man?

HIP. I simply cannot agree with you in this, Socrates.

c soc. Nor even I with myself, Hippias. But so it necessarily now appears to us, at least from the argument. However, as I was saying awhile ago, I keep wandering back and forth about this, and it never seems the same to me. It's not surprising that I or another private person should wander; but if even you wise men wander, at that point it's bad for us too, if we can't even cease our wandering by coming to you.

THE LACHES

COMMENT

Introduction (178a–181d)

The dramatic date of the *Laches* falls after the Battle of Delium in 424 B.C. and before the death of Laches in battle at Mantinaea in 418. Socrates, born in 469 B.C., was then about forty-five years old.

The dialogue has a notable cast of characters. Lysimachus and Melisias are, respectively, sons of Aristides the Just and the general Thucydides, leading statesmen of the previous generation, the generation of Themistocles. Laches and Nicias are Athenian military leaders of great distinction, whom Lysimachus and Melisias come to consult about whether their own sons should be trained to fight in armor; they wish distinction for their sons of a sort they have not themselves attained, a fact they blame on the neglect of their distinguished fathers. They are, in short, telling illustrations of the Socratic claim that the greatest statesmen of Athens were unable to transmit their virtue to others, including their own sons, and they are cited by name as evidence for this at *Meno* 94a–d, as part of an argument against the claim that virtue can be taught. They are, as it were, something in the nature of walking counterexamples.

Plato's audience would have immediately recognized irony in his choice of characters. There are other elements of irony as well. The main theme of the *Laches* is courage, and the dialogue raises attendant questions of whether courage is a virtue, and whether the virtues are one. It cannot be irrelevant that Laches, who led an expedition against Sicily in 427, was on his return accused of wrongfully appropriating funds entrusted to his care—embezzlement. The case was well enough known for Aristophanes to play with it in the *Wasps* (836–8, 894 ff.). Yet Laches was a brave man. He fought side by side with Socrates on the retreat from Delium, stemming a rout; Alcibiades, who won the prize for valor that

49

day, testifies to Socrates' courage (*Symposium* 220d–221b; cf. *Apology* 28e) and indirectly to Laches' courage too. Laches, in short, is a bluff old soldier who by ordinary standards was both courageous and a bit corrupt. He embodies in his own person the common-sense argument against the unity of virtue offered by Protagoras, namely, that it is possible to be courageous without being virtuous or just or wise (cf. *Protagoras* 349d–351b).

Nicias was a political ally of Laches, at least for a time: Laches moved in the Athenian Assembly in 421 the one-year truce Nicias negotiated with the Spartans. But the Peace of Nicias was afterward thought to work to Athens's disadvantage, and conversational byplay in the *Laches* suggests a considerable amount of latent personal tension, if not outright antagonism, between the two men (cf. 195a–b, e, 196a–b, 197c, 200a–c); that tension is exacerbated by the dialectic. Nicias led a second expedition against Sicily in 415, after Laches' death, and so became a central figure in the disaster which was the turning point in the Peloponnesian War. He opposed the Sicilian Expedition in the Assembly, but was chosen as one of its generals because of his caution with the impetuous Alcibiades. Lamachus was chosen general too, and he died in battle before Syracuse under circumstances of great bravery; he is mentioned at 197c as an example of courage, and the context is clearly meant to remind the reader of what happened in Sicily.

The reader is reminded of the Sicilian Expedition in other ways as well. Nicias's leadership was dilatory and superstitious; he failed according to his own definition of courage, as knowledge of what things to fear and what to be confident about. At a crucial moment before Syracuse, after an eclipse of the moon, he relied on the advice of seers rather than the clear requirements of strategy and delayed retreat, with catastrophic results;[1] it is not by accident that Laches should here taunt him with making the courageous man a seer (195e), or that Socrates should remind him that the law requires that generals govern seers, rather than seers generals (199a). Dramatic foreshadowing, and Platonic irony.

In the end, Nicias's army was destroyed and he himself put to the sword, "A man who, of all the Hellenes of my time, least deserved to meet such a calamity, because of his course of life that had been wholly regulated in accordance with virtue." So Thucydides (VII 86, trans. Smith). Plato's portrait in the *Laches* is different. Nicias is clearly both a distinguished and a decent man, but he does not know what courage is, or wisdom, or virtue. Despite his manifest admiration for Socrates, he relies

---

1. See Thucydides VII 50, and Plutarch's *Life of Nicias*.

on Damon (200b) and thus ultimately on the sophist Prodicus (197c–d) for his opinions. He looks, that is, to distinctions in the meaning of words, not to the nature of things.

Nicias and Laches Disagree about Fighting in Armor (181d–184c)

In the *Euthyphro*, Euthyphro undertook to prosecute his father for murder because it was the holy thing to do and the gods demanded it; his father and his relatives, and no doubt most ordinary Athenians, thought such prosecution unholy. In the *Laches* what is at issue is learning to fight in armor, as practiced by Stesilaus. Nicias thinks it is a useful thing for young men to learn. Laches does not think it useful, and even doubts that it is a subject of study. With the vote divided evenly, Lysimachus asks for Socrates' casting vote to break the tie.

Lysimachus's suggestion is not inapt. This lengthy section consists of two set speeches by Nicias and Laches, acknowledged leaders of opinion, offering advice to Lysimachus and Melisias about the education of their sons. The failure of those political leaders to agree with one another—or, as it will turn out when Socrates begins to ask questions, with themselves—is a representation in miniature of the Athenian political process at large. It may be added that Laches and Nicias, especially Nicias, speak with a strongly rhetorical turn of phrase; they meet privately and on familiar terms, but they have not quite laid aside their role as public men, nor their habit of making speeches at each other instead of asking and answering questions. It is not by accident that Lysimachus refers to the gathering as a βουλή—counsel and Council.

Fighting in Armor and Care of the Soul (184c–189d)

On the issue of whether his own son should be taught to fight in armor, Lysimachus will join whichever side the majority takes, and appeals to Socrates to provide a majority by voting. On the same principle, Mr. Pickwick shouted with the largest crowd in the elections at Eatanswill. Socrates offers a contrary proposition, and an analogy. The contrary proposition is that one ought to judge not by numbers but by knowledge. The analogy, supporting and supported by the proposition, is that of the trainer whose knowledge in preparing athletes for competition is superior to the opinions of a causal majority. the reasoning may be compared to *Crito* 47a–c.

The inquiry concerns the educational value of fighting in armor. But the counsel involved is not about fighting in armor, any more than counsel about applying salve to the eyes is about salve instead of the eyes, or than counsel about putting a bit on a horse is about the bit instead of the horse. In general, "When someone considers something for the sake of something (ἕνεκα του), the counsel (βουλή) is really about that for the sake of which he was considering, but not about what he was seeking for the sake of something else" (185d). When we consider fighting in armor, we do so for the sake of the soul of the young men. So the teacher we seek is expert, not about fighting in armor but about care of the soul.

In the *Protagoras*, subjects of study, μαθήματα, are the food of the soul, and the danger of sophistry is that food for the soul, unlike food for the body, cannot be carried away in a separate container; it must be learned and carried away in the soul itself, the soul thereby benefited or harmed. The underlying medical analogy refers us to the Socratic Proportion in the *Crito*, that justice is to the soul as health is to the body. Socrates there dismisses Crito's appeal to the opinion of the Many as a reason to escape, and offers the analogy of the trainer to show that the opinion of one man, if he but have knowledge, is superior to all the rest. The knowledge required is not of the body, but of "whatever it is of ours to which justice and injustice pertain" (48a)—the soul, though it is not there given its name. So here in the *Laches*, there is need for a teacher who is τεχνικός, skilled, expert, in service of soul.

That description, if it fits anyone, fits Socrates himself (cf. *Apology* 29d–30b), a fact made explicit in the *Gorgias* (521d), where Socrates is made to describe himself, quite un-Socratically, as the one true statesman in Athens, possessed of knowledge of what benefits and harms the soul. This, of course, is not the historical Socrates but Plato on Socrates.

The claim that when one considers A for the sake of B, one's counsel is about B and not about A, involves a claim of priority which is analyzed in the account of the Primary Friend in the *Lysis* (219d–220a), and in the *Gorgias* (467d). The examples given in the *Gorgias* include medicine for the sake of health and sailing for the sake of wealth, and it is easy to suppose that it is the relation of means to ends which is primarily in view, for health and wealth are purposes or aims to which medicine and sailing are means. But the *Laches* suggests that the principle is broader than this. Eyes are not the aim or purpose of salve, or horses of bits, or souls of subjects of study, though salve may benefit the eyes, bits horses, and studies souls. In general, means do not benefit ends, and ends are not benefited by means. Eyes, horses, and souls are not things at which action aims but things for whose benefit action is done; as the *Lysis* suggests

(219d), they move by being valued or loved. Put briefly, we can say of an action that it was done for the sake of a horse, even though it is nonsense to say that it is a means to the horse or that the horse is the aim or purpose of the action.

The "for the sake of something," which Aristotle later identified as the final cause, is not to be identified with the relation of means to ends, though it may include it. Perhaps, however, the distinction masks an underlying equivalence: if salve is applied to the eyes, it is applied to benefit the eyes, and benefit to the eyes, unlike the eyes, is an aim or purpose to which salve or the application of salve is a means. So it would seem that statements about what is for the sake of something can be translated without remainder into statements about what is to the benefit of something, and thus that "for the sake of something" can be reduced to the relation of means to ends after all. But this account actually shows that statement equivalences do not do duty for analysis of the underlying facts, and further that there is an issue of ontological priority which is not captured by logical equivalence. A being for whose good an action is done is not the same as something at which the action aims; and eyes can exist apart form the diseased state which salve benefits, whereas the diseased state and the benefit of the salve cannot exist apart from the eyes.

What Is Courage? (189d–190e)

As the *Euthyphro* asks what holiness is, so the *Laches* asks what courage is; but if the questions are the same in form, their purpose is different. Socrates asked what holiness is in order to determine whether a given action—Euthyphro's in prosecuting his father for murder—was holy. Socrates now asks what courage is because it is a virtue or excellence which can be present in souls, as sight and hearing are excellences which can be present in eyes and ears, and because, if we are to serve as counselors as to how best to attain virtue, we must know what it is.

The primary question of the *Laches* is not What is courage? but What is virtue? It is assumed (190c–d) that inquiry into the whole of virtue may be too big a job, and that since courage is a part of virtue, it will be easier to begin with that. The assumption that courage is a part of virtue, as in the *Euthyphro* holiness is a part of justice, is formally important for the dialectic of the *Laches*. Nicias's definition of courage as a kind of wisdom or knowledge will be refuted by showing that it makes courage not one part of virtue but the whole of it (199e).

The *Laches* brings together two main themes of Socratic inquiry and indicates how they are related. The first and major theme is the Socratic concern for the care and cure of souls: this was the central purpose of his mission to Athens (*Apology* 29d–30b) and the core of his reflection on justice and other virtues (*Crito* 47c–48a). The second theme, scarcely less important, appears at first glance less ethical than logical: it is Socrates' repeated and persistent use of the "What is it?" question, his search for definitions of the virtues.

The *Laches*, in its doctrine of βουλή, counsel (185d), shows the inner connection. We inquire into fighting in armor not for its own sake but for the sake of the soul and its excellence. so in taking counsel for the sake of the soul, we must ask in what its excellence or virtue consists. This question, central to the *Meno* and *Protagoras*, is deferred in the *Laches*, on the ground that virtue is a whole of which courage is a part, and inquiry may best proceed by considering a part. Only when we have determined what courage is can we determine whether fighting in armor, or various other practices and studies, will tend to produce courage.

Nicias remarks (187e–188a) that Socrates' questioning ultimately puts at issue the life of the person questioned. The pursuit of the definition of a virtue leads ultimately to that self-examination which is put as the main aim of Socratic inquiry in the *Apology:* the unexamined life is not worth living. To inquire into the virtues is to inquire into elements of excellence of soul, as a physician inquires into sight and hearing as the excellence of eyes and ears. The analogy is apt, since by the Socratic Proportion virtue is the health of the soul. But to inquire into excellence of soul is by implication to inquire into the excellence of one's own soul.[2]

This account involves a peculiar priority, which runs contrary to much modern ethical and logical theory. In Greek as in English, there is a distinction between courageous actions and courage as an excellence of soul. But, it will be said, courage of soul is a disposition to perform courageous actions, as solubility of salt is a disposition to dissolve, to become a solute. Before determining what courage is, we must first know what actions are courageous.

2. Richard Robinson refers to "the personal character of the elenchus," meaning roughly that the examiner must take the answer the respondent gives him, and remarks, "By addressing itself always to this person here and now, elenchus takes on particularity and accidentalness, which are defects. In this respect it is inferior to the impersonal and universal rational march of a science axiomatized according to Aristotle's prescription. Plato might urge, however, that elenchus is the means by which the irrational and accidental individual is brought to the appreciation of universal science, brought out of his individual arbitrariness into the common world of reason" (*Plato's Earlier Dialectic*, 2d ed., Oxford, 1953, p. 16). But this scarcely gives adequate weight to Laches' remark, which Robinson does not advert to: elenchus is a means to self-knowledge.

It is important to see that this precisely reverses the Socratic analysis. Actions are in themselves neutral, neither good nor bad; they take their value from their object, that for the sake of which they are done (cf. *Gorgias* 467e–468a). The *Laches* suggests that the worth of a practice such as fighting in armor must be estimated by reference to the soul and its excellence, and that courage is an excellence of soul. This is a reason for supposing that courage in souls is prior, ontologically, epistemologically, and in definition, to the courageousness of actions. It is misleading to say that courageous men are the kind of men who do courageous actions; on the contrary, courageous actions are the kinds of actions courageous men do. Issues of the value of actions are founded on moral psychology, and moral terms are not in any primary sense dispositional predicates.

Laches' First Definition: Courage Is Standing to Your Post (190e–192b)

Asked what courage is, Laches offers an example: courage is sticking to your post in battle. He characterizes himself by his answer, even as Nicias had said.

Socrates quickly demonstrates that this is too narrow: courage is shown not only in war but in perils at sea, disease, poverty, and politics, and in opposing not only pains or fears but also desires.[3] To ask what courage is, is to ask what is the same in all these. In the same way quickness, whether in running or flute playing or speaking or learning, is the power of getting a lot done in a little time. The "What is it?" question is a request for a definition, not for an example.[4]

Laches' attempt to define by example fails in not one but two ways. As an example, it does not and cannot give an account of a character common to all examples; on this point the *Laches* and the *Euthyphro* coincide. But also, because it is an example of an action, it does not indicate what, when added to the souls of the young sons of Lysimachus and Melisias, will make them better; in its concern for the soul as that for the sake of which actions and practices are to be valued, the *Laches* reaches an issue beyond the *Euthyphro*.

---

3. Against this, see *Nicomachean Ethics* III vi. This chapter is a meditation on various suggestions about courage offered in the *Laches*.

4. Cf. *Euthyphro* 5d, 6d–e; *Hippias Major* 300a–b; *Meno* 72c.

Laches' Second Definition: Courage Is
Perseverance of Soul (192b–194e)

Laches' first definition of courage, as standing to your post, indicated an action instead of an attribute of soul. In this respect his second definition, courage as perseverance of soul, is an improvement.

But the definition is too broad. Courage is seemly or noble; perseverance accompanied by wisdom or prudence (φρόνησις) is noble and good, but perseverance accompanied by folly is harmful and injurious. Laches is therefore led to agree that it is wise perseverance that is courage. But this won't do either, because the definition is not convertible. If courage is wise perseverance, not all wise perseverance—for example, that of the businessman or the doctor—is courage. So the definition is too broad. Again, Laches thinks it takes greater courage for a soldier to fight without wise calculation or the skill which art confers, or to dive down wells and persevere at it if one is unskilled at it: not all courage is wise. So the definition is also too narrow.

Laches' second definition has issued in perplexity. On the one hand, courage is good and foolish perseverance bad. On the other hand, wise perseverance does not imply courage, and foolish perseverance is sometimes more courageous than wise perseverance. And Laches, who believes he knows what courage is, is now angry at himself for not being able to say what he means.

The foundation of this perplexity is perhaps the distinction between courage and boldness or fearlessness: Nicias puts this distinction, though Laches objects to it (196d–197c). Socrates has implied a further distinction: the unskilled well-diver would not be unwise in diving if he did so for the sake of the soul.

Nicias's Definition: Courage Is a Kind of
Wisdom or Knowledge of What to Fear and
What to Be Confident About (194c–196c)

Nicias beings by appealing to Socrates' own admission that we are good in what we are wise about, bad in what we are ignorant of: goodness and wisdom are equivalent. If the courageous man is good, he is wise, and Socrates infers, with Nicias's approval, that courage is a kind of wisdom or knowledge. What kind of wisdom? Nicias answers that courage is knowledge of what to fear and what to be confident about (τὴν τῶν δεινῶν καὶ θαρρελέων ἐπιστήμην).

Laches, smarting from his own inability to answer Socrates' question, dismisses Nicias's definition. Arguing by analogy with the arts, he states that doctors know what to fear in disease, farmers in farming, and craftsmen generally know what to fear and what to be confident about in their respective arts. But this does not imply that they are courageous. Laches, in effect, is suggesting that Nicias's definition is too broad.

Nicias offers a reply which, if it relies on Damon and Prodicus, also makes a point with which Socrates must have agreed. Doctors know health and disease, but they do not know whether it is better for the patient to live or die. That is, as doctors they do not know what is to be feared and not feared. One may compare the modest ship's pilot of the *Gorgias* (511d ff.).

Nicias's reply suggests something of the ambiguity of the expression "what to fear" (τὰ δεινά). Are sickness and death fearful because we in fact fear them? Or are they fearful because they are evils and ought to be feared? Nicias holds that they sometimes ought not be feared, and therefore implies that they are sometimes not evil, or perhaps even good. It is an implication Socrates will return to.

Laches replies to Nicias with a bitter jibe: Nicias must mean that courageous men are seers, since only a seer can tell if someone is better off dead. Nicias, in a response heavy with dramatic irony, replies that seers can predict what is to come, but are no better judges than anyone else about what is good. And now Laches is stumped: Nicias has successfully defended his definition against Laches' attack.

Courage and Fearlessness (196c–197e)

Socrates next interposes in order to draw out an implication. If courage is a kind of knowledge, it is not something "any pig would know," nor would a pig be courageous. In general, Nicias must deny courage to wild beasts, to lions and panthers, boars and stags and bulls. And yet, as Laches is quick to point out, people do in fact call such animals courageous.

Nicias agrees that wild beasts are not courageous, nor anything else which is fearless by reason of lack of understanding—for example, children. Fearlessness and courage are not the same; what Laches and the Many call acts of courage, Nicias calls acts of confidence or daring (θρασέα). Socrates suggests that Nicias got his definition from Damon and Prodicus, and Laches attacks it as sophistical.

Courage as a Part of Virtue (197e–199e)

Socrates now offers a formal refutation of Nicias's definition. Nicias has agreed that courage is a part of virtue because there are other parts, such as temperance and justice. In the language of the *Euthyphro,* courage and temperance and justice are species of virtue as a genus: if courage is a part of virtue, then whatever is courageous is virtuous.

Socrates next fastens on Nicias's claim that courage is knowledge of what to fear and what to be confident about. Fear is expectation of future evils. So future evils are things to fear, future goods or things not evil are things to be confident about. So Nicias implies that knowledge of future goods and evils is courage, a consequence to which Nicias agrees.

But this raises a third point. In general, knowledge is not limited to the future but concerns past and present as well, a point Socrates argues by analogy with medicine, farming, and generalship, in contrast to the art of prophecy. So if knowledge applies to past, present, and future, and if courage is knowledge, then courage is not only knowledge of what to fear and what to be confident about, that is, of future goods and evils. Nicias's definition covers scarcely a third part of what is required. Courage, if Nicias is right in thinking that it is a kind of knowledge of good and evil, must be equivalent to virtue. But Nicias has agreed that courage is not virtue but a part of virtue. So he has not succeeded in saying what courage is.

It cannot be the case that courage is part of virtue, that courage is knowledge of good and evil, and that acknowledge of good and evil is virtue—unless, of course, part is equivalent of whole, and the virtues are one as being coimplicatory. But this is a suggestion the *Laches* does not entertain, and Nicias, on the basis of his own admissions, accepts that he has been refuted.

Conclusion (199e–201b)

At this point, Laches and Nicias squabble: the dialectic has been divisive. Socrates concludes that they have not found out what courage is, and need to find a teacher of it.

So the *Laches* ends in perplexity, ἀπορία. There is no indication that it is a "masked" dialogue, stating a satisfactory definition of courage which is then obscured by inconsistent agreements. On the contrary, the *Laches* ends without a definition: in particular, it does not settle the issue of whether courage is a natural disposition or a cognitive achievement; nor does it state or imply that virtue is knowledge, or that all the virtues are one. The reader is not asked to construct from the dialogue a definition of courage any more than he is asked in the *Euthyphro* to construct a definition of holiness. He is asked to follow an argument, stick to a point, and undertake to provide an answer to the question What is courage? for himself, and to do so for the good of his soul. The *Laches,* like other early dialogues, teaches not by telling the reader what to think, but by showing him how to begin to think, and why it is important to think. The Socratic aim is not indoctrination but education, the process of leading men who must see for their own sake to see for themselves.

TRANSLATION

LYSIMACHUS / MELISIAS / THEIR SONS / SOCRATES / NICIAS / LACHES

Introduction (178a–181d)

178a LYS. You've seen the man fighting in armor, Nicias and Laches. Melisias here and I didn't tell you at the time why we invited you to join us in watching, but now we will: for we believe we should be frank with you. Some people scoff at things like this, and if you ask

b their advice, they don't say what they really think but guess at the advice you want and speak contrary to their own opinion; but we believe you are sufficiently knowledgeable and will say simply what seems true to you. That's why we ask your advice in the matter about which we intend to consult you.

179a Well, the point I've been leading up to by way of this long preamble is this. Melisias and I have these sons here. That one is his, and bears his grandfather's name, Thucydides. This one is mine—he tool has the name of his grandfather on my father's side, for we call him Aristides. Well, we've decided to take the best possible care of them, now that they've become young men, and not do as most people do and let them do what they please, but especially at this point to begin to take care of them so far as we are able.

b Well, we know you also have sons, and we believed that you, if anyone, would be concerned about how they might be raised to become most excellent. But if after all you haven't paid much attention to this sort of thing, we remind you that it mustn't be

61

neglected, and summon you to exercise care for your sons jointly with our own.

You must hear why we decided this, Nicias and Laches, even if it takes a little longer. Melisias here and I dine together, and our
c lads with us. Well, as I said to begin with, we'll be frank with you: we can each tell the young fellows of many noble deeds done by our fathers in war and in peace, in managing the affairs of allies and those of the this city; but of our own deeds neither of us can speak. So we're embarrassed by this and blame our fathers for allowing us to be spoiled as young men while they attended to the
d business of others; we point this out to these young fellows, saying that if they neglect themselves and fail to obey us, they too will be without renown, but if they care for themselves, they may perhaps become worthy of the names they bear. Well, they say they'll obey; so we're considering what they should learn or practice to become good men.

Well, someone suggested as a study to us that it would good for
e a young man to learn to fight in armor, and recommended this fellow whose exhibit you've now watched, and bid us watch him. So we decided we'd go see the man and take you along, both as fellow spectators and, if you're willing, as partners and counselors in the care of our sons. So that's what we wish to discuss with you.
180a Well, at this point it's your part to advise us about this study and whether you think it should be learned or not, and about others if you have any study or practice to recommend for a young man, and to say what you'll make of our partnership.

NIC. I approve your plan, Lysimachus and Melisias, and I'm ready to take part in it. I suppose Laches here is too.

b LACH. You suppose right, Nicias. For what Lysimachus was just saying about his own father and Melisias's seems to me very well said indeed, in respect both to them and to us and to everyone who enters on the affairs of his city, because what he says pretty well applies equally to children and other things: public men neglect private affairs and manage them carelessly. This then is excellently said, Lysimachus, but I'm surprised you invite us to be coun-
c selors in the education of these young men but don't invite Socrates here. In the first place, he's of your own deme, and again, he always spends time where there's some noble study or practice for the young of the sort you seek.

LYS. How do you mean, Laches? Socrates here is concerned for things of this sort?

LACH. Very much so, Lysimachus.

d NIC. And I can state this as strongly as Laches. In fact, just recently
he recommended a music teacher for my son—Damon, a pupil
of Agathocles, who's quite accomplished not only in music but
in everything else worth spending time on for young men of
that age.

LYS. People my own age hardly get to know the younger generation
anymore, Socrates and Nicias and Laches: we spend so much time
at home due to old age. But if you can offer any good counsel to
e these fellow demesmen of yours, son o Sophroniscus, you must do
so. You ought to, for actually you're our friend through your
father. Your father and I were ever two friends and comrades, and
he died before we ever disagreed in anything. A memory came
back to me just now as we were speaking: these young men here
talk with one another at home and often mention Socrates and
praise him highly. I never thought to ask if they meant the son of
Sophroniscus. Well, tell me, boys, is this the Socrates you've mentioned so often?

181a SON Certainly that's him, father.

LYS. I'm delighted you're such a credit to your father, Socrates,
because he was the best of men, and especially because your own
concerns will be ours and ours yours.

LACH. Yes, Lysimachus, you really mustn't let go of the man, because
b I saw him in another place do honor not only to his father but to
his fatherland. He was with me on the retreat from Delium, and I
tell you that if the rest had only been like him, our city would have
stood upright and not taken such a fall.

LYS. Socrates, this is high praise indeed. You're praised now by men
to be relied on in these matters. Rest assured then that I'm delighted to hear you're held in such high regard, and consider me
c among those most kindly disposed to you. Well, you should have
visited us before and counted us your kindred, as is right; but
from this day on, now that we've found each other, you must share
our thoughts and get to know us and these young men here, so
that you and they may also preserve the friendship of our houses.
You'll do this, then, and we in turn will remind you. But what do
you say about the subject with which we began? What do you
think? Is this study, learning to fight in armor, suitable for young
men or not?

d SOC. Why, I'll try to give the best advice I can, Lysimachus, and to do
all you ask. But since I'm younger than these gentlemen (*Socrates*

indicates Nicias and Laches) and less experienced, I think it very right for me first to hear what they have to say and to learn from them. If I have anything to add, I'll at that point teach and persuade both you and them. But Nicias, why doesn't one of you begin?

Nicias and Laches Disagree about Fighting in Armor (181d–184c)

NIC. Nothing prevents it, Socrates. Indeed, I think this study is beneficial to young men in many ways. For one thing, it's good for them not to spend time elsewhere on the things young men like when they're at leisure, but on this instead; the body necessarily improves from it, for it's in no way inferior to other bodily exercise, or less strenuous. And at the same time this exercise and horsemanship especially befit a free man. For we are athletes in a contest, and in the matters in which we contend, only those are exercised who are exercised in the tools of war. Then too, this study will also be a benefit in combat when one might fight in ranks with many others, but its greatest benefit is when ranks are broken and single combat is required, either pursuing someone warding off attack or warding off attack when retreating oneself. A man who knew this would not suffer at the hands of a single opponent, and perhaps not even of many, but everywhere gain the advantage. Again, this sort of thing calls forth desire for another excellent study: anyone who learns to fight in armor would want to go on next to the study of tactics, the ordering of men in ranks, and once he grasps this and his ambition is stirred, he'll be eager for all that pertains to strategy, the art of the general. It's already clear that every study and practice involved in these subjects is noble and of great value for a man to study and practice, for which this study might serve as introduction. I'll add—and it's no small addition—that this knowledge would make any man more confident and courageous in war, and by no small amount. Nor let us disdain to say, even if one thinks it less important, that it will also make him more graceful where a man should appear more graceful, and in a place where at the same time he will appear more terrible to his enemies by reason of his gracefulness. So for my part, Lysimachus, as I say, I think it should be taught to the lads, and I've said why I think so. But if Laches has something contrary to say, I'd myself gladly listen.

LACH. Why Nicias, it's hard to say of any study whatever that it shouldn't be learned, because it seems good to know everything, and in particular this skill in arms, if it's really the subject of study

e   its teachers claim and Nicias says; but if it's not a subject of study and those who profess it are practicing a deception, or if it is a subject of study but not a very serious one, why learn it? I say this with a view to the following: I think if it amounted to anything, the

183a Spartans would not have ignored it; nothing else matters in life to them except to seek and practice whatever once learned and practiced gives them advantage over others in war. If they've ignored it, that very fact is something at least these teachers of it have not ignored, namely, that the Spartans are in earnest about this sort of thing beyond all other Greeks, and that anyone honored by them in it would make much more money from the rest, as tragic poets

b   do when honored by us. That's why anybody who thinks he's good at producing tragedy doesn't go on circuit outside the walls, putting on performances in other cities around Attica, but brings his work straight here and performs for this audience—reasonably enough. But, I see, these people who fight in armor believe Sparta is sacred and forbidden ground, not to be trod on even tip-toe; they skirt it and put on a show for everyone else instead, especially those who'd even themselves agree they have many superiors in warfare.

c   Then again, Lysimachus, I've met quite a few of these fellows in the work itself, and I see what they are. Indeed, we can look at it from that point of view: for as though to illustrate the point, not one of these experts in armor-fighting has ever yet become distinguished in war. And yet those who get a name for anything else do so from the practice of it. It seems these folk, compared to others, have in this respect been quite remarkably unfortunate.

d   For instance, take this fellow Stesilaus, whom you and I watched putting on a show in that great crowd and boasting about himself. I watched him elsewhere under real conditions put on a better show—though not voluntarily. The warship he was serving on rammed a merchantman, and he was fighting with a sickle-spear—another kind of weapon for another kind of fellow. Well, the rest of the story is hardly worth telling, except for the bit

e   of cleverness about the sickle attached to the spear and what resulted. As he was fighting, it caught somewhere in the tackle of the merchantman and got stuck. So Stesilaus pulled, trying to free it, but he couldn't—and ship was passing ship. So he ran along

184a   the side for a while hanging onto his spear, but when ship sheared
off from ship and drew him with it, still hanging onto his spear,
the spear pulled through his hand until all he had hold of was the
end of the shaft. There was laughter and applause from the crew
of the merchantman at the figure he made, and when somebody
threw a stone at the deck by his feet he let go of the spear, and at
that point even the crew of his own trireme could no longer contain their laughter at seeing that sickle-spear dangling from the
rigging.

b   Well, maybe there's something in this, as Nicias says, but my
own experience of it has been things like this. So as I said to begin
with, it's not worth trying to learn whether it's a study of small
usefulness, or whether they claim and pretend it's a subject of
study when it isn't. In fact, I think if a coward supposed he knew it,
he'd only become more rash because of it, and his cowardice
would become even more evident; but if he were courageous,
people would be on guard against him, and if he made even a
little mistake, he'd incur great prejudice. For pretensions to such

c   knowledge rouse jealousy, so that unless one is astonishingly superior in virtue to the rest, it's impossible to escape becoming a
laughingstock by claiming to have this knowledge. So that's about
what I think of taking this study seriously, Lysimachus. But as I
told you to begin with, don't let Socrates here go, but ask him to
advise us what he thinks about the subject before us.

Fighting in Armor and Care of the Soul (184c–189d)

LYS. Why, I do ask it, Socrates. In fact I think our council needs a
d   casting vote, as it were. It would scarcely be needed if these two
were in agreement, but as it is, Laches and Nicias vote on opposite
sides, as you see. So it would be good to hear also from you, and to
hear which of the two you vote with.

SOC. Really, Lysimachus? You intend to take whichever course the
majority of us favor?

LYS. Why, what else, Socrates?

SOC. Would you do this too, Melisias? If you took counsel about how
e   your son should exercise for a contest, would you be persuaded by
the majority of us, or by that man who'd been exercised and
trained by a good trainer?

MEL. Very likely the latter, Socrates.

SOC. You'd be persuaded by him rather than by the four of us?

MEL. Perhaps.

SOC. Because I suppose one must judge by knowledge, not by a majority, if the issue is to be judged properly.

MEL. Of course.

185a SOC. So too now, we should first consider this very thing: whether or not there is someone among us who is skilled in the subject about which we're taking counsel. If there is, we'll be persuaded by him though he be but one and dismiss the rest, but if not, we'll seek someone else. Or do you think it a small thing that you and Lysimachus are risking right now, and not your most important possession? For surely, regardless of whether sons turn out useful or the opposite, the whole house of the father will be governed according to how the children do turn out.

MEL. True.

SOC. So it needs considerable forethought?

MEL. Of course.

b SOC. How then would we consider what I just mentioned, if we wished to find out who among us is most skilled about a contest? Wouldn't it be one who has learned and practiced, and also had good teachers of it?

MEL. Yes, I think so.

SOC. Even prior to that, shouldn't we ask what it is we're seeking teachers of?

MEL. How do you mean?

SOC. Perhaps it will be more obvious this way. I don't think we agreed at the beginning what we're taking counsel about, in asking who among us is skilled and had teachers for the purpose and who did not.

c NIC. Aren't we considering fighting in armor, Socrates, and whether or not it should be learned by young men?

SOC. Of course, Nicias. But when someone inquires of someone about a drug for the eyes, and whether or not it should be used as a salve, do you think the counsel is then about the drug or about the eyes?

NIC. About the eyes.

d SOC. And if someone considers whether or not a bit should be applied to a horse, and when, he's surely taking counsel about the horse and not about the bit?

NIC. True.

SOC. In a word, then, when someone considers something for the sake of something, the counsel is about that for the sake of which he was considering, but not about what he was seeking for the sake of something else.

NIC. Necessarily.

SOC. So one must also consider the advisor, and ask whether he is expert in serving that for the sake of which we are considering what we are considering.

NIC. Of course.

e SOC. Well, we now claim to be considering a subject of study for the sake of the soul of these young men?

NIC. Yes.

SOC. So it must be considered whether any of us then is expert in service of soul and able to serve it well, and which of us has had good teachers.

LACH. Really, Socrates? Haven't you ever seen people who've become more expert without teachers than with them?

SOC. Yes, Laches, I have. But if they claimed to be good craftsmen, you surely wouldn't put trust in them unless they could show you some well-wrought work of their art—one, and more than one.

186a LACH. Well, that's true.

SOC. And so we also, Laches and Nicias—since Lysimachus and Melisias have summoned us into counsel about their two sons, eager that their souls become as good as possible—we also should show them who our teachers have been, if we claim we have them,
b teachers who, first, were good themselves and served the souls of many young people, and next, manifestly taught us. Or if any among us claims he did not have a teacher but all the same has works of his own, then he should speak and point out which Athenian or foreigner, freeman or slave, has acknowledgedly become better through him. But if neither is true of us, we should bid them seek out others, and simply not corrupt the sons of our comrades and risk incurring the most serious of charges from their closest relations.

c   Well, to speak first for myself, Melisias and Lysimachus, I say I have not had a teacher in this; and yet, I've desired the thing from my youth. But I can't afford the fees of the sophists, who alone announced that they could make me noble and good, and on the other hand, I'm incapable even now of discovering the art myself. But I wouldn't be surprised if Nicias or Laches has discovered or learned it; actually, they have greater means than I do, so they may have learned it from others, and at the same time they're older, so

by this time they may have discovered it themselves. I certainly
d   think they have the ability to educate men. For they'd never fearlessly declare what pursuits are beneficial and harmful for a young
man unless they were confident they adequately know. Now, in
others matters I have confidence in them, but I was surprised that
they disagreed with each other in this. So, Lysimachus, just as
Laches a moment ago urged you not to let me go but to question
me, so I now ask you in turn not to let Laches go, nor Nicias either,
but to question them, saying, "Socrates denies that he understand
e   the matter, or that he's adequate to judge which of you is speaking
the truth—for he has neither discovered nor learned this sort of
thing. But you, Laches and Nicias, will each please tell us the most
skilled person you've met in the nurture of the young, and
whether you know because you learned it from another or discov-
187a ered it for yourselves. And if you learned it, who your teachers in
either case were and who were their fellow practitioners, so that
should you lack leisure due to the affairs of the city, we may go to
them and persuade them with gifts or favors or both to care for
our children and yours, so that they won't disgrace their forebears
by turning out worthless. But if you understand because you've
discovered this sort of thing yourselves, please give an example of
others you've already cared for and made noble and good where
before they were worthless. For if you're now beginning to
educate for the first time, you must take care lest you put at
risk not a Carian slave,[1] but your own sons and the children of
b   your friends—lest, in short, as the proverb has it, you begin pottery on a big pot.[2] State then which of these you assert or deny to
pertain and apply to you." Ask them that, Lysimachus, and don't
let them go.

c LYS. I think Socrates speaks well, gentlemen. But it's for you to
decide, Nicias and Laches, whether you wish to be questioned and
render an account of such matters. As for myself and Melisias
here, we'd clearly be pleased if you were ready to go through an
account of everything Socrates asks; in fact, we began by saying
that we'd summoned you to counsel because we believe you're
concerned about such matters as this, as is natural, especially since
d   your sons are almost, as ours actually are, of an age to be educated.
So if it's all the same to you, please join Socrates in common in-

1. See *Euthydemus* 285c.
2. See *Gorgias* 514e.

quiry, rendering and receiving an account from each other. For
he's surely right to say that we're now taking counsel about our
most important possession. Do you agree to the inquiry?

NIC. I think you really know Socrates only through his father,
e   Lysimachus, and haven't associated with him except as a child, if
perhaps he followed along after his father and met you at temple
or some other gathering among the people of your deme. You
clearly haven't met him since he grew up.

LYS. Why, in particular, Nicias?

NIC. I don't think you realize that whoever is nearest Socrates and
188a joins him in conversation, even if the conversation perhaps begins
with something else, is necessarily drawn round and round by him
in argument without pause until he's trapped into rendering an
account of himself, and what kind of life he now leads and has led
in the past. Once he is entangled, Socrates will not let him go until
Socrates has well and thoroughly put all his ways to the test. I'm
used to the fellow, and I know what must be suffered at his
hands—yes, and still further, I well know I'll suffer it myself. I
b   delight in being near the man, Lysimachus; I think there's nothing
bad in being reminded of what I'm not doing or haven't done well.
On the contrary, a man necessarily lives the rest of his life with
more forethought if he doesn't avoid this but is willing, as Solon
says, to continue learning as long as he lives,[3] and doesn't assume
that old age by itself brings intelligence. For me, there's nothing
unaccustomed or unpleasant in being put to the test by Socrates;
c   indeed, I pretty well knew awhile ago that with Socrates present
the discussion would not be about the young men but about ourselves. So, as I say, for my part nothing prevents conversing with
Socrates in whatever way he wishes. But see how Laches here is
disposed in the matter.

LACH. I'm simpleminded about arguments, Nicias—or, if you will,
not simple but of two minds. Actually, I'd seem to some to love
argument and also to hate it. For when I hear a man discussing
virtue or any kind of wisdom, if he's genuinely a man and worthy
of the words he speaks, I am exceedingly delighted, because I look
d   at once to the speaker and what he says to see that they fit each
other and are in accord. A man like that seems to me entirely

---

3. "In growing old one is able to learn many things" (*Republic* VII 536c–d).

musical: he has not brought into most noble attunement[4] a lyre or an instrument of entertainment, but really brought into attunement his own life, a concord of words fitted to deeds quite in the Dorian mode[5]—the only mode which is solely Greek, as distinct from the Ionian or Phrygian or Lydian. Well, a man like that makes me delight in his utterance, makes me seem to everyone to

e   be a lover of argument—so eagerly do I accept what he says. But someone who does the opposite of this pains me, the more by so much as he seems to speak better, and he on the other hand makes me seem to hate argument. I have no experience of the arguments of Socrates, but before this I put his deeds to the test, I think, and there found him worthy of noble words and all frankness of

189a   speech. So if he has that too, I'm of one mind with the man; I'd be very pleased to be examined by such a person, and I wouldn't be distressed at learning. For I agree with Solon too, with only one addition. I'm willing as I grow older to be taught many things, but only by good men. Grant that my teacher is himself good, so that I may not appear hard to teach and displeased at learning. I don't care if the teacher is younger than I am, or not yet famous, or

b   anything of the sort. I invite you then, Socrates, to teach and refute me however you may wish, and to learn at least what I know. I've been disposed this way toward you since that day in which we passed through peril together and you gave proof of your own virtue, which a man must give if he intends to give rightly. So say what you like, and without regard to our difference in age.

c SOC. It seems I'll have no reason to blame any of you for not being ready to join in counsel and inquiry.

    LYS. But that's our task, Socrates—for I count you as one of us. Consider then in my stead and in behalf of the youngsters what we need to learn from these men here, and give counsel by conversing with them. Because nowadays I forget many things I intended to say because of my age, and I also forget what I heard, and if

---

4. ἁρμονίαν. Not "harmony," which suggests a combination of simultaneous notes to form chords, as distinct from melody or the tune. There is doubt whether Greek music admitted harmony in this sense. If it did, it was included in συμφωνία, concord.

5. ἁρμονία, stringing, a method of stringing, a scale. Greek music, based on the natural rather than the tempered scale, had many modes or scale sequences, which were understood to express distinctively different emotions and characters. The closest analogue in our own music is the distinction between major and minor: we do not expect a requiem in C major, nor a waltz in B minor. The Dorian mode was specifically grave and martial—Laches is a soldier.

d other arguments come in the middle, I don't remember them at all. So you must speak and explain among yourselves the subject we proposed; I'll listen and, along with Melisias here, I'll do what you think best.

What Is Courage? (189d–190e)

soc. Well, Nicias and Laches, we must be persuaded by Lysimachus and Melisias. Perhaps it's no bad thing to ask ourselves what we just undertook to consider, namely, who our teachers in this sort of education have been, or whom we've made better. But I suppose

e the following kind of inquiry bears on the same issue and is perhaps more nearly fundamental: if we happen to know of anything whatever that, being present to something, makes that to which it is present better, and if in addition we are able to make it come to be present to that thing, it is clear that we know the thing about which we might become advisors as to how one might best and most easily possess it. Perhaps you don't understand what I mean,

190a and you'll learn more easily this way. If we know that sight, when present to eyes, makes that to which it is present better, and if in addition we're able to make it come to be present to eyes, clearly we know what sight itself is, about which we may become counselors as to how one might best and most easily possess it. For if we don't know this very thing—what sight is, or what hearing is— we'd scarcely be worth mentioning as counselors and doctors of eyes or ears, and of how one might best possess hearing or sight.

b LACH. True, Socrates.

soc. Then, Laches, these two friends now summon us to counsel over how virtue may come to be present to their sons and so make them better in soul?

LACH. Yes, they do.

soc. Does this then first require knowing what virtue is? For surely if we didn't at all know what virtue happens to be, how could we become counselors for anyone as to how he might best possess it?

c LACH. In no way at all, it seems to me, Socrates.

soc. So we claim, Laches, to know what it is.

LACH. Yes, certainly.

soc. Then we could tell, presumably, what it is that we know?

LACH. Of course.

soc. Then let's not inquire straightaway about the whole of virtue, dear friend, for perhaps it's too big a job. Let's first look at some part to see if we have adequate knowledge. The inquiry will likely be easier for us.

d LACH. Why, let's do as you wish, Socrates.

SOC. Then which of the parts of virtue should we choose? Isn't it clear it's that to which learning to fight in armor is thought to be relevant? Most people surely think it relevant to courage, do they not?

LACH. Yes indeed, very much so.

SOC. Then let us first try to say what courage is, Laches. After that, we'll consider how it might come to be present in these young men,

e insofar as it can come to be present from practice and study. But try to tell what I ask: What is courage?

Laches' First Definition: Courage Is Standing to Your Post (190e–192b)

LACH. Why really, Socrates, it's not hard to say: if someone is willing to stay in ranks and ward off the enemy and not flee, rest assured he is courageous.

SOC. Excellent, Laches. But perhaps I'm at fault for not speaking clearly: you didn't answer the question I meant to ask, but a different one.

LACH. How do you mean, Socrates?

191a SOC. I'll tell you, if I can. This man you mention is courageous if he remains in ranks and fights the enemy.

LACH. So I claim, at any rate.

SOC. I do too. On the other hand, what about the man who fights the enemy while fleeing rather than remaining?

LACH. How fleeing?

SOC. As the Scythians are said to fight no less while fleeing than while attacking. And Homer surely praises the horses of Aeneas,[6]

b "how they understood their plain, and how to traverse it in rapid pursuit and withdrawal." And he lauded Aeneas himself for this, for his knowledge of fear, and said he was "author of fright."

LACH. Yes, and properly, Socrates, because he was talking about chariots, and you're talking about the tactics of Scythian horsemen. Cavalry fights that way, but Greek heavy infantry as I described.

6. *Iliad* viii 106–08, trans. Lattimore.

c SOC. Except perhaps Spartan infantry, Laches. For they say that the Spartans at Plataea, when they met troops using wicker shields, refused to stand and fight but fled, and when the Persians broke ranks, the Spartans turned to fight like cavalry and so won the battle.

LACH. True.

SOC. This then is what I meant just now, that I was at fault for your not answering properly because I didn't ask properly: for I wished

d to learn from you about those who are courageous not only in the heavy infantry, but also in the cavalry and every other form of warfare; and not only about those courageous in war but in perils at sea, and all who are courageous in disease and poverty and politics; and still again, those who are not only courageous against pains or fears, but also skilled to fight against desires or pleasures, both standing fast and turning to run away—for surely some people are also courageous in these sorts of things, Laches.

e LACH. Very much so.

SOC. Then they're all courageous, but some are possessed of courage in the midst of pleasures, others in the midst of pains or desires or fears. And others, I suppose, are possessed of cowardice in these same things.

LACH. Of course.

SOC. What is each of these two? That's what I was asking. Try again, then, to say, first, of courage: what is it which is the same in all these? Or don't you fully yet understand what I mean?

LACH. Not quite.

192a SOC. I mean this. Suppose I were to ask what quickness is, as we find it in running and lyre playing and talking and learning and many other things; we pretty well have it in anything worth mentioning in the actions of hands or legs, mouth and voice, or intelligence. Don't you agree?

LACH. Of course.

b SOC. Well, suppose someone asked me, "Socrates, what do you say it is which in all things you name quickness?" I'd tell him that I call quickness a power of getting a lot done in a little time, both in speech and in a race, and in everything else.

LACH. And you're surely correct.

SOC. Try then also to speak this way about courage, Laches. What power is it which, being the same in pleasure and pain and all the things we just now were mentioning, is then called courage?

Laches' Second Definition: Courage
Is Perseverance of Soul (192b–194e)

LACH. Well, it seems to me that it's a kind of perseverance of soul,[7] if one must say what its nature is through all cases.

c SOC. Of course one must, at least if we're to answer the question among ourselves. It appears to me, though, that not every perseverance appears to you to be courage. My evidence is this: I know pretty well, Laches, that you believe courage is a very noble thing.

LACH. Be assured that it is among the most noble.

SOC. Now, perseverance accompanied by wisdom is noble and good?

LACH. Of course.

d SOC. But what if it's accompanied by folly? In that case, isn't it on the contrary harmful and injurious?

LACH. Yes.

SOC. Then will you say this sort of thing is at all noble, if it's injurious and harmful?

LACH. No, at least not rightly, Socrates.

SOC. So you won't agree that this kind of perseverance is courage, since it's not noble, but courage is a noble thing.

LACH. True.

SOC. So wise perseverance, according to your account, would be courage.

LACH. It seems so.

e SOC. Let's see, then. Wise in respect to what? Everything, large and small? For example, if someone perseveres in spending money wisely, knowing that by spending he'll get more, would you call that courageous?

LACH. Certainly not.

SOC. But, for example, if someone is a doctor, and his son or someone else is taken with inflammation of the lungs and begs him to give food or drink, and he doesn't give in but perseveres in refusing?

193a LACH. That's not it either.

SOC. But take a man who perseveres in war and is willing to fight on a wise calculation, knowing that others will come to his aid, and suppose that he fights fewer and inferior men compared to those on his side, and still further that he has a stronger position. Would

7. καρτερία τις . . . τῆς ψυχῆς: perseverance, patient endurance, toughness of soul.

you say that the man who perseveres with this sort of wisdom and preparation is more courageous than the man willing to remain and persevere in the opposing camp?

b LACH. No, the man in the opposing camp is more courageous, it seems to me, Socrates.

SOC. Yet surely his perseverance is less wise than that of the other.

LACH. True.

SOC. So you'll say that the man with knowledge of horsemanship who perseveres in a cavalry fight is less courageous than the man without that knowledge.

LACH. It seems so to me.

c SOC. And the man who perseveres with skill in using the sling or the bow, or any other such art.

LACH. Of course.

SOC. And anyone willing to go down into wells and dive, and to persevere in this work without being skilled at it, or some other work of the same sort, you'll say is more courageous than those skilled in it.[8]

LACH. What else can one say, Socrates?

SOC. Nothing, if one supposes it's so.

LACH. But I surely do suppose it.

SOC. Moreover, Laches, people of this sort run risks and persevere more foolishly than those who do the same thing with an art?

LACH. It appears so.

d SOC. Didn't foolish boldness and perseverance appear to us before to be shameful and harmful?

LACH. To be sure.

SOC. But courage, it was agreed, is something noble.

LACH. Yes.

SOC. But now, on the contrary, we're saying that this shameful thing—namely, foolish perseverance—is courage.

LACH. We seem to be.

SOC. Then do you think we're right?

LACH. No, Socrates, I certainly don't.

e SOC. So by your account, Laches, you and I are not tuned in the Dorian mode: our deeds are not in concord with our words. In deeds, it seems, one might say we have a share of courage, but not I think in words, if he now heard us conversing.

LACH. Very true.

8. See *Protagoras* 350a, 359a ff.

soc. Well then, does it seem noble for us to be so situated?

LACH. Not at all.

soc. Well, do you wish us to be persuaded at least to this extent by what we're claiming?

LACH. To what extent? And by what claim?

194a soc. The claim that bids us persevere. If you wish, let's stand our ground and persevere in the inquiry, so that courage herself won't laugh at us for not seeking her courageously, if perhaps perseverance is often courage after all.

LACH. I'm not ready to give up, Socrates. And yet I'm not accustomed to such arguments. But a certain love of victory over these questions has taken hold of me, and I'm truly angry that I'm so
b   unable to say what I mean. For I do think I have a concept of what courage is; I don't know how it just slipped away from me, so that I can't capture it in a statement and say what it is.

soc. Well, my friend, the good hunter must follow the trail and not give up.

LACH. To be sure.

soc. Do you wish us then to call on Nicias here to join the hunt? He may be more resourceful than we are.

LACH. Yes, why not.

Nicias's Definition: Courage Is a Kind of Wisdom or Knowledge of What to Fear and What to Be Confident About (194c–196c)

c   soc. Come then, Nicias, and if you can, rescue friends storm-tossed and perplexed in argument. You see how perplexed we are. If you state what you believe courage is, you'll release us from perplexity and yourself establish in speech what you conceive.

NIC. Well, Socrates, I've been thinking for some time that you're not defining courage well because you don't use what I've already heard you say so well.

soc. How so, Nicias?

d   NIC. I've often heard you say that each of us is good in things in which he is wise, bad in those of which he is ignorant.

soc. Why, that's certainly true, Nicias.

NIC. Then since the courageous man is good, it's clear he's wise.

soc. Hear that, Laches?

LACH. Yes, and I don't at all understand what he means.

soc. I think I do. I think he means courage is a kind of wisdom.

lach. What kind of wisdom, Socrates?

e soc. Why don't you ask him?

lach. Very well, I will.

soc. Come then, Nicias, tell him what kind of wisdom courage is, by your account. Not, surely, the kind involved in flute playing.[9]

nic. Not at all.

soc. Nor again lyre playing.

nic. Of course not.

soc. Then what is this knowledge, or of what?

lach. A good question, Socrates. Let him say what he claims it is.

195a soc. Nic. I say it's this, Laches: knowledge of what things to fear and what to be confident about, both in war and everything else.[10]

lach. How absurdly he talks, Socrates.

soc. What do you have in view in saying this, Laches?

lach. Why, that wisdom is surely separate from courage.

soc. Nicias denies that.

lach. Yes, he does. He also babbles.

soc. Then let's instruct him, not abuse him.

nic. No, Socrates, I think Laches wants to show I'm also saying nothing,[11] because he just appeared that way himself.

b lach. Yes, Nicias, and I'll try to prove it. Because you really are saying nothing. Take doctors, for example. Don't they know what things to fear in diseases? Or do you think the courageous know? Or do you call doctors courageous?

nic. Not at al.

lach. No, nor farmers either, I dare say. And yet they surely know what things to fear in farming. And all other craftsmen know what to fear and what to be confident about in their own arts. But they aren't any the more courageous for it.

c soc. What do you think Laches is saying, Nicias? He certainly appears to be talking sense.

nic. Sense, yes. Truth, no.

soc. How so?

nic. Because he thinks doctors know something about sick people beyond being able to tell what's healthy and diseased. But surely that's only as much as they know. Whether it's more to be feared

9. Wisdom, σοφία, includes cleverness or skill in any kind of handicraft or art. The artist is σοφός, wise in his art.

10. Cf. *Protagoras* 359c ff.

11. μηδέν λέγοντα: either speaking falsely or talking nonsense.

for someone to be healthy rather than sick—do you believe doctors know that, Laches? Don't you think it's better for many people not to rise than to get up from their illness? Tell me this: do you claim that in each case it's better to survive and not for many preferable to be dead?

d LACH. I suppose that's so.

NIC. Then do you think the same things are to be feared by those better off dead and those better off alive?

LACH. No, I don't.

NIC. But do you give it to the doctors to know this, or to any other craftsman except him who knows what things to fear and not to fear, whom I call courageous?

SOC. Do you understand clearly what he's saying, Laches?

e LACH. I do. He calls sees courageous. For who else will know for whom it is better to live than to be dead? Well, Nicias, do you agree you're a seer, or that you're neither a seer nor courageous?

NIC. What's this? It's for a seer, your think, to know what things to fear and what to be confident about?

LACH. Of course. Who else?

196a NIC. Much rather the man I mean, dear friend. Because the seer needs only to know the signs of things to come, whether there will be death for someone or disease or loss of money, or victory or defeat in war or any other contest.[12] But which of these it is better for someone to suffer or not suffer—why is that for a seer to judge more than anyone else?

LACH. I don't understand what he means to say, Socrates: he makes clear that he doesn't mean a seer or a doctor or anyone else is courageous, unless he means it's some god. Well, it appears to me that Nicias is unwilling generously to agree that he's saying noth-

b ing, but twists back and forth to hide his own perplexity. And yet, you and I just now could have twisted that way too, if we wished not to seem to contradict ourselves. If this were a law court, there'd be some point in it; but as it is, in a meeting of this sort, why decorate oneself in vain with empty words?

c SOC. I think there's no reason at all, Laches. But let's see whether Nicias doesn't suppose he's saying something after all, and not just talking for the sake of talk. Let's inquire of him more clearly what he means, and if he appears to be saying something, we'll agree, but if not, we'll instruct him.

---

12. As a matter of art indicating historical fact, note how seriously Nicias takes the seer's claims to knowledge.

LACH. Well, if you want to inquire, Socrates, do so. I think I've perhaps found out enough.

SOC. Why, nothing prevents me: the inquiry will be common to us
both.

LACH. Of course.

Courage and Fearlessness (196c–197e)

d SOC. Tell me then, Nicias—or rather, tell us, for Laches and I share
the argument. You claim that courage is knowledge of things to
fear and be confident about?

NIC. I do.

SOC. But to know this doesn't belong to every man, when neither a
doctor nor a seer will know it or be courageous, unless he has this
very knowledge in addition. Didn't you say that?

NIC. Yes, I did.

SOC. So as the proverb has it, this really isn't something "any pig
would know," nor would a pig be courageous.

NIC. No, I think not.

e SOC. Clearly then, Nicias, you don't believe that even the Crommyo-
nian sow[13] was courageous. I don't say this in jest, but because I
think one who says this must either deny courage to any wild beast
or agree that a wild beast is so wise as to know what few men know
because it's difficult to understand, and claim a lion or panther or
some wild boar knows these things. (*Socrates turns to Laches*) But
one who claims courage to be what you do must assume that a lion,
a stag, a bull, and an ape are naturally alike relative to courage.

197a LACH. By the gods, you do speak well, Socrates. Answer this truly for
us, Nicias. Do you claim that these wild animals, which we all agree
are courageous, are wiser than we are, or do you dare oppose
everybody and deny that they're courageous?

NIC. No, Laches, I don't call wild beasts courageous, or anything else
which out of lack of understanding is fearless and foolish and

b   unafraid of what is to be feared. Do you suppose I also call all
children courageous, who fear nothing through lack of understanding? On the contrary, I think fearlessness and courage are
not the same. Of courage and forethought, I think, very few have
a share. But of boldness and daring and fearlessness accompanied
by lack of forethought, quite a few have a share—men, women

13. A monster slain by the Attic hero Theseus.

and children, and wild beasts. What you and most people call courage, then, I call boldness: what is wise concerning the things of which I speak, I call courageous.

c LACH. Look at how well he thinks he embellishes himself by his argument, Socrates; he tries to rob those whom everyone agrees are courageous of the honor.

NIC. But not you, Laches, so cheer up. For I say you're wise, and Lamachus[14] too, since you're both courageous, and many other Athenians as well.

LACH. I won't reply as I might, so that you won't claim I'm truly an Aexonian.[15]

d SOC. No, don't say anything, Laches. Actually, I don't think you're aware that he's received this wisdom from Damon, a friend of ours, and that Damon associates a great deal with Prodicus, who is supposed to be the best among the sophists in making distinctions among names of this sort.

LACH. Actually, Socrates, it befits a sophist to be clever in such subtleties, rather than a man whom the city thinks worthy to preside over her.

e SOC. Surely it befits a man presiding over the greatest matters to have a share of the greatest wisdom, my friend. It seems to me that Nicias deserves to be examined as to what he has in view in assigning this name "courage."

LACH. Then examine him yourself, Socrates.

SOC. I intend to, my friend. But don't at all suppose I'm releasing you from your partnership in the argument. Pay attention and join in considering what is said.

LACH. Very well, if it seems I should.

Courage as a Part of Virtue (197e–199e)

SOC. Of course it does. But you, Nicias, start again from the beginning: you know that we began our discussion by considering courage as a part of virtue?[16]

198a NIC. Of course.

14. Plato's audience would have recalled that Lamachus was a general on the Sicilian Expedition of 415, along with Nicias and Alcibiades, and died before Syracuse under circumstances of great bravery. This is the only place Lamachus is mentioned in Plato's dialogues.

15. Members of the deme Aexone were noted for their abusive wit.

16. Cf. 190b–c.

soc. Then again, you answered that it is a part, but that there are also other parts, which all together are called virtue?

nic. Of course.

soc. Then do you also say what I do? I call temperance and justice and certain others of that sort parts, in addition to courage.[17] Don't you too?

b nic. Certainly.

soc. Hold it right there, for we agree on this. But let's inquire about what things to fear and what to be confident about, so that you don't think they're one thing and we another. Now, we'll tell you what we believe: if you don't agree, you'll instruct us. We believe that what produces fear is fearful, but what does not produce fear is something to be confident about. Fear is produced not by past or present evils but by expected evils: for fear is expectation of evil to come.[18] Doesn't that seem so to you too, Laches?

c lach. Yes, very much so, Socrates.

soc. Then hear our claim, Nicias. We say that evils to come are to be feared, but things to come which are not evil, or are good, one may be confident about. Do you agree?

nic. In this, yes.

soc. And you call knowledge of these things courage?

nic. Exactly.

soc. Then let us inquire whether you concur with us about a third thing.

d nic. What's that?

soc. Soc. I'll tell you. It seems to me and to Laches here that, in respect to the various kinds of knowledge, there isn't one knowledge of the past, another of the present, another of what may and will be best in future: they're the same. Take health, for example: at all times there is no other knowledge of health than medicine, which, since it is one, observes what is and has been and will come

e to be in future. So similarly again farming, concerning things which grow from the soil. And no doubt you would yourselves testify that in warfare generalship best exercises forethought specifically about what will happen in future; nor does it suppose it ought to serve but rather to rule prophecy, the seer's art, because it better knows what happens and what will happen in war. And the law so orders: the seer doesn't rule the general but the general the seer. Shall we say this, Laches?

17. See, e.g., *Protagoras* 329c; *Meno* 88c.
18. Cf. *Protagoras* 358d.

199a LACH. We shall.

SOC. Then do you agree with us, Nicias, that the same knowledge understands the same things, future, present, and past?

NIC. I do: it seems true to me, Socrates.

SOC. Now, my friend, courage is knowledge of what things to fear and what to be confident about, you say?

b NIC. Yes.

SOC. But it was agreed that things to fear and things to be confident about are, respectively, future evils and future goods.

NIC. Of course.

SOC. But the same knowledge is of the same things, both of things to come and generally.

NIC. True.

SOC. So courage is not only knowledge of things to fear and to be confident about. For it understands not only future goods and evils, but those of the present and those of the past and things generally, as the other kinds of knowledge do.

c NIC. Yes, so it seems.

SOC. So your answer covered scarcely a third part of courage for us, Nicias; and yet we were asking what courage is as a whole. But as it is, it seems, by your account courage is not only knowledge of things to fear and be confident about but, as your present account has it, courage would pretty nearly be knowledge about all goods and evils and everything generally. Do you accept that revision, Nicias?

d NIC. I think so, Socrates.

SOC. Then, my friend, do you think that a courageous man would lack anything of virtue, since he would know all good things, and in general how they are and will be and have been, and evil things in like manner? Do you think he'd lack temperance, or justice and holiness, when to him alone it pertains to guard carefully against what is to be feared and what is not concerning both gods and men, and to provide good things for himself by knowing how to behave correctly toward them?

e NIC. I think there's something in what you say, Socrates.

SOC. So what you're now talking about, Nicias, would not be a part of virtue, but virtue as a whole.

NIC. It seems so.

SOC. And yet, we were saying that courage is one part of virtue.

NIC. Yes.

SOC. But that doesn't appear to be what we're saying now.

NIC. It seems not.

SOC. And so, Nicias, we haven't found out what courage is.

NIC. We don't appear to.

Conclusion (199e–201b)

LACH. Really, my dear Nicias, I thought you'd find it, since you dis-
200a   dained my answer to Socrates. I had high hope indeed that you'd
discover it by the wisdom you got from Damon.

NIC. Fine, Laches. You think it's at this point of no importance that
you yourself were shown just now to know nothing about courage,
but if I too am revealed as another such, you look to that. It makes
no difference at this point, it seems, that you along with me know
b   nothing of what a man who thinks he amounts to something ought
to have knowledge of. Well, you seem to me to do a very human
thing: you don't look at all at yourself but at others. I think I've
spoken suitably about the things we just now were discussing, and
if anything has not been adequately said, I'll correct it later with
the help of Damon—whom you apparently think it proper to
laugh at, and this without ever having laid eyes on Damon—and
with the help of others. And when I confirm the matter for myself,
I'll instruct you too and not begrudge it: for you seem to me to be
in very great need of learning.

c LACH. That's because you're wise, Nicias. Nevertheless, I advise
Lysimachus here and Melisias to dismiss you and me on the sub-
ject of educating the lads but, as I said to begin with, not to let go of
Socrates here. I my sons were of an age, I'd do the same thing.

d NIC. On that I too agree. If Socrates is willing to care for the youngsters, I'd seek no one else. Indeed, I'd gladly entrust Niceratus[19] to
him, if Socrates were willing; but when I mention something
about it to him, he keeps recommending others to me but refuses
himself. But see if Socrates will pay more heed to you, Lysimachus.

LYS. Yes, Nicias, it's surely only right. Indeed, I'd do many things for
him that I'd refuse to most others. What say you, then, Socrates?
Will you pay heed and share our eagerness that the youngsters
become as good as possible?

e SOC. It would be fearful indeed, Lysimachus, if I refused to share in
eagerness for anyone to become as good as possible. Now, if in the

19. Niceratus, son of Nicias, is present at the conversation in the *Republic* (I 327c). He was
put to death by the Thirty Tyrants.

present discussion I appeared to know, but these two here did not, it would be right to summon me specifically to this task. But as it is, all of us were equally in perplexity. How then choose any of us?

2018 Better then choose none. Since this is so, consider whether my advice is worthwhile. For I say, gentlemen—just among ourselves—that all of us jointly should first seek the best possible teacher for ourselves—for we need him—and afterward for the young men, sparing neither expense nor aught else. I do not advise that we allow ourselves to be as we now are. And if any of us is laughed at because at our age we think it right to go to school, I think we should quote Homer, who said, "Shame, for a man in need, is not a good quality."[20] So if anyone says anything, let's dismiss it; we'll be jointly concerned for our own selves and for the young men.

b LYS. What you say pleases me, Socrates. By as much as I'm the eldest, I'll in that degree most eagerly learn with the young. But please do this for me: you must come to my house at dawn tomorrow, so that we may take counsel about these very things. But for now, now let's end our meeting.

SOC. Why, I'll do it gladly, Lysimachus. I'll come to your house tomorrow, if god is willing.

20. *Odyssey* XVII 347, after Lattimore, quoted at *Charmides* 161a.

THE PROTAGORAS

COMMENT

Dramatic Introduction (309a–310a)

The scene is Athens. The date is approximately 435 B.C.,[1] in the sun-lit years before the outbreak of the Peloponnesian War. Socrates was then in his middle thirties, Pericles still alive and at the height of his power. Athens also was at her height, the most powerful city in Greece and the education of Hellas; the marble of her Acropolis, recently completed, gleamed like a jewel in the Mediterranean light. Plato, looking back on the scene from a vantage point of perhaps fifty years, is careful to let no shadow of things to come darken his portrait of what had been. The *Protagoras* is a sun-lit dialogue.

As the dialogue opens, Socrates is accosted by an unnamed friend who jocularly questions him about his relationship with the young Alcibiades. Socrates replies that he has just been with Alcibiades but paid him no heed; his attention was fixed on Protagoras of Abdera, who had come to Athens only two days before. Socrates has just left him, after a conversation Socrates now proceeds to narrate.

Narrative Introduction (310a–312b)

Socrates tells how Hippocrates, son of Apollodorus, knocked on his door that morning before first light to tell him that Protagoras has come to town. Hippocrates is so excited by the news and so eager to be introduced to him that the recent escape of one of his slaves occurs to him only as an afterthought.

1. The inference is based on the youth of Alcibiades (309a–b), who is just reaching manhood.

With good nature that few men waked from sound sleep could summon, Socrates mildly allows that he already knew that Protagoras was in town, and for several days, and he is surprised that Hippocrates should have only just heard. Why the excitement?

Hippocrates is excited because he hopes to become Protagoras's pupil, and he has come to Socrates to beg an introduction to the great man, preferably at once. Socrates remarks that it is a bit early to call, and suggests that they step into the courtyard of the house to walk and pass the time.

Once there, Socrates cross-questions Hippocrates about his purpose. Why study with Protagoras? A man studies with a physician to become a physician, with a sculptor to become a sculptor. Protagoras is a sophist, and Hippocrates wants to become his pupil. Does he then intend to become a sophist himself?

It has now become light enough to see Hippocrates blush. He would be ashamed to be known as a sophist.

The word *sophist* was not in use before the fifth century. If etymologically it meant someone who is skilled or wise, in actual use it had come to apply to a professional class of itinerant teachers who traveled from city to city offering instruction for a fee. Their stock in trade was the teaching of rhetoric, the art or knack of persuasion, and since this involved arguing both sides of an issue with equal advocacy, sophistry was associated with dishonest reasoning and moral skepticism. Aristophanes in *The Clouds* accused Socrates of being a sophist and of making the weaker argument stronger, and this was a matter of reproach at Socrates' trial. The *Protagoras* will adequately exhibit why one might form that belief. The *Gorgias* distinguishes between base rhetoric, a species of flattery aimed at giving pleasure to the audience without regard for truth, and philosophical rhetoric, aimed at truth and the good of the soul of the hearers without regard for pleasure.

Athens held sophists in ambivalent regard. The skill in speech they offered was admired and coveted; the speakers in Plato's *Symposium*, in their praise of Eros, exhibit their skill in rhetoric as a matter of pride. Yet sophistry was not an honorable profession: Hippocrates blushes for shame at the suggestion that he might become a sophist, as he would not have blushed at the suggestion that he might become a doctor or a sculptor, though both professions were beneath a gentleman. Protagoras himself will mention the odium attached to sophistry, though he thinks that a variety of ancient worthies, such as Homer, Hesiod, Orpheus, and Musaeus, were in fact sophists in disguise (316d). Prominent citizens in Athens in the fifth century were ashamed to leave writings behind them for fear of being called sophists by posterity (*Phaedrus* 257d), and Socrates will here treat with something very like ironical contempt the claim that a man who teaches virtue for money can also be a gentleman (348e–349c). Some part of this no doubt was social. Athens under Pericles was a democracy run by aristocrats; the day when the son of a sausage seller such as Cleon could run the city, if it was not far distant, had not yet come, and to an Athenian gentleman there was something common and banausic in teaching for pay.

Hippocrates has no wish to be known as a sophist, and Socrates, with his customary tact, alters the suggestion. Perhaps Hippocrates wishes to study with Protagoras as he studied reading and music and gymnastic, not in order to become himself a teacher, but for the sake of education and culture. Hippocrates agrees.

Sophistry and the Soul (312b–314c)

Hippocrates intends to submit his soul to a sophist for the sake of education. But what, after all, is a sophist? Socrates would be surprised if Hippocrates knows, and yet if he does not, he does not know to whom he is entrusting his soul, or whether the business is good or evil. The sophist deals in knowledge, no doubt. But what sort of knowledge?

Hippocrates has an answer: the sophist, as his name suggests, has knowledge of "wise things." But this, Socrates points out, can be said of painters and carpenters; painters, for example, are wise in the production of likenesses. In what is the sophist wise? What sort of skill has he got?

Skill, Hippocrates replies, in making one a clever speaker. But a clever speaker about what? Socrates asks. A musician will make you a clever speaker about music by teaching it to you, and he can teach it because he knows it. What is it of which the sophist has knowledge he can give to his pupil? And Hippocrates confesses he cannot answer.

Should he then study with Protagoras? He would not think of entrusting his body to someone he did not know was competent to care for it, such as a doctor or a trainer. If one is unwilling to risk harm to the body, much less should one risk harm to the soul. The sophist is a kind of huckster or merchant[2] of knowledge, and his wares have a danger which food and drink do not: they must be carried home in the soul after they have been purchased, instead of in a separate container.

This concludes Plato's introduction to the *Protagoras*. Questions have been raised which, in various forms, are also raised in the *Gorgias, Sympo-*

2. Cf. *Sophist* 223b–224d, and *Gorgias* 517d–3.

sium, Republic, Phaedrus, and *Sophist.* What is the nature of sophistry? What are its effects on the human soul? Most important of all, where does the true good of the soul lie? These questions are explored, not answered, in the dialogue which follows. In the *Gorgias,* sophistry and rhetoric are classed together as εἴδωλα, insubstantial images of lawgiving and statesmanship. The *Protagoras,* which begins by asking the "What is it?" question of sophistry, as other dialogues had asked it of holiness and temperance and courage, will fail of an answer. The *Gorgias* makes clear the reason: how can one define what is not real but only an imitation of what is real? It is doubtful that the question Socrates puts to Hippocrates about the nature of the sophist admits an answer except in terms of the nature of the philosopher.

Socrates' concern in the *Protagoras* for the soul recalls his description of his mission to Athens in the *Apology* (30a–b): "I go about doing nothing but persuading you, young and old, to care not for body or money in place of, or so much as, excellence of soul." The connotations of the word *soul* are not primarily theological: soul is the principle of life in men and animals. The noun ψυχή, soul, probably derives from the verb ψύχειν, to breathe, and the adjective ἔμψυχος, ensouled, means alive, living or, as a plural noun, living things. Not surprisingly, spirit, derived from Latin *spiro,* to breathe, is sometimes a translation for ψυχή. Aristotle, indeed, suggested that even vegetables have souls, characterized by reproduction, nutrition, and growth, as the animal soul is characterized by local motion and perception, and the rational soul by thought. The soul of a horse is more complete than the soul of an onion, in that it not only feeds and grows and reproduces but also perceives and moves, and less complete than the soul of a man, which is also rational. What is higher and more complete is more representative of its kind than what is lower and less complete, and if soul means life, we may also recall Aristotle's remark that the actuality or complete reality of life is mind. Mind, indeed, is another meaning of the word ψυχή, and often an excellent translation of it.

This does not of itself explain the Socratic doctrine of the soul, which is a moral doctrine: the soul is referred to in the *Crito* (47d–48a) as "whatever it is of ours to which justice and injustice pertain" and explicitly contrasted to the body as being of higher worth; it is for the good of his soul—surely not his body—that Socrates refuses to escape from prison and accepts his own sentence of death. The *Protagoras* implicitly identifies the soul with the self,[3] and in this anticipates Socrates' remark in the *Phaedo*—"Bury me if you can catch me."

3. Compare 313b 4, c 2–3 with 312b 8, 313b 1.

The Socratic doctrine of the soul must be understood in and through the Socratic Proportion, that justice or virtue is to the soul as health is to the body. The proportion is geometrical rather than arithmetical, dealing with equality of ratio rather than equality in number or magnitude, and in a moral context, equality not of merit or worth but of ratio of merit or worth.[4] The theme that virtue or justice is, analogically, the health of the soul runs through the whole of Plato's work.

With the Socratic Proportion runs the corollary that, as the relation of health to the body is a matter of knowledge, to be sought in the arts of the physician and trainer, so the relation of justice and virtue to the soul is also a matter of knowledge, the knowledge which Socrates claimed is philosophy and in the *Gorgias* identifies with statesmanship. Learning is to the soul as food is to the body; the sophist is to learning as the grocer is to food; the doctor and the trainer judge the worth of food. The introduction to the *Protagoras* suggests that, analogously, there is a physician of soul to judge the worth of learning.

A Foregathering of Sophists (314c–316b)

The sun has come up. Socrates and Hippocrates make their way to the house of Callias, son of Hipponicus, where Protagoras is staying. They have difficulty being admitted: the butler mistakes them for sophists.

Callias was a patron of the wise. His house is the finest in the city (337d), and he was reputed to have spent more money on sophists than all the rest of his fellow citizens combined.[5] Protagoras is not his only guest; Hippias of Elis and Prodicus of Ceos are there, along with many lesser lights and a retinue of followers.

It is here and before this audience that Protagoras will state his claim to teach virtue and make men good. Socrates with dry humor characterizes the scene in the house as they enter: Protagoras walking in the portico surrounded by a constantly maneuvering chorus, Hippias off to one side lecturing on astronomy, Prodicus still in bed covered with rugs and fleeces. Socrates is so impressed that he is twice inspired to quote Homer—the *Odyssey*, not the *Iliad*. The occasion calls for a touch of epic dignity.

This is not Protagoras's first visit to Athens (310e). He is the most famous teacher in Greece, now at the height of his fame, and he has made

4. Cf.*Gorgias* 507e–508a; *Timaeus* 31b–32c; *Laws* V 744x, VI 757–c; Aristotle, *Politics* 1301 b 29–35; *Nicomachean Ethics* V 1133 1b 15 ff.
5. *Apology* 20a. Cf. *Cratylus* 391c.

more money at his trade than the sculptor Phidias, who made a great deal, and any ten other sculptors combined.[6] He is perhaps now in his middle sixties; he has lived many years in his art and is old enough to be the father of anyone present (317c). When he dies, he will leave behind an undiminished reputation for excellence as a teacher and as a man.[7]

He has written a variety of books. One of them, *On Truth*, contained the famous dictum that "man is the measure of all things; of things that are, that they are, of things that are not, that they are not" (*DK* Fr. 1); Plato, quoting this in the *Theaetetus* (152a), interprets it to imply radical skepticism of the intellect.[8] A fragment which survives from Protagoras's *On Gods* shows something not only of his own temper but of the temper of his age: "Of gods, I cannot know whether they exist or not, nor what they are like in form. Many things prevent knowing—the obscurity of the subject, the brevity of human life" (*DK* Fr. 4). Plato here portrays Protagoras as a convinced defender of νόμος, custom, law, use and wont, prescription—a profoundly conservative skeptic, a defender of the established order of things on grounds of doubt. Socrates will find Protagoras a decent, kindly man, well stricken in years and dignity, an ornament to his profession. If he cannot defend against Socrates' peculiar examination, his failure will call his very profession into question.

Hippias of Elis is another famous sophist, much younger than Protagoras (317c; *Hippias Major* 282d–e). He was a man of many parts: diplomat (*Hippias Major* 281a), literary critic (*Protagoras* 347a), historian (*Hippias Major* 285d), authority on astronomy, geometry, calculation, the properties of letters and syllables, rhythm and harmony (*Hippias Major* 285c–d). He offered himself at Olympia to answer any question and was never stumped (*Hippias Minor* 363e ff.; cf. *Protagoras* 315c). He is also the inventor of an art of memory (*Hippias Minor* 368c, 369a; *Hippias Major* 285e).

Prodicus of Ceos is also a distinguished sophist, of more than human wisdom, a divine man (316a; cf. 340e; *Theaetetus* 151b), who travels from city to city and has become rich as the result of his art.[9] He is author of a famous moral discourse, *The Choice of Heracles*,[10] but is best known for his genius in distinguishing the meaning of words and determining the correctness of names.[11] Socrates, because he couldn't afford Prodicus's fifty-

6. *Meno* 91d.
7. *Meno* 91e. Cf. *Republic* X 600c–d.
8. Cf. *Euthydemus* 286c.
9. *Apology* 19e. Cf. *Republic* X 600e; *Hippias Major* 282e.
10. Cf. *Symposium* 177b; Xenophon, *Memorabilia* II i 21.
11. 337a, 340a, 341a, 358a, d. Cf. *Charmides* 163d; *Laches* 197d; *Euthydemus* 277e, 305c; *Meno* 75e; *Hippias Major* 282e.

drachma course on the subject, which provided a complete education, could attend only the one-drachma course, and doesn't know the truth about such matters (*Cratylus* 384b–c).

√ Can Virtue Be Taught? (316b—320c)

Socrates, after some delay, introduces Hippocrates to Protagoras as a young man anxious to become prominent in his city, and recommends him on grounds of wealth, birth, and ability. The recommendation is sufficient to cause Protagoras to recommend himself. Other men try to conceal the fact that they are sophists because of the odium and jealousy which attaches to the name. Not Protagoras: he admits frankly that he is a sophist, and that he educates men. Proud of his profession, he is willing to discuss it at length. The rest of the company, including Hippias and Prodicus and their followers, are summoned to provide an audience and take their seats in a circle around him.

Socrates asks Protagoras the questions he had earlier put to Hippocrates: What does he teach? What is to be gained by studying with him? Protagoras replies with a promise: Hippocrates will daily improve and become better.

This does not set Socrates' mind at rest. If Hippocrates took lessons in music or painting, he would no doubt be the better for it and improve every day in music and painting. In what does Protagoras mean to improve him? What does Protagoras teach?

Not what other sophists teach, Protagoras replies, with a glance at the polymath Hippias: most of them maltreat the young by forcing them back into the study of the arts[12] against their will, teaching them calculation, geometry, astronomy, music, and poetry. The student who comes to Protagoras will get precisely what he came to learn: good judgment in personal and civic affairs, so that he can order his private concerns wisely and be powerful in speech and action in his city. Protagoras undertakes to teach the political art, statesmanship, and to make men good citizens. That is, Protagoras promises to teach virtue, the excellence proper to a man.

The question whether virtue could be taught was a common subject of debate in the late fifth century in Athens, and the sophistic movement was itself divided in its answer. Protagoras was not the only sophist who made that claim; even Euthydemus and Dionysodorus were willing to give a course on the subject (*Euthydemus* 273d). But Protagoras was by far the

---

12. τέχναι, the first known use of the word in this sense.

most eminent professor, and the most convincing. Gorgias of Leontini, the only major sophist not present in the *Protagoras*, ridiculed the claim (*Meno* 95e) and held out to men only the promise of "that art which gains authority through speech," rhetoric (*Gorgias* 450e), an art of persuasion which might give men dominion in their cities.

The claim to teach virtue is the claim to teach the excellence proper to a man and a citizen: virtue in its public aspect is politics. Socrates demurs: he had not supposed such things could be taught, or at least the majority of men do not think so. When the Athenians gather in the Assembly, they seek the advice of experts—builders, shipwrights, and so on—on matters which they think require professional skill. But in affairs of state, everyone has an equal voice—smith or merchant, rich man or poor—and no one looks for professional skill in the subject, or asks whether the speaker has been properly instructed. The reason is they doubt that politics or statesmanship can be taught.

This is an argument from popular opinion. To it Socrates joins another, offered in the *Meno* (92e–94e). It is that virtuous men cannot transmit their excellence even to their own sons. Virtue cannot be taught, since if it could be taught, virtuous men would teach it.

The issue between Socrates and Protagoras has now been stated; it has yet to be fairly joined. At the beginning of the dialogue, with Hippocrates, Socrates asked what Protagoras as a sophist might teach. Protagoras has promised to teach virtue. If Socrates thought sophistry dangerous to the soul, Protagoras holds out the promise of a good which Socrates himself claimed to be of highest benefit. Socrates had characterized the sophist as a huckster of learning. If Protagoras is right, he is in fact a physician of soul.

This division of opinion sets the stage for the remainder of the dialogue. Protagoras will next offer a speech which is also a sales talk (see specifically 328b–c). Socrates will then ask Protagoras, since he supposes virtue can be taught, whether virtue is one or many; and after a lengthy exhibition of sophistical technique applied to a poem by Simonides, the question is put again: whether temperance, wisdom, courage, justice, and holiness are five different names for the same thing, or whether each of these names answers to a certain nature and reality peculiar to itself (349b–c). Socrates and Protagoras, in their discussion of this issue, reach an impasse, and the *Protagoras* ends in a confession of bewilderment. The dialectic has become tangled because Socrates and Protagoras have tried to say whether virtue can be taught before first discovering what it is (360e–361d). The *Meno* begins abruptly, with precisely that question in view.

The Speech of Protagoras (320c–328d)

Protagoras replies to Socrates' objection that virtue cannot be taught first with a μῦθος, a story, and then with a λόγος, an argument. The μῦθος makes two main points: first, that the various arts are to human survival as the various natural powers are to the survival of animals; second, that the political art is an art, and necessary for human survival.[13]

Once upon a time there were only gods; animals and men had not been made. When the destined time arrived to bring them forth into the light, the gods shaped and compounded them within the earth from earth and fire, and charged Prometheus and Epimetheus, Forethought and Afterthought, with the task of distributing to the animals their δυνάμεις, their natures and powers. Epimetheus took it upon himself to do this. To some he gave speed, to others strength, or armor, or wings, or hair and hide to shield them, for he intended that no race of things should be extinguished. But he squandered his stock of powers, and when it was time for men to be brought forth, he had nothing to give. Man was left naked and unarmed.

It was Prometheus who saved the situation, stealing from the gods their own prerogatives, fire and the arts, and giving them to men so that they might survive. So man had a share of divine apportionment and became the only animal who acknowledged gods and erected altars because of his kinship to the god—a kinship derived not, surely, from being made in the divine image but, as the text directly states, from human use of divine possessions, fire and the arts.

Other animals were much stronger, so that men were forced to band together for protection and to live in cities. But they quarreled and wronged each other because they did not have the art of politics, with the result that they were dispersed again and in danger of extinction. Zeus, to prevent their destruction, sent Hermes to bring them δίκη and αἰδώς, right and reverence or shame, so that there would be proper order in their cities and associations bound by friendship. Though other arts such as medicine had been distributed to only a few men, Zeus decreed that these gifts be given to all, for otherwise a city cannot exist.

This is why people summon experts to advise them on technical matters, while in matters of civic wisdom everyone has a voice. Men in cities are guided by justice and temperance: all men must partake or have a

13. For further discussion, see G. B. Kerford, "Protagoras' Doctrine of Justice and Virtue in the *Protagoras*," *Journal of Hellenic Studies* 73 (1953), pp. 42–45, and "Plato's Account of the Relativism of Protagoras," *Durham University Journal* (1949), pp. 20–26.

share (μετέχειν) of this virtue, if cities are to exist at all.[14] So in some sense wisdom and temperance are arts in which all men are expert. But men also believe that virtue can be taught, as the institution of punishment shows.

The practice of men in matters of blame and punishment shows that they think virtue can be taught. We do not punish men for being ugly or short or weak in strength; those things come by luck or nature. But we do blame and punish them for being unjust and impious. Punishment is not inflicted because or for the sake of the past wrong; that, Protagoras thinks, would be the mere blind unreasoning vengeance of a wild beast, though in fact wild beasts do not exact vengeance, and it is part of the very essence of legality that punishment should be imposed for, and only for, the violation of a rule; suffering inflicted for any other reason, whatever else it may be, is not legal punishment. Protagoras identified the justification of punishment in individual cases with what he thinks ought to be its institutional aim: to correct and deter, to prevent future wrongs. This involves a fallacy of division, confusing the justification of a rule of law with the justification of given actions determined by that rule: the legal order punishes theft to deter it, and Jones because he has committed theft; the rule is justified by its purpose, but the punishment by Jones's breach of the rule.

Protagoras infers that the institution of punishment presupposes that virtue comes by education, whence he infers that Socrates is wrong in supposing that ordinary men deny that virtue can be taught, and wrong in thinking that their refusal to call on moral experts to advise them proves they do.

Protagoras abandons μῦθος and turns to λόγος in order to answer Socrates' second objection, that good men are unable to teach their virtue to their sons. This is a mistake: they do teach them. The whole of social life is a process of teaching virtue, for the excellent reason that without virtue there can be no social life. Children from their earliest years are taught to distinguish just from unjust, beautiful from ugly or noble from shameful. If they fail in their lessons, they are straightened by punishment like warped and twisted wood. The whole of their education, both in gymnastic and in music and literature, is directed toward this, and the process continues under the laws of their city all their lives. Why then do the

14. Notice that Protagoras here speaks of justice and temperance as though they were a single virtue, as he will again at 324e–325a. He will further assume at 323e–324a that political virtue has many opposites. The issue of the unity of virtue which will occupy the rest of the *Protagoras* begins here, and is directly connected with the question of whether Protagoras knows what he is talking about in claiming to teach virtue.

sons of good men turn out badly? The answer is that they do not turn out *that* badly; the most unjust man one could find would stand out as a craftsman in the art of justice if compared to someone never educated by society.

But virtue, after all, may be found in varying degree, and Protagoras claims as his own peculiar gift the ability to assist men in becoming fully noble and good—in becoming, in a word, gentlemen: he is not one to talk himself out of a job. Here is an earnest of his confidence in his ability to improve his students: if they do not think his instruction is worth his fee, they need pay only what they think it was worth.[15]

Protagoras then has shown that virtue is teachable, and that the Athenians think it so. If there is in his speech some gentle ribbing on Plato's part—for example, the delicious description of fur as provided to animals not only to protect against the seasons sent by Zeus, but "so that each would have the same for his very own personal self-grown mattress" (321a)—it also contains a lively myth, an argument which genuinely joins issue with Socrates' objections, and a plausible account of Protagoras's role as a teacher of virtue. Grote sums up the speech:[16]

> What virtue is, Protagoras neither defines nor analyzes, nor submits to debate. He manifests no consciousness of the necessity for analysis: he accepts the ground already prepared for him by King Nomos: he thus proceeds as if the first step had been made sure, and takes his departure from hypotheses of which he renders no account. . . . To Protagoras, social or political virtue is a known and familiar datum, about which no one can mistake: which must be possessed in greater or less measure, by every man as a condition of the existence of society: which every individual has an interest in promoting in all his neighbors: and which every one therefore teaches and enforces upon every one else. It is a matter of common sense or common sentiment, and thus stands in contrast with the special professional accomplishments; which are confined only to a few—and the possessors, teachers, and learners of which are each an assignable section of the society. The parts or branches of virtue are, in like manner, assumed by him as known, in their relation to each other and to the whole. This persuasion of knowledge, without preliminary investigation, he adopts from the general public, with whom he is in communion of

15. Compare the story told by Diogenes Laertius (IX 55): Protagoras sued his pupil Euathlus for his fee, but Euathlus refused because he hadn't won a case yet. Protagoras replied, "Why, I win the fee. For if I win, I get it because I win; and if you win, I get it because you win."

16. *Plato and the Other Companions of Socrates*, vol. 2, 3d ed., London, 1875, 72–73.

sentiment. What they accept and enforce as virtue, he accepts and enforces also.

With felicitous invention, Protagoras offers the conventional wisdom: he is telling his audience what they want to hear, which is what they already believe. In the *Gorgias,* sophistic rhetoric is described as a species of flattery.

Protagoras has been made to give an excellent speech—so excellent that some scholars have supposed it the work of the historical Protagoras,[17] and many more that it represents his beliefs.[18] There are obvious difficulties in the way of this. The myth of Prometheus and Zeus is hard to reconcile with the agnostic views of the historical Protagoras, who expressly refused to discuss the existence or nonexistence of gods (*Theaetetus* 162d–e). Nor is it clear how the ethical claim that right and reverence are gifts of Zeus, fundamental to the existence of cities, comports with the epistemological subjectivism ascribed to the historical Protagoras in Plato's *Theaetetus* (151e): "Man the Measure." Plato thought Protagoras meant by this that what seems true is true for him to whom it seems so (*Theaetetus* 170a). The historical Protagoras would have been skeptical about Hippias's attainments in "the arts," mathematics, for according to Aristotle (*Metaphysics* III 997b 32–998a 3; cf. 999b 3), Protagoras undertook a refutation of the geometers on the ground that no perceptible thing admits of lengthless points and breadthless lines: so much for tangents.[19] It is a skepticism of the intellect which has its roots, by way of reaction, in Elea, in Parmenides' and Zeno's skepticism about plurality and the truth claims of perception.

In the *Theaetetus* (161c–e), "Man the Measure" is taken to imply that no one can be wiser than anyone else, and that there is no justification for anyone setting up as a teacher and asking pay for it, since each of us is the measure of his own wisdom. Socrates constructs a defense for Protagoras against this objection (166c–167d), and in that defense, F. M. Cornford and others have claimed to find doctrines of the historical Protagoras:[20]

> In this central section there is no reason to doubt that Socrates is doing what he professes to do—defending Protagoras' thesis as Pro-

17. So, for example, J. Adam and A. M. Adam, *Platonis Protagoras,* Cambridge, 1893, pp. xxi–xxii. Grote remarked: "I think the discourse one of the most striking and instructive portions of the Platonic writings: and if I could believe it was the composition of Protagoras himself, my estimation of him would be considerably raised" (*Plato,* vol. 2, p. 47n1).

18. So, for example, W. K. C. Guthrie, *A History of Greek Philosophy, vol. 3. The Fifth-Century Enlightenment,* Cambridge, 1969, pp. 265–68; cf. 166–75, 181–91.

19. See T. L. Heath, *Mathematics in Aristotle,* Oxford, 1949, pp. 204–05.

20. F. M. Cornford, *Plato's Theory of Knowledge,* London, 1935, pp. 72–74.

tagoras, if he were alive, would himself have defended it. The form of the argument is necessarily adapted to the context; but the contents are, in all probability, Protagorean. Protagoras was the first to claim the title of "Sophist," with its suggestion of a superior wisdom. He must have reconciled this claim with his doctrine that all opinions are equally true, and can only have done so by arguing, as he does here, that some opinions are "better," though not truer, than others, and that his own business, as an educator, was to substitute better opinions for worse. The analogy of the husbandman substituting sound and healthy sensations in plants is an archaic touch, suggesting that Plato may be drawing on Protagoras' own writings. Protagoras' special profession was to educate men and make them good citizens; and he taught the art of Rhetoric, which was to enable the public speaker to offer good counsel to the assembly in an effective form. He must have held the corresponding view, here stated, about the laws and customs of States, considered as the judgments or decisions of the community. Such laws and customs are "right" for that community so long as it holds them; but a wise statesman can try to substitute others that are "better" or "sounder." We may conclude that Plato is here fairly reproducing the standpoint of the historic Protagoras.

Perhaps Cornford neglects the depth of skepticism. No doubt Plato in the *Theaetetus* could state Protagoras's position as apt for analysis and criticism, but the *Theaetetus* also suggests what Aristotle afterward explicitly maintained, that Protagoras meant by "Man the Measure" to deny the law of contradiction.[21]

> The saying of Protagoras is like the views we have mentioned; he said that man is the measure of all things, meaning simply that that which seems to each man also assuredly is. If this is so, it follows that the same thing both is and is not, and is bad and good, and that the contents of all other opposite statements are true, because often a

21. *Metaphysics* XI 1062b 11–20; cf. IV 1009a 6 ff. Cf. *Cratylus* 385e–386e, 429d; *Euthydemus* 285d–286e. Protagoras held that there are two accounts opposite to each other concerning any subject matter (*DK* 80A 20, B 6a), a claim that presumably led in the next generation of sophists to the *Dissoi Logoi*, or *Double Arguments*, an anonymous sophistic treatise, written in Doric, appended to manuscripts of Sextus Empiricus and usually dated to the end of the fifth century. The sixth chapter is concerned with whether virtue is teachable, and replicates certain of the arguments put in the *Protagoras*—for example, Socrates' claim that virtue cannot be taught because good men have not taught it to their own sons. See Guthrie, *Fifth-Century Enlightenment*, pp. 317–20. Protagoras also undertook to make the worse or weaker argument better or stronger (Aristotle, *Rhetoric* II 1402 23), a charge brought against Socrates by Aristophanes and the Old Accusers at his trial—the wolf and the dog.

> particular thing appears beautiful to some and the contrary of beautiful to others, and that which appears to each man is the measure.

Aristotle here calls attention to one of the more pleasant properties of contradiction, namely, that it implies everything and nothing, allows both assertion and skepticism, dogma and doubt.

It may or may not be true that Plato's version of Protagoras's speech in the *Protagoras* accurately represents the beliefs of the historical Protagoras, as distinct from a sophistical ἐπίδειξις or exhibition for purposes of rhetorical display; if Protagoras denied the possibility of contradiction, it is difficult to assign content to the notion of accuracy. Certainly the speech needs to be reconciled with "Man the Measure" as it bears on rhetoric and advocacy: if the historical Protagoras might have given the speech Plato offers him, he might also have given another speech contradicting it point for point.

If the speech in the *Protagoras* is taken to represent Protagoras's own beliefs, or some of them, is it then philosophy? To understand it as a philosophical statement perhaps misses the point. Its author was Plato, who thought that sophistry was merely an image, a deficient resemblance of philosophy. How then shall we read the speech? Socrates himself has told us in his comparison of sophists to hucksters: it is the speech of a salesman who does not understand the worth, for good or ill, of what he sells, but is earnest in the selling of it. Protagoras is portrayed as selling learning, offering to teach virtue for a fee. This is accurate to the intent and presumably the method of the historical Protagoras. But if Protagoras teaches virtue, does he then know what virtue is? At no point does he address that issue, or undertake to render an account, or explain how his teaching contributes to the good of the soul.

It is a main purpose of the dialogue which bears his name to demonstrate that Protagoras does not in fact know what virtue is. The most distinguished of sophists offers a speech which is a mere εἴδωλον of philosophy, the love of wisdom and knowledge. In the *Sophist*, a late dialogue which may be understood in part as a comment on the *Protagoras*, the Eleatic Stranger assumes that the sophist, like the angler, is possessed of an art and makes him subject to a series of divisions: he first appears as a hired hunter of rich young men; he is next a merchant-importer of learning as nourishment for the soul; third, a retailer of these same wares; fourth, a salesman who sells products of his own manufacture; fifth, an athlete in debate who practices eristic. If he also appears as a purifier of the soul from conceits that block the way to understanding—an appearance that suggests Socrates—he is afterward a controversialist who instructs others in controversy, and finally a kind of spurious imitator who takes refuge in the darkness of not-being. If we map the portrait of Protagoras in the *Protagoras* onto this account, we find that it fits well.

The Unity of Virtue (328d–334c)

The conversation now turns to the main dialectical issue of the *Protagoras*, one which was to occupy Plato's thought to the end of his life.[22] That issue is the unity of virtue. Discussion of the problem will be suspended for a time by an interlude devoted to interpreting a poem by Simonides (334c–349a); it is then restated (349b) and pursued without interruption to the end of the dialogue.

What is meant by the unity of virtue? It is often supposed that Socrates, in the *Protagoras*, maintains against Protagoras that the virtues are one in definition—unity indeed—and that the definition of virtue is knowledge. It is maintained, that is, that the various species of virtue are identical with their genus, and that the genus is to be defined in terms of one (but not all) of its species; for knowledge, in the *Protagoras*, is wisdom,[23] and wisdom is a virtue. This is a strange result and, perhaps not surprisingly, raises problems of interpretation which have never been resolved. It derives support from Aristotle:[24]

> Socrates in one respect was on the right track while in another he went astray; in thinking that all the virtues were forms of practical wisdom he was wrong, but in saying they implied practical wisdom he was right. . . . Socrates, then, thought the virtues were rules or rational principles (for he thought they were, all of them, forms of scientific knowledge), while we think they *involve* a rational principle.

Aristotle in effect suggests that the virtues are one in definition, synonyms, or, as Socrates here puts it (329c–d, 349b), different names for the same thing. But Socrates also envisages another kind of unity, not of definition but of power or function. This sort of unity turns on the issue of detachability: on the question of whether a man may be just and not holy, or temperate and not just, or courageous and not wise. To the view that the virtues are one in definition, synonyms, may be opposed the view that they differ in definition but are one in that they are mutually implicative, so that to have any is to have all.

22. Cf. *Laws* XII 963a ff.
23. Cf., e.g., 330b 4 and 330a 1.
24. *Nicomachean Ethics* VI 1144b 16–29, trans. Ross. Cf. VII 1145b 22–30, 1147b 15–18.

Let us recall the dialectical context. Socrates begins by complimenting Protagoras on the persuasiveness of his speech; formerly he thought that there is no human art by which good men become good, but now he thinks there is. Only one small point troubles him. He would not raise it if Protagoras were only an orator, like Pericles and the rest, for orators are like books; they cannot answer questions or ask any of their own, and if you ask them a question they give you a speech, never a brief reply. But Protagoras is known for his ability to answer questions briefly, and to accept for purposes of argument the answers he receives, a thing few men can do. And Socrates would like Protagoras, if he pleases, to answer questions now. Protagoras said that virtue can be taught, that Zeus has given justice and reverence to men, and that justice, temperance, and holiness are all virtues. Socrates now wishes him to speak more precisely. Is virtue on thing, and justice, temperance, and holiness parts of it, or are those things all names for one single thing? Protagoras replies that the answer is easy: virtue is one thing, and the virtues Socrates has mentioned are parts of it. Socrates then asks whether they are parts like the parts of the face, mouth and nose and eyes and ears, or like the parts of gold, in which there is no difference between the parts or between the parts and the whole except size. Protagoras replies they are parts like the parts of the face.

In the *Euthyphro* (11e–12e), Socrates asks Euthyphro to tell whether the holy is part of the just, as reverence is part of fear and even number part of number. If the holy is part of the just, it should be possible to state what part, as the even is that part of number divisible by two. Socrates' question may be paraphrased, not inaccurately, as the question whether holiness is not a species of which justice is the genus. But though "part" and "whole," μέρος or μόριον and ὅλον, are ordinary Greek for species and genus, Socrates' language is here very concrete: features of the face are parts of the whole face, but eyes, ears, and nose are not species of face as a genus. Yet Protagoras accepts Socrates' suggestion. An analogy, after all, is not an identity.

Still, the analogy of the face may well seem peculiar in another aspect. One cannot understand what eyes, ears, and nose are without understanding that they are parts of the face, and one cannot define a species without mentioning its genus. But it may be urged that one also cannot understand what a face is without understanding that it contains eyes, ears, and nose. The peculiarity of the analogy is this: it suggests that the relation of genus to species is such that, in grasping the genus, one will thereby grasp the species which fall under it. To understand the nature of the whole is to understand that it contains certain kinds of parts.

Aristotle supposed that species are richer than genera and genera more empty than species, as lacking a difference, and the assumption that predicates may be arranged in an abstractive hierarchy has colored most subsequent thought on definition. The account fits neatly with the species and genera of natural kinds—man, ox—with which Aristotle was most concerned. It fits less neatly with mathematical and moral terms. If triangles are plain rectilinear three-sided figures, it follows that there are scalene, isosceles, and equilateral triangles, according to the ratios of their sides: the genus implies the species. If numbers are pluralities of units—the Euclidean definition—it follows that there are two kinds of number, odd and even, according as the plurality is or is not evenly divisible by two: once again, the genus implies its species. Perhaps a similar relation holds for moral terms. Perhaps if one comes to understand what virtue is, one thereby understands that wisdom, temperance, justice, courage, and holiness are virtues.

Socrates' example bears directly on this. To be an eye or a nose is to be part of a face; to be a face is to contain mouth, eyes, ears, and nose. If features of the face are analogous to species, and the face to a genus, this suggests a symmetry of implication rather than an asymmetry between species and genus. It suggests that to understand the nature of the whole is to understand that it contains certain parts, and to understand those parts is to understand that they are parts of that whole.

Protagoras agrees that the parts of virtue are more like parts of the face than parts of gold. Socrates proceeds to his next question: are the parts detachable? That is, can different people come to partake of different parts of virtue? Or, if they have one part, must they not have all? Protagoras thinks the virtues are detachable, that men may be courageous but not just, just but not wise. He agrees that courage and wisdom, like justice, temperance, and holiness, are parts of virtue, and thinks that wisdom is its most important part. If so, this calls into question another feature of the Aristotelian account of species and genera, the exclusiveness of species: a member of one species cannot also be a member of another. Once again, this doctrine fits neatly with natural kinds: a man is not a horse. But a just man, surely, may also be a wise one.

Protagoras supposes that when men come to partake of parts of virtue, some may have one and others another. The virtues are detachable: men may be brave but unjust, or just but unwise. Each part is distinct from any other, both in itself and in its own proper and peculiar δύναμις, its power or function.

Protagoras then is committed to a conjunction: that the virtues differ in definition and are detachable. To prove that they are not detachable is to falsify the conjunction. It is also to prove that he was mistaken in accepting the parts of the face as a simile for the virtues.

This bears on what has gone before. At the beginning of the dialogue, Socrates had expressed to Hippocrates doubt as to what Protagoras, as a sophist, could teach: Protagoras is a merchant-importer of knowledge, recommending indiscriminately wares which, once taken into the soul, may prove poisonous. Protagoras, on the other hand, claims to teach virtue; if he is right, he is not a huckster but a physician of soul. But if Protagoras cannot defend his thesis about the virtues, he does not to know what virtue is. That is, he does not know what it is he claims to teach.

To understand the role of Socrates in the *Protagoras,* one should recall the *Sophist,* whose divisions stumble across a man who purifies the soul from deceit.[25] The *Protagoras* illustrates what the *Sophist* describes. The method of purification is elenchus, refutation, and in applying that refutation, Socrates seems at times much like a sophist himself: dialectic often resembles eristic.[26] But the inner reality is different: those who purify the soul from deceit resemble sophists as dogs resemble wolves, the tamest and gentlest of animals and the fiercest (*Sophist* 231a). It is important to the *Protagoras* to contrast sophistic education with Socratic education, to the disadvantage of the former; that purpose could not have been served by portraying the greatest of sophists as taken in by mere snares of words. Protagoras's difficulty is logical, not verbal. It arises from failure to distinguish two ways in which the virtues may be one: in definition and in function. This need not be left to conjecture; it is shown by analysis of the arguments themselves.

Socrates in the *Protagoras* offers four arguments against the claim that the virtues differ in themselves and in their function. The first (330b–332a) maintains the unity of justice and holiness; the second (332a–333b), the unity of temperance and wisdom; the third (333b–334c) is interrupted without reaching its conclusion; it would have maintained the unity of justice and temperance. There follows a digression on Simonides, after which the question is restated (349b–d) and pursued without interruption through the remainder of the dialogue; Socrates in the final section proves the unity of courage and wisdom or knowledge.

The Unity of Justice and Holiness (330b–332a)

In the first elenchus, Socrates and Protagoras agree that justice "is a thing," and the persons of the argument then shift. Socrates imagines that he and Protagoras are to become respondents to a new interlocutor

25. *Sophist* 230b–d.
26. Cf. *Sophist* 225c–d; *Protagoras* 329b, 334e, 335b.

(330c). The device of an imaginary interlocutor is found in other early dialogues, though it is perhaps not quite accurate to call the interlocutor imaginary: he is the λόγος, the argument itself (cf. 361a).

The first question asked by the argument is whether this thing justice is itself just or not just.[27] Socrates replies that it is just, and Protagoras agrees. They also agree that this implies that justice is of a sort to be, or such as (οἷον), a just thing,[28] and this is also true of holiness: Protagoras and Socrates agree that holiness "is something," that is, that it exists; for it can scarcely be that anything else would be holy, if holiness itself is not a holy thing. Existence is implicated with causality.

The argument next (330e) recalls the claim (330a–b) that the parts of virtue are not of a sort to be such as each other. This, Socrates holds, was Protagoras's claim, not his own. What will Protagoras say if the argument goes on to inquire whether holiness is not such as to be a just thing or justice such as to be a holy thing, but such as to be an unholy thing? Can holiness be not just, and perhaps then (ἀλλ' . . . ἄρα) unjust, that is, what is not holy (τὸ ἀνόσιον)?

The suggestion that justice is a holy thing and holiness a just thing suggests a cognate accusative: the adjectives are cognate in sense but not in form, and the appropriateness of their use is attested by Socrates' claim that holiness and justice are the same in themselves or in their function.[29] Given that this is so, nothing is just if holiness itself is not a holy thing, that is, not a thing; the same applies, *mutatis mutandis*, for justice. So justice is such as holiness, and holiness such as justice.

Protagoras admits that justice has a certain resemblance to holiness— for everything has some resemblance to everything else. this is even true of things which are quite opposite: what is white in a way resembles what is black, and what is hard what is soft. Even the parts of the face, which were agreed to be different in δύναμις and not such as each other, resemble each other in some way or other. But it is improper to call things which are like only in some small respect alike, or to call things which are unlike only in some small respect unlike. Protagoras, however, is unwilling to agree that justice and holiness are alike only in a small degree; nor yet will he admit that they are related as Socrates seems to think.

Protagoras, undertaking to reply to Socrates' refutation, has in effect taken refuge in vagueness—in an answer that sounds like anything and

27. ἄδικον, either unjust as the opposite of just, or not just (cf. 331a 9). Opposition, as distinct from negation, is first explicitly dealt with at 332a–333b, anticipated at 331d 5.

28. οἷος, *qualis*, of which sort, (such) as, is a relative pronoun correlative to the interrogative ποῖος, indefinite ποιός, of what sort, of some sort.

29. Cf. *Charmides* 161a: "Temperance is a good, since it makes those things to which it is present good, but not bad."

may mean nothing. The reader may well sympathize, for the purport of Socrates' questions seems unconscionably obscure.

The first requirement for understanding the argument is to recall its point. Socrates is not, as is often supposed, undertaking to prove that justice and holiness are the same or "most like"; very probably (ἤτοι . . . γε)[30] justice is the same as holiness or most like it (ὁμοιότατον),[31] but it is beyond question (μάλιστα πάντων) that justice is of a sort to be such as holiness, and holiness of such sort as justice—that is, they are the same in function or power.

What is the power or function (δύναμις) of a virtue? The force of the word δύναμις, which may itself mean the force of a word, suggests that the δύναμις of a virtue, as distinct from the δύναμις of the name of a virtue, is its power of introducing a property. Protagoras had earlier been led to grant that holiness is a holy thing on the ground that it could scarcely be that anything else would be holy, if holiness itself were not by nature such as to be a holy thing. That is, if holiness is not a holy thing, nothing is holy; if anything is holy, holiness is a holy thing. To follow the argument, one must attend not to preconceived notions about the logical form of statements but to the facts Socrates means to describe. Holiness is that by which other things are holy; in similar vein, Socrates will shortly suggest that temperance is that by which (instrumental dative, 332b 1) or due to which (ὑπό + genitive of agent, 332d 7) temperate men and actions are temperate. Its office is its force.

To say, then, that holiness and justice are such as each other, that holiness is a just thing and justice a holy thing, is to say that each introduces the other; but if the presence of one implies the presence of the other, then the two virtues are not detachable.

Socrates has offered a telling blow to Protagoras's position—which is why Protagoras, in his reply, is forced to qualify it. he will not grant that justice is a holy thing and holiness a just thing, but only that justice has a certain resemblance to holiness; after all, even the parts of the face, which differ in function and are not such as each other, resemble each other "in a way." This is a new tune, and Socrates has forced Protagoras to sing it.

Justice is a holy thing and holiness a just thing: Socrates suggests this but he does not prove it, and when Protagoras balks at accepting it, he allows the argument to drop, to be resumed again after a long interlude at 349a. Socrates will there undertake to show that the virtues are not de-

30. Smyth, *Greek Grammar*, 2d ed., 2858.
31. Greek is more generous than English with the superlative, which may often best be translated as a strong comparative—"very much like it."

tachable, and that Protagoras is wrong to think that men may be courageous but not just, or just but not wise. The present passage is a prelimi-
nary statement of the problem.

"Self-Predication"

This stretch of argument in the *Protagoras* has long been thought subject
to the logical vice of assuming that a characteristic has what it is, "self-
predication." Grote described the propositions that justice is just and
holiness holy as "strange,"[32] suggested that they must either be mere
tautology or else an impropriety of speech, and quoted Hutcheson, *On the
Passions* (i 234): "None can apply moral attributes to the very faculty of
perceiving moral qualities: or call his moral Sense morally Good or Evil,
any more than he calls the power of tasting, sweet or bitter—or the power
of seeing, straight or crooked, white or black." Gregory Vlastos cited it as
the chief example of self-predication in Plato:[33]

> In the *Protagoras* (330c–d) we get an even more striking text which,
> since first noticed by Goblot in 1929, has become the star instance of
> Self-Predication in Plato. Here Socrates roundly declares that justice
> is just and holiness holy. "What other thing could be holy, if holiness
> isn't holy," he asks, indignant at the idea that anyone could gainsay
> that holiness is holy.

It will be evident that the claim that justice and holiness are self-predicable
is absurd: it is moral agents, not moral virtues, which are capable of having
virtues and vices. The claim that justice cannot be unjust is then also
absurd: only what is capable of being unjust is capable of being just. That
holiness is holy has nothing whatever to do with whether anything else is
holy, or whether anything else is just. "Self-predication" is dialectically
sterile. The point of Socrates' argument is to show that justice is such as
holiness and holiness such as justice. That justice is just and holiness holy
not only does not establish this but is irrelevant to establishing it.

  Nor does Socrates claim that justice is just and holiness holy, for this
distorts the structure of the underlying Greek. A predicate adjective
agrees with its subject noun in gender, number, and case. But Socrates
uses not a cognate predicate adjective but a cognate adjective equivalent

32. Plato, vol. 2, p. 76 and note d.
33. "The Third Man Argument in the *Parmenides*," in R. E. Allen, *Studies in Plato's Metaphysics*, London, 1965, pp. 249–50, repr. from *Philosophical Review* 63 (1954), pp. 319–49. Cf.
Richard Robinson, *Plato's Earlier Dialectic*, 2d ed., Oxford, 1953, p. 234; C. C. W. Taylor,
Plato: Protagoras, Oxford, 1976, p. 112.

to a predicate noun. In ἡ ὁσιότης ὅσιον (330e 1), for example, ὅσιον is neuter nominative; since ὁσιότης is feminine, the literal translation cannot be that holiness is holy.

The literal translation might be that holiness is holiness. Greek usage differs from English in that syntactical adjectives may function as abstract substantives: δίκαιον and ὅσιον, with or without the neuter article, may be equivalent to δικαιοσύνη and ὁσιότης. But the context suggests that ὅσιον is in apposition with πρᾶγμα understood (see 330c 4–5, though see also 331c 4). If so, the proper translation is then that holiness is a holy thing: ὅσιον is a predicate adjective equivalent to a predicate noun, exactly as Socrates has shown.[34]

The use of a cognate predicate noun is pleonastic, in analogy to the cognate accusative, which repeats the idea contained in the main verb, whether transitive or intransitive. Accusatives may be cognate in both sense and form, or only in sense. In the first case, the cognate accusative has the same root as its corresponding verb: πολλὴν φλυαρίαν φλυαροῦντα, talking much nonsense, ἀρχὴν ἄρχειν, to hold an office, γραφὴν γράφεσθαι, to lay an indictment. The second kind of cognate accusative is an extension of the first: the accusative, though of different root, expresses a meaning akin to the verb: thus νίκην νικᾶν, to win a win, but μάχην νικᾶν, to win a fight. In English, one can fight a fight, but not win a win; the Greek use of cognate accusatives is far more extensive than English will comfortably allow, though English preserves, like a fly in amber, make a match, bake a batch.

The cognate accusative is matched by a cognate nominative. At *Protagoras* 324e, ἡ ἀπορία ἣν σὺ ἀπορεῖς has the force of "the perplexity which perplexes you." At *Laws* X 894a, γίγνεται δὴ πάντων γένεσις, becoming of all things becomes; at *Laches* 187b, κίνδυνος κινδυνεύηται, risk is risked; at *Phaedrus* 229d, λέγεται . . . ὁ λόγος, the tale . . . is told. Such examples are often treated as cognate accusatives in disguise, the direct object of the active verb becoming the subject of the passive—if they fight a battle, a battle is fought by them. This, however, is by no means always an adequate explanation of cognate nominatives: in Platonic Greek, love loves, thought thinks, the argument argues, without the slightest suggestion of passivity, or for that matter, "personification." Again, a cognate accusative may be used with adjectives; specifically, a neuter adjective may represent a cognate accusative, its noun being implied in the verb: μεγάλα

34. This accords with ordinary Platonic usage. Abstract nouns and collective nouns may take a neuter predicate adjective used as a noun. καλὸν ἡ ἀλήθεια, *Laws* 663e; ἀθάνατον ἄρα ἡ ψυχή, *Phaedo* 105e. The primitive force of the neuter singular is collective and thus abstract. See Goodwin, *Greek Grammar*, Boston, 1900, 925.

ἁμαρτάνειν (sc. ἁμαρτήματα), to commit great faults, αἰσχροὺς φόβους φοβοῦνται (360b), brave men do not fear shameful fears.

Cognate constructions, without modifying adjective, are in general pleonastic and therefore eliminable—if you fight a fight, you fight. ἡ ὁσιότης ὅσιον (330e 1), that holiness is a holy thing, or by nature such as to be holy (d 6), is strained English but natural Greek, a cognate predicate noun. The pleonasm is used to emphasize that holiness is something, πρᾶγμα τι (330d 4). This is clearly an existence claim, implicated with causality. The sentence "It could scarcely be that anything else would be holy, if holiness itself is not a holy thing" reduces to "It could scarcely be that anything else would be holy, if holiness itself is not something." That is, the existence of holiness is a condition for other things being holy, a relation which will be expressed by the instrumental dative (332b 1) and the genitive of agent (332d 7). The cognate construction implies that it is not only mistaken but manifest nonsense to suppose that holiness is by nature such as to be not holy, or unholy, as Protagoras, who is no metaphysician, agrees. You don't win a loss.

Socrates' further suggestion that justice is a holy thing and holiness a just thing represents the derivative use of a cognate adjective equivalent to a predicate noun; the adjectives are cognate in sense but not in form, and their use rests on his claim that holiness and justice are the same in themselves or in their function. If this is so, it could scarcely be that anything else would be just, if holiness itself is not something; the same applies, *mutatis mutandis,* for justice. So justice is such as holiness, and holiness such as justice.

The "star instance of self-predication in Plato" rests on a misunderstanding of Greek idiom.

The Unity of Temperance and Wisdom (332a–333b)

Socrates now offers a second argument. There is something called folly, and it is the opposite of wisdom. When men behave rightly and beneficially, they are temperate, and it is by temperance (instrumental dative) that they are temperate. People behave foolishly by folly, and Protagoras agrees that behaving foolishly is the opposite of behaving temperately.

There follows an ἐπαγωγή, a leading on or induction. What is done foolishly is done by foolishness; what is done temperately is done by temperance; what is done by strength is done strongly, by weakness weakly, with quickness quickly, with slowness slowly. In general, whatever is done in like manner is done by the same thing, and what is done in opposite manner is done by the opposite.

Socrates next proceeds to argue, by ἐπαγωγή once more, that no oppo-

site has more than one opposite. There is something beautiful, which has
no opposite except the ugly; something good, which has no opposite
except the evil; something high in pitch which has no opposite except the
low. In general, each opposite has only one opposite, not many.

Protagoras has agreed to all this, and it is now time to add things up.
He has agreed that each thing has one opposite, not many; that what is
done in an opposite way is done by opposites; that what is done temperately is done by (ὑπό + genitive of agent) temperance; that what is done
foolishly is done by folly; and that these are opposite beings. But Protagoras has also agreed that folly is the opposite of wisdom, and that one
thing has only one opposite. So he must abandon either the claim that one
thing has only one opposite, or the claim that temperance is different
from wisdom (333a–b).

This second elenchus has often been treated as merely verbal, but it
anticipates arguments from opposites used later to refute definitions in
the Academy,[35] and it has a foundation in common sense. It is reasonable
to claim that folly and wisdom are opposite, because sometimes the presence of one entails the absence of the other, and sometimes the absence of
one entails the presence of the other. It is reasonable to deny that a
temperate action can be foolish (cf. *Charmides* 160e–161b), or that an act
of folly can be temperate. Socrates' argument does not prove the unity of
temperance and wisdom, but offers considerations which incline the intellect: it suggests that temperance and wisdom are not detachable.

The Unity of Justice and Temperance (333b–334c)

Much against his will, Protagoras admits the difficulty Socrates has put,
and Socrates without pausing starts another argument, which Protagoras
will not allow him to conclude. Can a man who does injustice, Socrates
asks, be temperate in respect to what he unjustly does?

Protagoras replies that he himself would be ashamed to admit that,
though most people in fact believe it; he agrees to defend the view of the
Many so that Socrates can test the argument.

To be temperate is to be reasonable; and if reasonable men commit
injustice, it is because they are well advised in respect to what they unjustly
do. But they are well advised only if they fare and do well (εὖ πράττουσιν)
as the result of their injustice.

Next step: some things are good, and they are beneficial to men. But
here Protagoras demurs; he perhaps sees where the argument tends and
does not want to be driven to admit that either temperance is an evil or

35. H. F. Cherniss, *Aristotle's Criticism of Plato and the Academy*, Baltimore, 1944, pp. 36–37.

injustice is a good. Instead, he offers an essay on the relativity of goodness. Some good things are not useful to men but beneficial to horses, or
cattle, or dogs. Some are beneficial only to trees, or good for the roots but
not the branches. So various a thing is the good, and varied in kind.

Interlude: Questions and Speeches (334a–338e)

Provoked and harassed, unable to answer Socrates' peculiar questions,
Protagoras has abandoned short answers and launched into a speech. The
effect is to disrupt and very nearly conclude the discussion. Socrates
politely asks Protagoras to return to short answers, and when Protagoras
refuses, Socrates gets up to leave. The μακρολογία of rhetoric is a kind of
witchcraft, producing persuasion without rendering an account, as Protagoras's speech has already shown; little questions and short answers,
κατὰ βραχὺ διαλέγεσθαι, are of the essence, for Socratic dialectic rests on
mutual agreements, not speech and counterspeech.

Socrates is detained by his audience. Callias lays hold of his arm and
begs him to stay, defending Protagoras's right to speak in the way that
seems best to him. Alcibiades, young and contentious, urges that if Protagoras is to deny Socrates short answers, he should confess himself inferior to Socrates in argument. Critias asks Prodicus and Hippias to join him
in asking that the discussion continue. And at this point, Prodicus, perhaps not unhappy to be appealed to as an authority in a matter touching
Protagoras, helps matters along with a demonstration of right naming.

Next Hippias speaks. Protagoras had praised νόμος at the expense of
φύσις, convention or custom or law at the expense of nature, and condemned education in "the arts," arithmetic, astronomy, geometry, and
music. Hippias, who teaches the arts, takes this opportunity to condemn
νόμος and praise φύσις. He also recommends neither long speeches nor
short answers but medium speeches, with a referee to keep watch, presumably on mediumness. by a happy choice of metaphors, Socrates is to
loosen his reins while Protagoras is to refrain from stretching out his
reefing ropes and setting all sail; they are each to steer a middle course,
which, it appears, is only partly at sea.

The proposal, if not the metaphor, is applauded by everyone except
Socrates, who rejects it. Gauging his audience, he offers an argument
calculated to delight them. There can be no arbiter: for if the arbiter is
inferior to disputants, it is wrong for the inferior to oversee the superior;
if the arbiter is the equal of the disputants, he will do exactly as they do and
be superfluous; the arbiter can scarcely be superior to the disputants,
since no one is wiser than Protagoras.

Socrates next turns the tables with a counterproposal. If Protagoras does not wish to answer questions, let him ask them, and Socrates will answer, provided that when Protagoras has finished questioning, Socrates will have the right to question Protagoras. The whole company will oversee the discussion. There is forensic cunning in this. Socrates' proposal is at least speciously fair, and the good judgment of the audience has been quietly flattered: he has got the jury on his side. His suggestion is instantly approved and Protagoras, against his will, gives in: he will ask questions and then render an account to Socrates with short answers.

Part of the purpose of this interlude is structural. Plato often uses interludes as Shakespeare used clowns, to break the tension of the drama, to suspend action for a time so that the effect of action will be more sharply felt. Protagoras has failed to come to grips with the question of the unity of virtue. That question will be repeated at 349b and pursued through the rest of the dialogue; indeed, at the surface level at least, it is the main theme of the dialogue. This interlude marks the fact that it has been left unanswered and, preparing the way for its repetition, emphasizes its importance.

It does more. It indirectly restates the question with which the dialogue began: is Protagoras, or any sophist, competent to teach virtue? Protagoras has been unable to answer Socrates' peculiar questions about the nature of virtue, and came close to losing his temper because of it; this suggests that Protagoras does not understand what virtue is. What does the sophist teach? Can Protagoras teach virtue as he claims, if he does not know what it is he is teaching? or know that his teaching benefits rather than harms the souls of his pupils? Is Protagoras a physician of soul or, as Socrates has suggested, a merchant-importer of knowledge, indiscriminately commending a set of wares with no real notion of their worth? The interlude has been generated by failure to give short answers to questions; it implies a short answer to such questions as these.

From this point on, the tone of the *Protagoras* shifts. The discussion turns toward parody—parody on the part of both Plato and Socrates. Protagoras's speech was marked by force and dignity; he spoke directly to Socrates' first questions in a well-organized way, with balance of phrase and loftiness of conception and diction. Plato, among other marks of genius, had a precise and nearly infallible ear, and when Prodicus and Hippias speak, the ear turns openly satiric. Prodicus undertakes to settle a serious disagreement over the form of the discussion with a series of trivial distinctions between largely irrelevant words; he is a pedant, and it is idle to plead in his behalf that one man's pedantry is another man's scholarship. Hippias, a noted polymath whom Plato delighted in portraying as obtuse, uses an abstract theory whose meaning is dubious—the contrast between nature and convention—to recommend a suggestion which is wholly impractical, and seasons his wit with an atrocious concoction of metaphors. From this point on, Plato's characterizations become parody, and in that parody there is a strain of intellectual contempt.

If Plato has begun to parody, so has Socrates. The argument he uses to show that it would be improper to have an arbiter in the discussion is of a pattern Protagoras himself is known to have used. And Socrates wins the audience to his side as though it were a jury, in a way nicely calculated to excite the admiration of any sophist. Socrates, in short, has put his tongue in his cheek and begun to out-Protagoras Protagoras.

The element of parody will become increasingly prominent as the dialogue proceeds. But it is a mistake to suppose for that reason that the dialogue is meant as a mere *jeu d'esprit*. Behind the play of wit loom serious questions—of the moral worth of sophistry, of the nature of virtue, of the true good of the human soul. In dealing with those questions, the *Protagoras* means much more than it says.

What is at issue is more than an argument between two men. It is an issue of two cultures or, more accurately, two ways of life. It is not without symbolic force that at the end Protagoras will fall silent and Socrates will question and answer himself.[36] The λόγος, the argument, will itself become party to the discussion,[37] thought criticizing the thinker.

The Poem of Simonides

Protagoras Questions Socrates (338e–342a)

Life often imitates literature. The poets were the traditional moral teachers of Greece, and the interpretation of poetry was part of the stock in trade of the sophists, and specifically Protagoras (cf. 339a). After all, the poets too were "wise" and taught virtue; Protagoras regards them as his predecessors and, as his treatment of Simonides suggests, his rivals, for they were sophists too (cf. 316d).

So Protagoras will take up the question Socrates has raised and discuss it with reference to poetry, specifically to a poem of Simonides which

36. 353c–357e. Cf. *Gorgias* 506b–507c.
37. 361a–c.

Socrates admires and has carefully studied.[38] Protagoras thinks it contains a glaring inconsistency: Simonides says it is hard for a man to become good, but reproves Pittacus for saying that it is hard to be good.

The effect of this objection on Socrates is to stun him as though he'd been struck a blow; he becomes blind and dizzy from the effect of the words. In need of help, he appeals to Prodicus, with his expertise in distinguishing the meaning of words, to come to the aid of Simonides. Is it, Socrates asks, the same thing to be and to become, and Prodicus answers with a single word: "different."[39] Prodicus proves that he can give short answers—none shorter—even if Protagoras cannot.

With this agreement, Socrates establishes his defense. Simonides thinks it is hard to become good, whereas Pittacus thinks it is hard to be good. Since to be and to become are not the same, Simonides has not contradicted himself. And Socrates caps this excellent bit of literary criticism with a quotation from Hesiod, that it is difficult to become but easy to be virtuous.

This suits Prodicus, but Protagoras returns to the attack. Socrates' correction, he says, contains a worse error than the one he meant to correct: the poet would be foolish to say it is easy to possess virtue when everyone agrees it is the hardest thing of all. Once again Socrates appeals to Prodicus and the ancient lineage of his wisdom. What, Socrates asks Prodicus, did Simonides mean by hard?

"Bad," says Prodicus, and Socrates applies the appropriate interpretation. Simonides was blaming Pittacus for saying it is hard to be good because he thought Pittacus meant it was bad to be good. This explanation so pleases Prodicus that he drops his devotion to brevity and adds an

---

38. Plato's quotations from Simonides' poem (Fr. 4, Page edition) are the only source for it we have, and there has long been debate about the poem's structure and meaning. Adam and Adam's account of it (*Plato: Protagoras*, Cambridge, 1893, Appendix I) remains useful. See also Leonard Woodbury, "Simonides on *Arete*," *Transactions of the American Philological Association*, 1953, pp. 135–63; C. M. Bowra, *Greek Lyric Poetry*, 2d ed., Oxford, 1961; and A. W. H. Adkins, *Merit and Responsibility*, Oxford, 1960.

39. There is a difficulty of translation here. Pittacus has said that it is hard to be (ἔμμεναι) good, while Simonides has said that it is hard to become (γενέσθαι) good, and the distinction between being good and becoming good is one of which Socrates will shortly make a great deal. Why then does Protagoras assume that Pittacus and Simonides were saying the same thing? Because γενέσθαι in Greek may be used as equivalent to the verb to be, a feature which, with its ambiguity, cannot be preserved in translation. Simonides did not have this overlap in view, any more than he had in view the distinction between being and becoming which Socrates foists on him with the help of Prodicus. His reason for holding that it is hard for a man to become good in truth is that only god can have that privilege (341e, 344e); so he presumably condemned Pittacus for saying that it is hard for a man to be good on the ground that it was not hard but impossible.

explanation of his own: Simonides, a Cean like himself, was reproaching Pittacus, a poor Lesbian, for not knowing how to distinguish words correctly.

But Protagoras is unconvinced: Simonides, he thinks, meant by hard not bad but difficult. Socrates, whose standards of literary criticism are flexible, quickly agrees and cites internal evidence to support Protagoras's view. Prodicus must have been joking. But Socrates, if the audience wishes, will give his own interpretation of the poem. And the company, nothing loath, urges him on.

The Speech of Socrates (342a–347a)

Socrates begins with a brief account of the origin of φιλοσοφία, the love of wisdom. The most ancient roots of wisdom—sophistry—were in Crete and Sparta, though the people there pretend to be ignorant and conceal their wisdom. Their wisdom is the source of their power, and when they wish to take lessons from their wise men, their sophists, they expel all foreigners for the sake of secrecy; they also forbid their young people to travel abroad so that they won't unlearn what they've been taught at home. Not only are the Cretans and Spartans wise, but their wisdom is noted for its brevity; a man's ability to speak briefly is a mark of education. Compare the Seven Wise Men of Greece: Thales of Miletus, Pittacus of Mytilene, Bias of Priene, Solon of Athens, Cleobulus of Lindus, Myson of Chen, and Chilon of Sparta. The first fruits of their wisdom were the sayings Know thyself and Nothing too much. Ancient φιλοσοφία had this style of laconic brevity. So much for Protagoras's inability to give short answers.

This bears on Simonides' purpose in his poem. Pittacus offered the saying "It is hard to be good." Simonides, wishing to get a name for wisdom, realized that if he could overthrow the saying, he'd win fame among the men of his day, so he composed his whole poem to refute the saying of Pittacus. Socrates proceeds to analyze the poem in such a way as to support this remarkable interpretation. The element of satire is unmistakable in the strained grammatical analysis, and not least in the fact that Socrates, the proponent of short answers, has now answered Protagoras with a speech.

Socrates interjects into the interpretation of Simonides the principle that no man errs willingly, and that all wrongdoing is involuntary (345d–e). But he immediately goes on to suggest that bad men act voluntarily (346a) and that good men—Simonides, for example—often compel themselves to praise bad men. As Adam and Adam remark, "Socrates' exposition of the poem is intended to shew by a practical demonstration that poetry does not teach virtue because in poetry there is no knowledge."[40]

Interlude (347a–348c)

Having practiced on Simonides an exegetical technique which out-sophists the sophists, Socrates proceeds to dismiss literary criticism as worthless; poets cannot be questioned about what they mean, and the Many, in discussing them, argue about something they cannot test.[41] People talk about the poets for lack of ability to speak for themselves, as common folk invite flute-girls to drinking parties for lack of ability to converse. The right way to proceed is to meet in familiar intercourse and put one's self and the truth to the test, by rendering and receiving accounts of one's own.

This account of literary criticism, on Socratic principles, is inescapable. If dead poets cannot render an account of their work, live ones, as Socrates remarks in the *Apology* (22a–c; cf. *Meno* 99c, e), scarcely do better. Poets are said to be seized by a kind of divine madness induced by the Muses and akin to possession (*Phaedrus* 245a; cf. *Ion* 534b–c, 536c, 542a), though in fact they are also compared to rhetoricians (*Gorgias* 502c). In a quite literal sense, they do not know what they are talking about, and interpreting them cannot lead to knowledge. For that, dialectic, question and answer, is required.

The Unity of Virtue Revisited (348c–349d)

Shamed into answering by Alcibiades, Protagoras allows Socrates to resume questioning. Socrates begins with a disclaimer: he has no purpose except to inquire into what he is himself perplexed by, and he has turned to Protagoras because Protagoras publicly proclaims that he educates men and teaches virtue. The search for essence continues.

Socrates briefly recapitulates the argument to this point. The question was this: are wisdom, temperance, courage, justice, and holiness five

40. *Plato: Protagoras*, p. xxvi.

41. "Agreement on the proper interpretation of the piece seems no closer today than when Protagoras pointed out to Socrates the apparent 'contradiction' between Simonides' words at the beginning of the first and the beginning of the second stanzas. Nevertheless, most interpreters do agree that Simonides was making an important statement concerning the nature of man." Walter Donlan, "Simonides, Fr. 4D and P. Oxy. 2432," *Transactions of the American Philological Association*, 1969, p. 71.

names for a single thing, or is there a proper and peculiar reality (τις ἴδιος οὐσία) underlying each of these names, and each a thing having its own power (δύναμις) and one not such as (οἷον) another? Protagoras had said they are not names for one thing: each name applies to a thing peculiar to it, though all are parts of virtue; they are not parts like the parts of gold, which are similar to each other and to the whole of which they are parts; they are parts like the parts of the face, dissimilar to the whole of which they are parts and to each other, each having a proper and peculiar power.

Protagoras now thinks that four of the virtues resemble each other—he was shaken by Socrates' earlier arguments—but that courage is vastly different from the rest. The proof of this is that there are men who are preeminently courageous who are also unjust, unholy, intemperate, and unwise. Protagoras has made this claim before (329e), and not unreasonably: one thinks of Laches, the brave soldier who was also an embezzler.[42]

Even in this short answer to Socrates, however, Protagoras has broken the rules of debate. He had previously agreed to a disjunction: either the parts of virtue are all alike as pieces of good are all alike, or the parts of virtue are unlike both in themselves and in their functions, as the parts of the face—eyes, ears, nose—are unlike. He chose the latter. He cannot, therefore, within the frame of his previous agreement, claim that some of the virtues are like each other and others are not, and the fact that he does so indicates a failure in argument.

But through Protagoras has failed to keep to his own agreement, he sees clearly that he must defend detachability or wreck his argument. If a man can be courageous and unwise, then it is not the case that courage implies wisdom or knowledge.

The Unity of Wisdom and Courage (349e–351b)

Begin, then, with the assumption that one can be courageous but unwise. Protagoras supposes that courageous men are confident or daring or bold—all three adjectives translate θαρραλέος. Socrates leads him to agree that virtue is an excellence (καλόν τι), something beautiful or noble, and excellent as a whole; one cannot say that some part of it is defective or ugly or shameful (αἰσχρόν). It follows that since courage is a virtue, it cannot be a defect.

Socrates next proceeds to an induction. Those who dive boldly or

---

42. One may also think of *Politicus* 306a ff. where the Eleatic Stranger maintains the detachability of courage and temperance; it is clear that the Stranger is talking about action considered apart from the state of the soul of the agent.

daringly or confidently into wells possess the art of diving, but to possess an art is to possess knowledge. Those who are bold or daring or confident in cavalry fighting possess the art of horsemanship; those who are daring or bold or confident skirmishers possess the art of the peltast. In general, those who have knowledge are more daring or bold or confident than those who lack it, and more daring or bold or confident after they learn than before (350a). But some men behave daringly or boldly or confidently in these matters without knowing anything about them. Such men, Protagoras agrees, are overconfident and therefore not courageous, for courage is not a defect, and daring or boldness or confidence without knowledge is a defect. Such men behave as if they were mad. And Protagoras goes on to agree that the wisest are most courageous.

Socrates now has what he needs to draw his conclusion. Since those who are wise are confident or daring or bold, those who are wise are courageous. Therefore, wisdom or knowledge is courage. The virtues are not detachable; for those who are courageous are wise, and those who are wise are courageous.

The argument is of astonishing brilliance. Protagoras began by assuming that courage is detachable from other virtues: one can be courageous without being just or temperate or pious or wise. Since wisdom implies knowledge, Protagoras has assumed (i) that courage does not imply knowledge or wisdom (349d 2–8). Protagoras goes on to agree (ii) that the courageous are daring or bold or confident (350c 7–8), and further (iii) that those who are daring or bold or confident and do not have knowledge are not courageous (350c 1–2).

Now, (ii) and (iii) in conjunction imply that those who are courageous have knowledge: knowledge (or wisdom) is a necessary condition for courage. This contradicts (i). On the other hand, if (i) and (iii) are taken in conjunction, then those who have knowledge are courageous: knowledge is a sufficient condition for courage.

The reader may perhaps forgive a lapse into symbolism, as a crutch for those of us less able in reasoning than Socrates himself; the account sacrifices some degree of elegance for greater perspicuousness. Let C = those who are courageous, D = those who are daring or bold or confident, K = those who have knowledge or wisdom. Then, eschewing quantifiers, if:

(ii) $C \supset D$
(iii) $(D \;\&\; \sim K) \supset \sim C$
then: $C \supset K$.

This contradicts (i). On the other hand, (i) and (iii) in conjunction imply that those who have knowledge are courageous, that knowledge is a sufficient condition for courage. If:

(i) $\sim$(C $\supset$ K)
(iii) (D & $\sim$K) $\supset$ $\sim$C
then: K $\supset$ C

It may be uged that K $\supset$ C follows from $\sim$(C $\supset$ K) as one of the paradoxes of material implication; so (iii) is compatible with but adjunctive to (i) and the conclusion. But the argument may in fact be made still stronger. For if we assume, as is reasonable, that 350c 1–4 states not only that (D & $\sim$K) $\supset$ $\sim$C, but also that (D & K) $\supset$ C, then, given $\sim$(D $\supset$ C) (350b 1–6), it follows without more ado that K $\supset$ C, and C $\equiv$ K. That is, if daring and knowledge imply courage, and it is not the case that daring implies courage, then knowledge implies courage, and courage implies knowledge. The proof may be checked by a simple truth table.

For those who prefer their quantifiers chewed: if $\sim$(x) (Cx $\supset$ Kx) and (x) (Cx $\supset$ Dx) and (x) ((Dx & $\sim$Kx) $\supset$ $\sim$Cx), then (x) (Cx $\supset$ Kx). Given the additional premise (x) ((Dx & Kx) $\supset$ Cx), then (x) (Kx $\supset$ Cx), and therefore, (x) (Cx $\equiv$ Kx). The argument proceeds by natural deduction and subordinate proof.

Dialectically, if Protagoras denies that courage implies knowledge, he must affirm that knowledge implies courage; whether or not he denies that knowledge implies courage, he must affirm that courage implies knowledge. In either case, his detachability thesis collapses.

This refutes Protagoras's claim that courage is detachable from the other virtues, and therefore his claim that the virtues differ among themselves both in nature and in function. If wisdom and courage are equivalent, each introduces the other; if each introduces the other, they do not differ in function. Perhaps then they also do not differ in nature: equivalence, substitution *salve veritate*, if it is not identity, is a necessary condition for identity. Socrates' argument provides adequate ground for saying that wisdom or knowledge is courage (350c). Protagoras has suffered the argumentative equivalent of being hit by a truck; his very denial that the courageous are wise helps prove that wisdom is courage.

Faced with a conclusion that follows validly from premises he has himself admitted, Protagoras attacks the truth of the conclusion instead of reexamining the agreements which imply it.[43] He then slides off the

43. To anticipate the history of logic a little, Protagoras realizes that universal affirmative propositions cannot be converted *simpliciter*. He has granted, he says that, courageous men are daring, but not that daring men are courageous: C $\supset$ D does not imply D $\supset$ C. But Socrates' argument does not require D $\supset$ C for its validity, and in fact requires that it be false. Protagoras has flatly misunderstood the argument.

point, appealing to logical analogy to deny Socrates' claim that wisdom is courage: one might just as well argue that wisdom is strength, for the strong are powerful as the courageous are confident, and those who have learned how to wrestle are more powerful than those who have not, and more powerful after they've learned than before, so if wisdom is courage, wisdom is strength; but this does not follow, for as the confident are not thereby courageous, so the powerful are not thereby strong. Power or confidence derive from knowledge or madness or passion, as distinct from physical strength, but courage from nature and right nurture of soul.

All this, of course, is irrelevant, and Socrates rightly ignores it. But the task of dialectic is to proceed according to what the respondent admits to be true, and it is by a different argument that Socrates will lead Protagoras to agree, or more accurately cease denying, at 360d–e, that courage implies wisdom, on the ground that intemperance is ignorance and courage is knowledge of what is and is not to be feared.

"Conceptual Analysis"

We live in an age which talks much of logic—as well it should, if philosophy consists in the study of statement-relations—and that talk has affected talk about Plato, including talk about the *Protagoras*. It is not quite twenty-five years since Vlastos announced the value of "more sophisticated methods of conceptual analysis in platonic exegesis"[44] and suggested that because of those methods we can now understand Plato better than he understood himself; indeed, it seemed that Plato often misunderstood himself. Still, "only a puerile critic would make immunity to logical error the measure of a philosopher's greatness." Vlastos praised the new methods because they are fecund: their use much increased the volume of articles and books on Plato, which Vlastos thought a good thing.

Certainly the production of books and articles has proceeded apace. And if the "techniques of logical and semantic analysis" are neutral and do not involve philosophical assumptions of their own, what results from using those techniques may be free of anachronism. On the other hand, if those techniques involve debatable philosophical assumptions—for example, the neo-Kantian assumption in quantification theory that assertions of existence reduce to assertions that predicates are sometimes true—then this style of exegesis is far from neutral: it transposes into Ain't Nobody Here But Us Chickens. The use of "more sophisticated

44. *Plato*, vol. 1, New York, 1971, p. 2.

techniques of conceptual analysis" then involves anachronism, and its fecundity gives reason to consider whether Gresham's Law does not apply to scholarship. Indeed, one might see the reduction of existence to truth as a neo-Kantian attack on the possibility of metaphysics, carried forward by historians who "interpret" metaphysicians into nonsense. Ain't Nobody Here But Us Chickens, that is, transposes into the Trojan Horse.

The argument of *Protagoras* 349d–350c is of philosophical importance. The issue is whether a man can be courageous but unwise; most people believe that true, and the question is of interest to moral philosophy, for Socrates provides cogent reason to believe that it is not true. But the results of applying the techniques of "conceptual analysis" to his argument have been something less than encouraging.

Vlastos himself, in an introduction to Ostwald's revision of Jowett's translation of the *Protagoras*, discussed Socrates' argument in a section entitled "How Good Is His Logic?" He did not accurately identify the premises of the argument, seemed unaware of enthymeme, appeared to suggest that allowing letters to stand for propositions was by itself revelatory of "logical form," and at no point lifted his eyes to consider the philosophical importance of the argument, or that the conclusion that courage implies wisdom and is more than animal spirits just might be true. Vlastos had said, "I must preface this analysis by making clear that my knowledge of logic is elementary. This should encourage readers who know little or no modern logic, and put on their guard those who know a great deal."[45]

The passage continues to have a curious history. Despite its intrinsic philosophical interest and its importance to the argument of the *Protagoras*, Terence Irwin does not deal with it, though he touches on some of its premises;[46] Martha Nussbaum, in her discussion of the *Protagoras*,[47] ignores it. C. C. W. Taylor devotes eleven pages of logical analysis to the argument, concluding—if I have followed him—that the argument is invalid and Socrates is confused. The argument is of course valid, a fact which Taylor might have seen had he embraced the assumption, which is also a heuristic principle, that Plato's text makes sense. Taylor's account of the argument analyzes meaningful statements into logical formulae which are not well formed, unless some unstated bracketing convention is assumed, and instead of the horseshoe of material implication, which despite its paradoxes can be truth-functionally defined, uses an arrow

45. Gregory Vlastos and Martin Ostwald, *Plato: Protagoras*, new York, 1956, p. xxxi, n. 25.
46. Terence Irwin, *Plato's Moral Theory*, Oxford, 1977, chap. 4.
47. Martha C. Nussbaum, *The Fragility of Goodness*, Cambridge, 1986, chap. 4.

without defining what the arrow stands for.[48] Perhaps, then, this is not logic but an εἴδωλον of logic, the mote and the beam.

That Virtue Is Knowledge (351b–360e)

The concluding argument of the *Protagoras* is perhaps the most remarkable in all this remarkable dialogue. The proximate dialectical *demonstrandum* is that courage is not detachable from wisdom or knowledge. This follows as a corollary of a far more powerful argument, that knowledge is a sufficient condition for temperance, or perhaps more generally, that virtue is knowledge. The knowledge in question is knowledge of good and evil, which is taken to be knowledge of the relative weight of pleasures and pains, present and prospective. The argument presupposes the hedonic equation of pleasure and goodness. Socrates will show on the premise of hedonism that intemperance is ignorance, and that no man is courageous but unwise.

In the *Meno,* Socrates borrows a method from the geometers and undertakes to inquire by hypothesis, asking what a proposition implies. Socrates perhaps in the *Protagoras* also borrows from the geometers, but to different effect: his argument is a dialectical analogue of geometrical analysis and synthesis.

Analysis is a method of discovering proofs of theorems or solutions to problems; it proceeds by asserting a proposition as given and reducing it, by successive stages, to a conclusion whose truth-value is known; *reductio ad absurdum* is a particular kind of analysis which reduces to a conclusion known to be false. Analysis is characteristically followed by synthesis, which not only acts as a check on the accuracy of the analysis, but consti-

---

48. Perhaps, it will be suggested, it stands for a conditional if-then, rather than material implication. But there are many if-thens. There is the contrary-to-fact conditional—εἰ with the protasis, ἄν with the apodosis, verb imperfect indicative of aorist—which is false if the protasis is true, that is, if the condition is fulfilled. There is the present-general conditional—ἐάν or ἄν with the subjunctive in the protasis, present indicative in the apodosis—which is false if the protasis is false, that is, if the condition is not fulfilled. There is the future-less-vivid conditional, should/would—εἰ with the optative in the protasis, ἄν with the optative in the apodosis—in which no truth-value or fulfillment of the condition but some element of relevance—causal, intensional, contextual—is distinctly supposed. And there are so many more that the grammar books often simply speak of "mixed conditionals," and let it go at that. English is a more analytic (or more eroded) language than Greek, but if grammatical flags have been lost, the complexity of the conditional remains. Taylor's arrow, if it is meant to stand for a conditional, does not indicate what kind of conditional, and is undefined.

tutes an actual proof or solution to the problem.[49] Logically, analysis and synthesis run horseshoes between the same propositions in opposite directions, and thus issue in equivalence. Definitions of analysis and synthesis are interpolated into Euclid XIII 1–5, and Heath supposed them to be Pythagorean, that is to say, pre-Platonic.[50]

Socrates will here assume as a given that pleasure and goodness are equivalent, as though that which is sought were already done. In exactly the same way he assumes that knowledge is a sufficient condition for temperance or continence. Instead of deducing consequences from these two propositions as from a hypothesis, Socrates elicits from Protagoras and the Many, the majority of men, denial of the first proposition, and from the many, though not Protagoras, denial of the second proposition, and in both cases shows that by their denial they assume what they deny. That is, there are two analyses, which issue in a sequence of dialectical reductions to absurdity. They stand as lemmata for the final proof that courage is not detachable from knowledge. Because the argument is dialectical, because it has to do with what the parties to it believe and what they mean, certain of its propositions are both intentional and intensional—"You say p but you mean q"—so the argument cannot be reduced to extensional or truth-functional relations.

The results of the analysis of the proposition that knowledge is a sufficient condition for temperance or continence are used in a synthesis, that is, a proof, of that same proposition (358b–d), a proof in which the equivalence of pleasure and goodness is an essential premise. No synthesis, however, is provided for the equivalence of pleasure and goodness. That is, there is no proof beyond a reduction to the opinion of the Many.

It may be, then, that the first readers of the *Protagoras* were meant to recognize, and would have recognized, that Socrates is using a dialectical variant of a mathematical form of inquiry and proof. If so, his argument as directed toward Protagoras is not without irony, even sarcasm: for Protagoras published a refutation of the geometers, denying that their

49. Socrates uses a dialectical analogue of synthesis in using the hedonic equation of pleasure and goodness to prove that virtue is knowledge or, more precisely, that knowledge is a sufficient condition for temperance. Significantly, there is no synthesis of the hedonic equation itself.

50. T. L. Heath, *The Thirteen Books of Euclid's Elements*, 2d ed., New York, 1956, i 137–42; cf. iii 442–43. See also Heath, *History of Greek Mathematics*, Oxford, 1921, vol. 1, pp. 371–72, 291, and vol. 2, p. 400. The present discussion of analysis and synthesis is based on Heath's account, which was questioned by Cornford in "Mathematics and Dialectic in the *Republic*, VI VII," *Mind*, n.s. 41, 43–47, but successfully defended by Richard Robinson in "Analysis in Greek Geometry," *Essays in Greek Philosophy*, Oxford, 1969. It is further support for Heath's account that it should so neatly fit, *mutatis mutandis*, the *Protagoras*.

reasoning, with its lengthless points and breadthless lines, dealt with reality,[51] and this coheres with the contempt for mathematics he expresses at 318d–e. Perhaps it also coheres with Zeno's rejection of the possibility of finite magnitude, a rejection which has implications for the development of a metric of pleasure.

The Hedonic Equation (351b–e)

Socrates now elicits Protagoras's agreement that some men live well (εὖ ζῆν), others badly. No man lives well if he lives in misery and pain; if a man lives out his life pleasantly, he has lived well. So to live pleasantly is good, and to live unpleasantly is bad. This implies that to live pleasantly and to live well are equivalent.

Protagoras agrees that to live well is to live pleasantly, but only on a condition: "Yes, if he lives pleasantly with excellent, or beautiful, or noble, or good things" (351c). Socrates questions him. Surely Protagoras does not agree with οἱ πολλοί, the Many, who call some pleasant things bad and some painful things good; on the contrary, things insofar as they are pleasant are good, and insofar as they are painful bad. But Protagoras is doubtful: "Relative not only to my present answer but to the rest of my whole life, I think it safer to reply that some pleasant things are not good, and again, some painful things are not bad, and some are, and there is a third kind which is neither good nor bad" (351d). He had earlier denied that one can be temperate and do injustice, though the Many, most people, the majority, claim it to be true (333b–c); but he is perhaps not quite consistent in this, for he also thought men may be courageous but unjust, or just but not wise (329e), and in his speech had put forward the Many as moral authorities.

Socrates suggests that things which either partake of pleasure[52] or cause pleasure are pleasant; since pleasure is a good thing, things which cause pleasure are pleasant, and things which are pleasant are good. "I'm asking whether pleasure in itself is not a good thing."

In the *Republic* (II 357d–c), Glaucon distinguishes goods that we choose for their own sake, such as harmless pleasures without further consequences, from goods which we choose only for their consequences, such as exercise and being healed and making money; both classes are to be distinguished from things which are good both in themselves and in their consequences, such as understanding, sight, and health. The difference between Thrasymachus and Socrates is that Thrasymachus, along

---

51. Aristotle, *Metaphysics* III 998a3. Cf. Diogenes Laertius IX 55.

52. Socrates is imitating Protagoras's language in his myth, where μετέχειν δικαιοσύνης (323a 6; cf. 322d 2, 5), "to partake of justice," means "to be just."

with the Many, thinks that justice is only instrumentally good, whereas Socrates thinks it is good not only in its consequences but in itself (358a). Measured against this distinction, the gap between living justly and living pleasantly cannot be bridged.

Socrates has suggested that the Many, in claiming that there are good pains and bad pleasures, are mistaken: just insofar as things are pleasant, they are in that respect good, unless something else follows from them; things are in like manner bad just insofar as they are painful. So pleasure in itself is always a good thing. Since this is meant to contradict the view of the Many that some pleasures are bad and some pains are bad, it must imply that all pleasures, whatever their source, are good. Socrates' account treats pleasure and pain in abstraction from their context: pleasure in itself is good, pain in itself is evil. This is hardly an incontrovertible claim, if the pleasure taken in wrong action is an inducement to repeat it, and the pain of right action an inducement not to repeat it.[53]

Protagoras restates this as the claim that pleasant and good are the same. That is, minimally, they are equivalent, as introducing each other: whatever is good is pleasant, and whatever is pleasant is good. Call this the hedonic equation.[54] It is to be distinguished from the view that pleasure is a good and pain an evil, which is compatible with the claim that there are other goods better worth choosing, and evils more to be avoided.

In putting forward the hedonic equation, Socrates has not adopted a theory but offered the first step in a dialectical analysis: for he will shortly prove that the Many, who say that some pleasures are not good, in fact assume that pleasure is the good. Protagoras agrees that the question should be examined, and if pleasant and good prove to be the same, he will concede it. Since Socrates began the argument, he should lead the inquiry.

Protagoras claims he would live differently if he adopted hedonism. John Stuart Mill in *Utilitarianism* suggested that the principle "that pleasure, and freedom from pain, are the only things desirable as ends" is "a theory of life," a theory with practical consequences for moral choice.

53. Compare Mill in *Utilitarianism:* "Let, then, pleasure be defined as feeling which the sentient individual at the time of feeling it implicitly or explicitly apprehends to be desirable;—desirable, that is, when considered merely as feeling, and not in respect of its objective conditions or consequences, or of any facts that come directly within the cognisance and judgement of others besides the sentient individual."

54. Since "pleasant" may mean not only pleasure but what is productive of pleasure, "good" presumably may mean not only what is good in itself but what is instrumentally good. This wrecks the hedonic equation and therefore the argument which will depend on it, since what is productive of pleasure may be unpleasant—medical treatment, for example. Socrates' equation is ambiguous according to a distinction he himself has introduced, unless we understand pleasant to mean pleasure in and by itself, in abstraction from what produces it.

George Grote, perhaps the ablest of all commentators on the *Protagoras* and certainly the most sympathetic, found in it virtually the whole of Bentham's hedonism, as distinct from his utilitarianism:[55]

> I perfectly agree with the doctrine laid down by Sokrates in the Protagoras, that pain or suffering is the End to be avoided or lessened as far as possible—and pleasure or happiness the End to be pursued as far as attainable—by intelligent forethought and comparison; that there is no other intelligible standard of reference, for application of the terms Good and Evil, except the tendency to produce happiness or misery: and that if this standard be rejected, ethical debate loses all standard for rational discussion, and becomes only an enunciation of the different sentiments, authoritative and self-justifying, prevalent in each community.

Living Well

Hedonism is the doctrine that pleasure is the ultimate human good and the chief aim of human striving. In short, hedonism is teleological: it defines goodness in terms of a goal and identifies that goal with pleasure. In this it both agrees and disagrees with the chief tenet of Socratic ethics, which defines goodness in terms of a goal and identifies that goal with justice or virtue. There is no evidence in dialogues other than the *Protagoras* that Socrates ever argued that pleasure and goodness are equivalent. On the contrary: Socrates consistently argues that they are not equivalent, on the ground that there can be bad pleasures and good pains.

The touchstone of Plato's moral theory in the early and early middle dialogues is the *Crito*. In the *Crito*, as in the *Protagoras*, Socrates assumes that life has an aim or purpose, and that the aim is not merely to live but to live well (εὖ ζῆν). But whereas Socrates in the *Protagoras* suggests that to live well is to live pleasantly, in the *Crito* he suggests that to live well is to live justly. The *Crito* does not use the word *soul* but refers to "whatever it is of ours to which justice and injustice pertain" (47d–48a), and contrasts this to the body as of higher worth. Life is not worth living if that of ours which is benefitted by justice is harmed by injustice. Socrates' argument in the *Crito* is an example of the Socratic Proportion: that Justice is to the Soul as Health is to the Body. Granting that soul is of greater worth than body, the question of whether Socrates should escape reduces to the question of whether it is just or unjust for him to do so (48b–d; cf. *Apology* 29c–30c). This is equivalent to the question whether escape will harm or benefit the

55. *Plato*, vol. 2, pp. 81–82.

soul. It is for the good of his soul, not, surely, of his body, that Socrates refuses to escape from prison and accepts his own sentence of death.

The *Crito* almost certainly represents the reasoning of the historical Socrates. It is probable that Socrates could have escaped, and that he refused; if he refused, he had reasons; if he had reasons, the *Crito* may be taken to present them.

The account of living well in the *Crito* is not only distinct from but incompatible with the hedonic equation of the *Protagoras*. As a matter of common sense, the aim of pleasant living precludes voluntary acceptance of a death sentence on grounds of justice. To a hedonist, justice is another's good and may well be one's own harm, for what is useful or good is what contributes to one's own pleasure. Justice has only instrumental value in attaining pleasure, and it is therefore in general better to do injustice than to suffer it. In the *Crito,* Socrates argues that one must never do injustice or return injustice for injustice, and that one must therefore never work injury or do evil in return for having suffered it. To do injustice is to harm others in respect to their proper excellence, as escape from prison harms the proper excellence of the Laws of Athens; it is thereby to harm one's own soul. Justice is not a means to living well, but constitutive of living well. It is therefore always better to suffer injustice than to do it, a proposition flatly incompatible with hedonism (49d):

> Look to this, Crito. Do not agree against your real opinion, for I know that few men think or will ever think it true. Between those who accept it and those who do not, there is no common basis for decision: when they view each others' counsels, they must necessarily hold each other in contempt. So consider very carefully whether you unite with me in agreeing that it can never be right to do injustice or return it, or to ward off the suffering of evil by doing it in return, or whether you recoil from this starting point. I have long thought it true and do still. If you think otherwise, speak and instruct me.

Hedonism is teleological in that pleasure is the end, and virtue, to the degree that it is good, a means to that end. Socratic moral theory is teleological in that virtue is the end, intrinsically good in and of itself, good for its own sake. It is constitutive of and not merely a means to goodness of soul.

The hedonic equation is not only inconsistent with the moral theory of the *Crito*: It is also inconsistent with Socrates' account of his mission to Athens in the *Apology* (30a–b), motivated by care for the souls of his fellows; it is therefore inconsistent with the concern for the soul and the danger to it of sophistry which Socrates expresses to Hippocrates at the beginning of the *Protagoras* (312b–314c), where he identifies the soul with the self. Socrates' analysis of living well in terms of hedonism continues the element of parody which marks the interlude at 334a–338e, including the parody which he offers, in comment on Simonides, of his own principle that no one voluntarily does wrong (345d–e, 346a).

Ancient Hedonism

The hedonism Socrates expounds in the *Protagoras*, if it involves parody, has nevertheless proved over time to be conceptually fertile. Aristotle anticipates Bentham in remarking that "the study of pleasure and pain belongs to the province of the political philosopher; for he is the architect of the end, with a view to which we call one thing bad and another good without qualification";[56] but Aristotle then turns to consider the claim, derived from Plato's *Philebus*, that the best thing cannot be pleasure, because pleasure is not an end but a process and therefore essentially incomplete.

As a moral theory, hedonism has often been thought true because it seems to be based on immediate experience and seems to provide an empiricist basis for ethics: "Pain and pleasure, at least, are words which a man has no need, we may hope, to go to a Lawyer to know the meaning of." So Bentham. Hedonism seems to offer in moral matters a guide to the perplexed, to provide an objective and verifiable foundation for moral judgment. But Henry Sidgwick, analyzing more closely, found the matter more obscure (*The Methods of Ethics*):

> When we speak of a man doing something "at his pleasure" or "as he pleases," we usually signify the mere fact of voluntary choice: not necessarily that the result aimed at is some prospective feeling in the chooser. . . . Now, if by "pleasant" we merely mean that which influences choice, exercises a certain attractive force on the will, it is an assertion incontrovertible because tautological, to say that we desire what is pleasant [p. 42]. . . . But if we take "pleasure" to denote the kind of feelings, above defined, it becomes a really debatable question whether the end to which our desires are always consciously directed is the attainment by ourselves of such feelings" [p. 44]. . . . In fact, the doctrine that pleasure (or the absence of pain) is the end of all human action can neither be supported by the results of introspection, nor by the results of external observation and inference: it rather seems to be reached by an arbitrary and illegitimate combination of the two" [p. 53].

56. *Nicomachean Ethics* VII 1152b 1–3, trans. Ross.

Concerning the nature of pleasure, the ancient schools divided over an issue which is left unclear in the *Protagoras*: whether pleasure and pain are contraries, in that one should be conceived to be the privation of the other, or whether they are distinct feelings or sensations which may coincide or coexist. It is tolerably certain that the Cyrenaic school began with Aristippus of Cyrene, an immediate member of the Socratic circle (cf. *Phaedo* 59c); accounts of his association with Socrates are provided by Xenophon in several places in the *Memorabilia*.[57] Aristotle dismissed Aristippus as a sophist, allied with Protagoras in his skepticism of mathematics (*Metaphysics* II 996a 32–35), and does not mention him in his own discussion of pleasure in the *Nicomachean Ethics* (VII 11–14). Still, the view that pleasure is the good found a home in the Academy, for it was sponsored by Eudoxus.[58] The account of Aristippus offered by Diogenes Laertius preserves a good deal of Hellenistic gossip and scandal-mongering, but often has the ring of truth. The following account probably derives mainly from the Stoic historian of philosophy Panaetius:[59]

> Those then who adhered to the teaching of Aristippus and were known as Cyrenaics held the following opinions. They laid down that there are two states, pleasure and pain, the former a smooth, the latter a rough, motion, and that pleasure does not differ from pleasure, nor is one pleasure more pleasant than another. The one state is agreeable, the other repellent to all living things. . . . Our end is particular pleasure, whereas happiness is the sum total of all particular pleasures, in which are included past and future pleasures. . . . That pleasure is the end is proved by the fact that from our youth up we are instinctively attracted to it, and, when we obtain it, seek for nothing more, and shun nothing so much as its opposite, pain. . . . The removal of pain, however, which is put forward in Epicurus, seems to them not to be pleasure at all, any more than the absence of pleasure is pain. For both pleasure and pain they hold to consist in motion, whereas absence of pleasure like absence of pain is not motion, since painlessness is the condition of one who is, as it were, asleep. . . . Pleasure is good even if it proceed from the most unseemly conduct. . . . For even if the action be irregular, still, at any rate, the resultant pleasure is desirable for its own sake and is good.

57. E.g. II i, III viii.
58. *Nicomachean Ethics* X 1172b 9–25.
59. *D.L.* II. 86 ff., trans. R. D. Hicks. See further Henry Sidgwick, *History of Ethics*, 6th ed., London, 1931, pp. 32–33.

For Aristippus, then, pleasure is not equivalent to absence of pain: pleasure and pain consist in motion, smooth or rough, and the absence of the one does not imply the presence of the other. Pleasure is positive enjoyment, pain active suffering. If this is true, one on occasion may feel neither pleasure nor pain, or feel a mixture of pleasure and pain at the same time.[60] This is in fact the doctrine of Plato's *Republic* and *Philebus* in respect to bodily pleasures; one thinks of Socrates in the *Phaedo*, rubbing his recently fettered leg and offering an Aesopian fable about how pleasure and pain are joined at the head.

Epicurus offered a different theory: his concept of pleasure is negative, the absence of pain, and his hedonism less a goal of life than a means to salvation. Philosophy, he thought, "is a practical activity, intended by means of speech and reasoning to secure a happy life by saving mankind from the two great terrors which might disturb their lives, the dread of arbitrary interference of divine beings in the world and the fear of punishment of the soul after death."[61] The great Epicurean fears, that is, are divine providence and immortality—the eschatology of the great myth of the *Gorgias,* and the foundation of *Laws* X—and the primary aim of life is serenity, undisturbedness, ἀταραξία. The result is an ascetic hedonism which has much in it of the sheltered garden and little enough of the stews and the fleshpots:[62]

> When we say, then, that pleasure is the end and aim, we do not mean the pleasures of the prodigal of the pleasures of sensuality, as we are understood to do by some through ignorance, prejudice, or wilful misrepresentation. By pleasure we mean the absence of pain in the body and trouble in the soul. It is not an unbroken succession of

60. Sidgwick (*The Methods of Ethics,* 7th ed., London, 1962, p. 124) argued for a hedonistic zero: "If pleasure, then, can be arranged in a scale, as greater or less in some finite degree; we are led to the assumption of a hedonistic zero, or perfectly neutral feeling, as a point from which the positive quantity of pleasures may be measured. And this latter assumption emerges still more clearly when we consider the comparison and balancing of pleasures with pains, which Hedonism necessarily involves. For pain must be reckoned as the negative quantity of pleasure, to be balanced against and subtracted from the positive in estimating happiness on the whole; we must therefore conceive, as at least ideally possible, a point of transition in consciousness at which we pass from the positive to the negative." The arithmetical analogy is dubious: the sum of plus 10 and minus 10 is the same as the sum of plus 1 and minus 1, yet it seems unmeaning to claim that the sum of very intense pleasures and pains is equal to the sum of very mild pleasures and pains, and false to claim that it amounts to a perfectly neutral feeling. And if we may feel pleasure and pain at the same time, it is surely mistaken to define pain as the negative quantity of pleasure: less pleasure does not imply more pain and, even if pathologically, more pain does not always imply less pleasure.

61. Cyril Bailey, *The Greek Atomists and Epicurus,* Oxford, 1928, p. 233.

62. Epicurus, *Letter to Menoeceus,* trans. Hicks. See also Sidgwick, *History of Ethics,* pp. 86–90.

drinking-bouts and of revelry, not sexual love, not the enjoyment of the fish and other delicacies of a luxurious table, which produce a pleasant life; it is sober reasoning, searching out the grounds of every choice and avoidance, and banishing those beliefs through which the greatest tumults take possession of the soul. Of all this the beginning and the greatest good is prudence.

So for Epicurus pleasure is a goal or end, but that end is not positive enjoyment but absence of pain; temperance is the foundation of all virtue.[63] It is a doctrine which would pass to Rome in great poetry, the *De rerum naturae* of Lucretius. Socrates in the *Protagoras* nowhere pronounces on this issue; he does not say what pleasure is. But pleasure and pain are treated as contraries if good and evil are contraries, and the aim of life is described as peace of soul (356e). There are many echoes of the *Protagoras*, conceptual and linguistic, in both Cyrenaic and Epicurean thought: the dialogue was seminal in the subsequent history of Hedonism.

Utilitarianism

Hedonism has been associated with utilitarianism, the doctrine that in all cases, good and evil are to be determined summatively, as the greatest good of the greatest number. So, for example, John Stuart Mill in chapter II of *Utilitarianism*:

> The creed which accepts as the foundation of morals, Utility, or the Greatest Happiness Principle, holds that actions are right in proportion as they tend to promote happiness, wrong as they tend to produce the reverse of happiness. By happiness is intended pleasure, and the absence of pain; by unhappiness, pain, and the privation of pleasure. To give a clear view of the moral standard set up by the theory, much more requires to be said; in particular, what things it includes in the ideas of pain and pleasure, and to what extent this is left an open question. But these supplementary explanations do not affect the theory of life on which this theory of morality is grounded —namely, that pleasure, and freedom from pain, are the only things

63. Sidgwick used his notion of a hedonistic zero to deny this: "I have by implication denied the paradox of Epicurus, that the state of painlessness is equivalent to the highest possible pleasure; so that if we can obtain absolute freedom from pain, the goal of Hedonism is reached, after which we may vary, but cannot increase, our pleasure. This doctrine is opposed to common sense and common experience" (*Methods of Ethics*, p. 125). But if the hedonistic zero is a piece of faulty analysis, and if the best we can hope for in the vagaries of this changeful life is serenity of soul, Epicureanism and Stoicism, with their ideal of undisturbedness, hold out a goal which experience and common sense have often been led to approve.

desirable as ends; and that all desirable things (which are as numerous in the utilitarian as in any other scheme) are desirable either for the pleasure inherent in themselves, or as means to the promotion of pleasure and the prevention of pain.

But this is a marriage of inconvenience. Grote criticized Mill for confusing the greatest happiness of the agent and the greatest happiness of the greatest number, and claimed the doctrine of the *Protagoras* is true but incomplete (pp. 82–83; cf. 123):

> The doctrine of Sokrates in the Protagoras requires to be enlarged so as to comprehend these other important elements. Since the conduct of every agent affects the happiness of others, he must be called upon to take account of its consequences under both aspects, especially where it goes to inflict hurt or privation upon others. Good and evil depend upon that scientific computation and comparison of pleasures and pains which Sokrates in the Protagoras prescribes: but the computation must include, to a certain extent, the pleasures and pains (security and rightful expectation) of others besides the agent himself.

But it is more than a matter of incompleteness, given that hedonism, defined in terms of the interests of the individual, and utilitarianism, defined as the greatest good of the greatest number, are on occasion incompatible. For utilitarianism represents an attempt at a theory of justice, conceived as arithmetical equality: each counts for one and none for more than one, as Bentham put it. The pleasure of the agent is of no greater, and no less, importance than the pleasure of those affected by his actions. Yet this seems to remove the main prop of hedonism, which is egoistic.

Bentham was a psychological hedonist: we are so made psychologically that, as moth flies to flame, we inevitably choose the experience which promises to be most pleasant.[64] "Nature has placed mankind under the governance of two sovereign masters, pain and pleasure. It is for them alone to point out what we ought to do, as well as to determine what we shall do. . . . They govern us in all we do, in all we say, in all we think: every effort we can make to throw off our subjection will but serve to demonstrate and confirm it." So begins *The Principles of Morals and Legislation*. Yet

64. The phrase "psychological hedonism" was coined by Sidgwick in *The Methods of Ethics*: it is the thesis that "volition is always determined by pleasures or pains actual or prospective" (p. 40), or that the end of action "is definitely determined for me by unvarying psychological laws" (p. 40), and that pleasure is "the actual ultimate end of my action" (p. 41).

Bentham's psychological hedonism is unclear. It may mean that we are so constituted as to pursue only the pleasures of the moment; Callicles in the *Gorgias* comes close to suggesting this, and there is reason to think it was the Cyrenaic view; but it is clearly false, for one may forgo present pleasures to attain future ones. Or it may mean that we are so constituted as to pursue the sum of pleasures over a period of time, the pleasant life in the long run; Socrates in the *Protagoras* comes close to suggesting this, but it also is clearly false, since one may forgo greater good for the pleasures of the moment. Bentham, like Socrates, would no doubt have argued that in either case the common factor is pleasure.

If Bentham was a psychological hedonist, he was also a utilitarian: whether an action is right or wrong is determined by its consequences, and the value of its consequences is measured by the pleasure and pain not only of the agent but of all sentient beings. Bentham accordingly argued that not only men but animals have rights which ought to be respected; they have rights not because they are rational or possess the gift of speech, but because they suffer. This is an important and admirable result, yet as Sidgwick pointed out (*Methods of Ethics*, pp. 84–85), it is difficult to reconcile with psychological hedonism: "From Bentham's psychological doctrine, that every human being always does aim at his own greatest apparent happiness, it seems to follow that it is useless to point out to a man the conduct that would conduce to the general happiness, unless you convince him at the same time that it would conduce to his own." In attempting to reconcile psychological hedonism with utilitarianism, there is an inherent conflict between individual and social good—a conflict, if you will, between interest and duty.

Bentham saw this and tried to solve the problem by holding that, since the policy most conducive to general happiness is not always conducive to the happiness of the individual, the conflict between one's own good and the public good must be resolved by the legislator in the use of sanctions, and specifically punishment. By the use of sanctions, self-regarding individuals might be made to act as if they were other-regarding, and the latent conflict between the good of the individual and the good of society overcome. In this way, the father of liberalism gave a philosophical justification for tyranny: the legislator is also a man who will act in his own interest and order the motives of others accordingly; government is moved by the self-interest of those who govern, unsanctioned by their own laws. Legal positivism and a legally unlimited and illimitable sovereign are the legitimate offspring of Benthamite utilitarianism. So, it may be said, is Marxism. The brocard of the *Communist Manifesto*, "From each according to his abilities, to each according to his needs," is a rewriting of the principle of utility and its implicit collectivism. The legal philosophy of communism, like liberalism, has been unremittingly positivist: law may have any content, and so long as the state endures, the sovereign is illimitable.

There is no necessary implication between hedonism and utilitarianism. One may suppose that moral obligation or duty is to be defined in terms of the greatest good for the greatest number without supposing that pleasure is the good; one may suppose that pleasure is the good, the goal of one's own life, without caring except instrumentally about the good of others. Utilitarianism is a distinctively modern theory, and the criterion it offers—that we ought to pursue the greatest good for the greatest number, and therefore on Benthamite grounds that we ought to pursue the greatest pleasure, ours or another's—is implicitly inconsistent with psychological hedonism. Both Aristippus and Epicurus suppose that the goal of life is each individual's own pleasure; nor is there anything in the statement of hedonism in the *Protagoras* to suggest otherwise. Psychological hedonism implies psychological egoism. In any case, whether hedonism as a theory of the good describes how men in fact behave or prescribes how they ought to behave—that is, whether hedonism is offered as a psychological theory or an ethical theory—is a distinction which the hedonism of the *Protagoras* renders vacuous: to say that there is a duty to pursue pleasure, or that one ought to pursue pleasure, one's own or another's, is to say that it is good to pursue pleasure; to say that it is good to pursue pleasure is to say that it is pleasant to pursue pleasure, and this is not an ethical claim, though it is often false. The distinction between psychological and ethical hedonism is one which can be consistently drawn only if one is not a hedonist.

The Authority of Knowledge (352a–353b)

Socrates now proceeds to state a second proposition to be solved by dialectical analysis. Protagoras must uncover more of his thought. Specifically, how does he regard knowledge?[65] Protagoras agrees with Socrates that wisdom or knowledge is the ruling principle of human life. The Many think that knowledge is a poor slave to be dragged about by the passions— by anger and pleasure and pain, sometimes by love, often by fear. They are mistaken. Knowledge is a thing of power and authority: if one once knows good from evil, he cannot but do what knowledge commands. Both Socrates and Protagoras agree to this, and their agreement is compelled, for Socrates has already argued the unity of wisdom and temperance on

65. 352b–c.

the ground that they have folly as a common opposite[66] (332a–333b), while Protagoras claims to teach virtue, and if virtue is teachable, it must be knowledge. If knowledge cannot be overcome by fear, this suggests that knowledge is a sufficient condition for courage.

The Many, however, think men may know what is best but refuse to do it, and the reason, they claim, is that they are bested or worsted or overcome (ἡττωμένους) by pleasure or pain—the common-sense notion of intemperance—or mastered (κρατουμένους) by anger, love, and fear. So, for example, Euripides' Medea claimed that though she knew it was wrong to murder her children, her fury was stronger than her thought.[67] It is an extreme case of the self divided in conflict of motives, and Henry Sidgwick, at least, regarded the possibility of such conflict as a plain deliverance of ordinary moral consciousness (*Methods of Ethics*, p. 39):

> This conception of Reason as an external authority, against which the self-will rebels, is often irresistibly forced on the reflective mind: at other times, however, the identity of Reason and Self presents itself as an immediate conviction, and then Reverence for Authority passes over into Self-respect; and the opposite and even more powerful sentiment of Freedom is called in, if we consider the rational Self as liable to be enslaved by the usurping force of sensual impulses.

But if Socrates and Protagoras are right against the Many, the rational self cannot be usurped by sensual impulses and men are never unfree.

Aristotle took Socrates' argument to amount to denial of ἀκρασία, incontinence:[68]

> Now we may ask how a man who judges rightly can behave incontinently. That he should behave so when he has knowledge, some say is impossible; for it would be strange—so Socrates thought—if when knowledge was in a man something else could master it and drag it about like a slave. For Socrates was entirely opposed to the view in question, holding that there is no such thing as incontinence; no one, he said, when he judges acts against what he judges best—people act so only by reason of ignorance. Now this view plainly contradicts the observed facts.

Though Aristotle nowhere mentions the *Protagoras* by name, this passage

66. That is, that ἀφροσύνη is the opposite both of σοφία and of σωφροσύνη, 333b—the play on words is untranslatable.

67. *Medea* 1078–80.

68. *Nicomachean Ethics* VII 1145b 22 ff., trans. Ross. Cf. 1147b 15; *Eudamian Ethics* 1216b 2ff.

contains a verbal echo of 352c, and his account of Socratic ethics depends directly on that dialogue: Socrates not only thought that knowledge was not to be dragged about like a slave and that ἀϰρασία is impossible; he also thought that courage was knowledge (*E.N.* III 1116b 4–5) and that the virtues are φρονήσεις, forms of practical wisdom (VII 1144b 18), a term which Socrates also uses as equivalent to knowledge or wisdom in the *Protagoras*—for example, at 337c and 352c.

Following Aristotle, many commentators have read the *Protagoras* as evidence for a "Socratic Paradox" that virtue is knowledge, in the sense that knowledge implies virtue. This is certainly a proposition to which Protagoras himself is committed—though he will end up denying it, inconsistently, in the special case of courage. For Socrates, on the other hand, the assertion of the authority of knowledge is proleptic: he will prove to the Many that on their own assumption, ἀϰρασία or incontinence is impossible, and prove it by assuming hedonism.

Keeping to Plato's own vocabulary, we may say that Socrates offers a denial of ἀϰολασία, intemperance; so Protagoras has agreed that knowledge implies temperance. But if this is so, intemperance implies ignorance, and no one voluntarily—that is to say, willingly and wittingly—does wrong by reason of intemperance. One might distinguish incontinence from intemperance, ἀϰρασία from ἀϰολασία, on the ground that the incontinent man knows what is good but does the opposite, whereas the intemperate man does not know what is good; but in the context of the hedonic argument, this distinction will prove not to make sense. For present purposes, one need not distinguish intemperance from incontinence.

It seems a plain deliverance of the moral sense that we have left undone those things which we ought to have done, and we have done those things which we ought not to have done—and done them in some sense knowingly. If this is true, and if the hedonism of the *Protagoras* implies that it is false, then that hedonism must itself be false: hedonism founders on the fact of ἀϰρασία. And not only hedonism, if Aristotle is right, but Socratic moral theory as well. But in this we shall find that Aristotle is wrong.

Reply to the Many (353c–354e)

To sum up the agreements so far: Socrates and Protagoras agree against the Many that knowledge implies temperance; Protagoras and the Many agree against Socrates that pleasure and goodness are not equivalent. Socrates will next show that though the Many say that knowledge does not imply temperance, they in fact believe that pleasure and goodness are equivalent.

Socrates interrogates the Many in an imaginary dialogue. What do they mean by "being overcome by pleasure"? The Many hold that men are mastered by food or drink or sex, which are pleasures, and recognize them as bad (πονηρά) but nevertheless pursue them. Why are they bad? Because they produce present pleasure? Or because they cause disease and poverty and other subsequent ills? The Many would reply that they are not bad because of the immediate pleasure they produce, but because they eventuate in pain and take away other pleasures.

Again, the Many claim that some good things are painful—for example, physical training, warfare, and medical treatment through cautery and surgery and drugs and starvation. These things are good not because they produce immediate pain but because they eventuate in pleasure and relieve and avert pain. So the Many pursue pleasure as good and avoid pain as evil: they think pleasure is bad only when it takes away greater pleasures or produces pain greater than the pleasure, and that pain is good only when it gets rid of greater pain or produces pleasures greater than the pains. In effect, the Many's mouth has been stopped: if they called pleasure bad with respect to something else besides pleasure and pain, or called pain good looking to some other end, then they could tell what it is: but they can't (354c–d). In this they differ from Socrates, who has suggested to Hippocrates that it is the good of the soul, which consists in justice and virtue. The Many are, in effect, psychological hedonists, and this because they are unaware of the primacy of justice and virtue. They are psychological hedonists out of ignorance.

The Many have now been shown, by an informal *reductio ad absurdum*, that in denying the hedonic equation, they in fact accept the hedonic equation: their denial rests merely on the distinction between immediate pleasures and pleasures which are more remote. So the Many agree that pleasure and goodness are equivalent. This constitutes a dialectical analysis of Socrates' hedonic equation: for denial of the equation has been reduced to acceptance of the equation. If not-*p* then *p*, then *p*. It is important to realize that the reduction required by the analysis rests on the inability of the Many to state an alternative to hedonism. Socrates stated that alternative in conversation with Hippocrates.

Protagoras had rejected the opinions of the Many as not worth considering, on the ground that they say whatever happens to occur to them (353a); but his agreement with the Many has at this point been elicited at every step of the way.

The hedonism of the Many is the foundation of the account of popular virtue—the virtue of the Many—offered in the *Phaedo* (68d–69a) in contrast to the philosopher's love of wisdom. Ordinary men are courageous through a kind of cowardice, temperate through a kind of intemperance: "they are afraid of being deprived of other pleasures, and desire them, so they refrain from some because they are mastered by others. Yet they call being ruled by pleasures intemperance." Popular or demotic virtue, in short, is a means to an end, namely pleasure, good in its consequences but not in itself.[69] The good life reduces to arithmetical proportion, a calculation of the balance of pleasure over pain which is summative, consisting in addition and subtraction of commensurable measures.

Arithmetical proportion may be contrasted with the claim in the *Gorgias* (507e–598a) that heaven and earth and gods and men are bound together by community and friendship, orderliness, temperance and justice; Callicles recommends the life of a robber because he has forgotten that geometrical equality or proportion has great power among both gods and men; he recommends excess because he has forgotten geometry.[70] The claim may best be understood by contrast. Arithmetical proportion produces equality of multitude or magnitude; geometrical proportion produces equality of ratio. Applied to moral psychology, geometrical proportion implies the satisfaction of some desires instead of others, in ratio to their merit; this is opposed to the arithmetical claim of all desires for equal satisfaction—Bentham's claim that, quantity of pleasure being the same, pushpin is as good as poetry. If geometrical proportion is fundamental to moral psychology, there must be a natural order of desires within the human soul, some superior to others, some in need of chastening or perhaps extirpation. This is why Socrates claims against Callicles

69. But see Mill, *Utilitarianism*, chap. IV. Thucydides (II 53, trans. Jowett), describing the effects of the plague, tells how it introduced ἀνομία, anomy, lawlessness, to the point of taking someone else's funeral pyre to burn one's own corpses: "There were other and worse forms of lawlessness which the plague introduced at Athens. Men who had hitherto concealed their indulgence in pleasure now grew bolder. For, seeing the sudden change,—how the rich died in a moment, and those who had nothing immediately inherited their property,—they reflected that life and riches were alike transitory, and they resolved to enjoy themselves while they could and to think only of pleasure. Who would be willing to sacrifice himself to the law of honour when he knew not whether he would ever live to be held in honour? The pleasure of the moment and any sort of thing which conduced to it took the place both of honour and of expediency." The *Phaedo* suggests that this is a shift not from virtue to hedonism but from deferred pleasure to the hedonism of the present moment: eat, drink, and be merry, for tomorrow we may die.

70. One might indeed suggest that he has also forgotten arithmetic. Given that the satisfaction of any desire is pleasant, the doctrine that all desire is for pleasure is trivially true. But trivial truths often lead to untrivial consequences. If pleasure is the good, and a concomitant of fulfillment of desire, perhaps all desires should be satisfied—the catamite—and we should let our desires multiply so that our pleasure will multiply—the curlew. This is the hedonism of Callicles in the *Gorgias,* and it is akin to madness, as Socrates with his analogy of the leaky jars shows (493a–494a). Callicles has forgotten not only geometry but even how to add and subtract. The *Gorgias* offers not one but three accounts of justice: as geometrical proportion; as arithmetical proportion; as the denial of any proportion at all.

that goods are not the same as pleasures, nor evils the same as pains (497a, d). The moral arguments of the *Protagoras* and the *Gorgias* differ, and one way of understanding the difference is to ask whether arithmetical or geometrical proportion is primary in living well.

George Grote, of the second generation of Utilitarians after Bentham and well versed in the history of hedonism, held that Socrates in the *Protagoras* "lays out one of the largest, most distinct, and most positive theories of virtue, which can be found in the Platonic writings."[71]

> Virtue, according to this theory, consists in a right measurement and choice of pleasures and pains: in deciding correctly, wherever we have an alternative, on which side lies the largest pleasure or the least pain—and choosing the side which presents this balance. To live pleasurably, is pronounced to be good: to live without pleasure or in pain, is evil. Moreover, nothing but pleasure, or comparative mitigation of pain, is good: nothing but pain is evil. Good, is identical with the greatest pleasure or least pain: evil, with the greatest pain: meaning thereby each pleasure and pain when looked at along with its consequences and concomitants. The grand determining cause and condition of virtue is knowledge: the knowledge, science, or art of correctly measuring the comparative value of different pleasures and pains. Such knowledge (the theory affirms), wherever it is possessed, will be sure to command the whole man, to dictate all his conduct, and to prevail over every temptation of special appetite or aversion. To say that a man who knows on which side the greatest pleasure or the least pain lies, will act against his knowledge—is a mistake. If he acts in this way, it is plain that he does not possess the knowledge, and that he sins through ignorance.

This summarizes the concluding argument in the *Protagoras* with considerable precision.

The Hedonistic Calculus (354e–356c)

Having questioned the Many, Socrates now proceeds to answer a question himself. The Many, unlike Socrates and Protagoras, deny that knowledge implies temperance, because they claim that men are overcome by pleasure. What does it mean to be overcome by pleasure? The answer is, it doesn't mean anything at all.

71. *Plato*, vol. 2, pp. 78–79.

The Many have agreed to the hedonic equation. They can still take back their agreement, if they can say that the good is something other than pleasure and the evil something other than pain. But if they accept pleasure and the avoidance of pain as sufficient for a human life, the notion that men are overcome by pleasure is absurd.

The absurdity of being overcome by pleasure follows from the hedonic equation. Assume that good = pleasant, and evil = painful: whatever is good is pleasant, and whatever is pleasant is good; whatever is evil is painful, and whatever is painful is evil.[72] Then by substitution, to say that a man does evil knowing it to be evil because he is overcome by pleasure, is to say that he does what is evil knowing it to be evil because he is overcome by what is good. Or again, that he does what is painful knowing it to be painful, because he is overcome by pleasures which don't weigh enough (ἀναξία) to conquer. This is manifestly absurd.

Given the hedonic equation, pleasures and pains can be compared in value only in respect to excess or defect of pleasures and pains: difference in worth is difference in degree. So if someone objects that what is immediately pleasant or painful differs in value from what is subsequently pleasant or painful, the reply must be that they differ only in pleasure and pain (356b–c). To claim that a man may refuse to do what he knows is good because he is overcome by immediate pleasure implies both that he refuses to do what he knows is good because he is overcome by immediate good, and that he refuses to do what is pleasant because he is overcome by immediate pleasure. Like a man skilled in weighing, one must add pleasures and pains both near and far and state which is greater: if pleasures exceed pains, the action is to be done; if pains exceed pleasures, the action is not to be done. So much, then, for intemperance, ἀκολασία.

The Nautical Almanac

The Many proceed by a hedonic calculus, weighing pleasures against pains. The ultimate criterion is quantity of pleasure, and both reflection on action and estimation of ends proceeds by addition and subtraction. This assumes that pleasures and pains are commensurable with each other.

This reasoning anticipates Bentham, who in constructing a theory not only of morals but of legislation held that, since pleasures and pains are the instruments of the legislator, it behooves him to understand their force or value (*Principles of Morals and Legislation*, chap. IV). For the indi-

72. The identity is one of equivalence, substitutibility *salva veritate*, and is intensional but not intentional: if whatever is good is pleasant, and good means pleasant, it does not follow that the Many believe (without instruction or Socratic questioning) that this is true.

vidual, the value of a pleasure must be judged by its intensity, its duration, its certainty or uncertainty, its propinquity or remoteness. In estimating the tendency of any act by which pleasure is produced, two other circumstances must be taken into account: its fecundity, the chance it has of being followed by other pleasures, and its purity, or the chance it has of not being followed by sensations of the opposite kind. These last, Bentham thought, are properties of the act, not of pleasures and pains in themselves. To these, the legislator must add the further criterion of extent, the number of people who will be affected by the action. According to these criteria, one must sum pleasures on the one hand, pains on the other, and compare them to decide if the act has or has not utility. It will be evident that, except for the concern for the principle of utility—that is, the greatest good of the greatest number—Bentham's position is an elaboration of the hedonistic calculus of the *Protagoras*. Sidgwick remarked (*Methods of Ethics*, p. 42): "If the actual ultimate springs of our volition are always our own pleasures and pains, it seems prima facie reasonable to be moved by them in proportion to their pleasantness and painfulness, and therefore to choose the greatest pleasure or least pain on the whole."

This was questioned by John Stuart Mill, who argued that pleasure must be valued according to not only its quantity but its quality. A pig satisfied is inferior to Socrates dissatisfied, and this because a beast's pleasures do not satisfy a human being's conception of happiness:[73]

> It is quite compatible with the principle of utility to recognise the fact, that some *kinds* of pleasure are more desirable and more valuable than others. It would be absurd that while, in estimating other things, quality is considered as well as quantity, the estimation of pleasures should be supposed to depend on quantity alone. . . . A being of higher faculties requires more to make him happy, is capable probably of more acute suffering, and certainly accessible to it at more points, than one of inferior type; but in spite of these liabilities, he can never really wish to sink into what he feels to be a lower grade of existence.

Quantity of pleasure being equal, pushpin is not as good as poetry. But this implies that pleasures, in being weighed against each other, must be measured by some criterion other than pleasure. Sidgwick, in this faith-

---

73. *Utilitarianism,* chap. II. This suggestion ill accords with Mill's psychological hedonism: "Desiring a thing, and finding it pleasant, are, in the strictness of language, two modes of naming the same psychological fact." "Pleasure is a kind of feeling which stimulates the will to actions tending to sustain or product it . . . pain is a kind of feeling which stimulates to actions tending to remove or avoid it."

ful to the *Protagoras,* made the appropriate response (*Methods of Ethics,* pp. 94–95):

> It seems to me that in order to work out consistently the method that takes pleasure as the sole ultimate end of rational conduct, Bentham's proposition must be accepted, and all qualitative comparison of pleasures must really resolve itself into quantitative. For all pleasures are understood to be so called because they have a common property of pleasantness, and may therefore be compared in respect of this common property. If, then, what we are seeking is pleasure as such, and pleasure alone, we must evidently always prefer the more pleasant pleasure to the less pleasant: no other choice seems reasonable, unless we are aiming at something besides pleasure. . . . No doubt we may mean something else: we may mean, for instance, that they are nobler and more elevated, although less pleasant. But then we are clearly introducing a non-hedonistic ground of preference.

Since all pleasures have the common property of pleasantness, to grade pleasures in terms of their quality is to introduce a standard of choice-worthiness other than pleasure itself.

The Art of Measurement (356b–358c)

Protagoras had claimed that virtue is an art, and that he could teach it. Socrates now explains, on the basis of the hedonic equation, what that art must be. It is an art of weighing pleasures and pains. A brief induction shows such an art is needed: the same magnitude appears larger when near, smaller when more distant; so similarly for frequencies (τὰ παχέα, "thicknesses") and multitudes, and the volume of sounds. If our welfare required us to choose only things of large dimension and avoid the small, our salvation in life would the be art of measurement (ἡ μετρητικὴ τέχνη, 356d 4), not the power of appearance (ἡ τοῦ φαινομένου δύναμις), for the latter leads us to make mistakes, whereas the art of measurement would correct the appearance (φάντασμα), make clear the truth, and cause the soul to abide in it, preserving our lives. Or suppose our salvation depended on the choice of odd or even, and when it was necessary to choose the more and when the fewer, whether near or far. Knowledge would be required of the art of measurement as it is concerned with excess and deficiency—that is, the art of arithmetic.

But we have now found that the salvation of life depends on right choice of pleasures and pains—more and fewer, greater and smaller, nearer and more remote; measurement is required for this; and that measurement must be an art or kind of knowledge. The nature of that art must be left for another time.[74]

Suppose then that the Many ask what the experience of being overcome by pleasure can be. (357e–e). In fact, it is ignorance, failure to use the art of measurement. Men err and do wrong for lack knowledge about how to add and subtract pleasures and pains—that is, by the hedonic equation, goods and evils. Intemperance implies ignorance.

Protagoras and Hippias and Prodicus are physicians of ignorance. But because the Many suppose that "being overcome by pleasure" is something other than ignorance, they try to save money by refusing to send their children to the sophists, or go themselves, because they think it can't be taught. And thus they fare badly (κακῶς πράττειν) both in private and public.

Grote remarks:[75]

> When some pleasures are called evil, that is not on account of anything belonging to the pleasure itself, but because of its ulterior consequences and concomitants, which are painful or distressing in a degree more than countervailing the pleasure. So too, when some pains are pronounced to be good, this is not from any peculiarity in the pain itself, but because of its consequences and concomitants: such pain being required as a condition to the attainment of health, security, wealth, and other pleasures or satisfactions more than counterbalancing. Sokrates challenges opponents to name any other end, with reference to which things are called good, except their tendency to prevent or relieve pains and to ensure a balance of pleasure: he challenges them to name any other end, with reference to which things are called evil, except their tendency to produce pains and to interrupt or destroy pleasures. In measuring pleasures and pains against each other, there is no other difference to be reckoned except that of greater or less, more or fewer. The difference between near and distant, does indeed obtrude itself upon us as a misleading element. But it is the special task of the "measuring science" to correct this illusion—and to compare pleasure or pains, whether near or distant, according to their real worth: just as we learn to rectify the illusions of the sight in regard to near and distant objects.

74. An art of this sort is discussed by the Eleatic Stranger at *Politicus* 283 ff., of whom it should be remarked that, as his name implies, he speaks as an Eleatic and not as a Platonist. It is not the least objection to utilitarianism that such a metric is specious.

75. Pp. 79–80.

Such an art, if it is not temperance or justice, would be an image of it, for it asks us to forgo the satisfaction of some desires in favor of others, and thereby ranks them. It offers an answer to the question of how to live a human life: not all desires are to be satisfied; some are to be satisfied and others not. Perhaps there is an underlying incoherence in this, if those desires are to be satisfied which yield greatest pleasure, and if pleasure consists in or is a concomitant of satisfaction of desire. The result would be an empty circle, a moral theory which offers a goal which is quite literally vacuous. The greatest sum of pleasure, or balance of pleasure over pain, cannot be a goal if pleasure is not a goal. So perhaps there is no art of arithmetical measurement after all.

Significantly, the *Gorgias* argues that the virtues are one, and the good man happy (506c–507c). The unity of the virtues implies their complication, and all are shown to be equivalent (not to wisdom but) to temperance. The fact that all virtues depend upon proper order of soul implies that the presence of temperance, or any virtue, requires the presence of the rest. To live well is to live justly and temperately, wisely and courageously. The moral arguments of the *Protagoras* are to the moral arguments of the *Gorgias* as sophistry is to philosophy, as εἴδωλον or image is to οὐσία or reality. The pursuit of pleasure as good is a deficient imitation of living well.

The Art Analogy

Socrates, by reducing intemperance to ignorance, makes temperance knowledge of an art of measurement whose aim is to weigh pleasant and unpleasant consequences, and to distinguish between the apparent and the real. That Socrates thought that virtue is knowledge, and that to know the good is to do it, is a widely accepted account of Socratic doctrine.

In English as in Greek, the association of knowledge with capacity or ability or power is primitive. Both *can* and *know* are derived from the same root, found in German *können*. Shakespeare's Queen Gertrude, describing the drowning of Ophelia, relates how for a little while the air in her garments buoyed her up:

> Which time she chanted snatches of old tunes;
> As one *incapable* of her own distress,
> Or like a creature native and indued
> Unto that element.

Similarly, Chaucer's Franklin, a simple man, confesses,

> I ne can no termes of astrologye.

The use of ἐπίσταμαι with the infinitive to indicate capacity is familiar Platonic Greek; it has the meaning and grammatical form of the English "know how to" and the infinitive with *können* and *savoir*.

The corresponding noun ἐπιστήμη corresponds also to this meaning —knowing how, if you will, as well as knowing that. Thus the brothers in the *Euthydemus* (294a ff.) claim to have ἐπιστήμη about everything: they reason that since nothing can have opposed attributes, and since it is admitted that they know some things, they cannot not know or be ignorant of anything. So they know the number of stars in the sky, and the grains of sand on the seashore, and they know how to do everything—to dance, to vault swords, to cobble and sew: since their knowledge is universal, they have ἐπιστήμη about all these things. The connection of art and knowledge, τέχνη and ἐπιστήμη, occurs throughout the early and early-middle dialogues.

It is often supposed that the art analogy implies that virtue is knowledge: those men are virtuous who possess the art of intelligent living, and we may call their skill either virtue or knowledge. And so, it is inferred, to speak of a man's knowledge as being overcome by passion or desire is to talk nonsense: when a man acts against his better judgment he shows that, despite his professions, he does not know how to live correctly and therefore does not have knowledge. Pleasures and fears, passions and desires, are a material element, patient to the knowing soul. Virtue uses them as a potter uses his clay, and the man who cannot work clay is no potter.

In the *Gorgias* (500e ff.; cf. 503e), the defining character of art as distinct from knack and experience, τρίβη and ἐμπειρία, is that it inquires into the nature of its object and the cause of its behavior, and is able to render an account. If virtue is knowledge, then Socrates' mission as an ethical teacher was, in effect, to raise men from moral ἐμπειρία to moral τέχνη. It is characteristic of ἐμπειρία that it is inarticulate; one can perform, but one cannot render an account of how or why one performs. The artist, on the other hand, knows what to do and to say; he can render an account of his work, because he has knowledge.

That virtue is knowledge may be supported by the further premise that all men wish for the good (*Meno* 77b–78a). For unless this were so, the knowledge which is virtue would be only a capacity or ability. The ability to be virtuous is not virtue, any more than the ability to play golf is golfing. The ability to be virtuous is actualized due to the βούλησις, the true wish of the soul for its own good. (Cf. *Gorgias* 466d ff.: "If a man does something for a purpose, he does not wish the thing he does, but that for the sake of which he does it.") βούλησις is the rational wish of the self for its own good, and that wish is constant, a necessity of human nature.

This is a reason for claiming that virtue is analogous to an art, in that knowledge is a necessary condition for virtue. But it is also a reason for denying that virtue is an art. Art involves capacity to produce opposite effects: to know the good in a given field is to know the bad and to be able to produce it. A doctor, skilled in healing, is best able to harm; a cobbler can artistically produce a pair of shoes that will not fit. But virtue is not a capacity to produce opposites: the virtuous man cannot be vicious. An art is an instrument, a means to attaining an end. Virtue is not a means to an end, but an end in itself. Because this is so, virtue is not an art. Virtue has to do not only with knowledge but with true wish. Put otherwise, virtue pertains to the rational will.

A consequence of this is put in the *Hippias Minor* (373c–376d; cf. *Crito* 44d). By arguing from analogy with the arts, Socrates concludes that only the good man, if anyone, can voluntarily, willingly and wittingly, do wrong, and that it is better to do wrong intentionally than unintentionally. This result necessarily follows, if virtue is an art, and it is a *reductio ad absurdum* of that claim.[76] That all wrongdoing is involuntary, however, is a conclusion Plato continued to accept to the end of his life (*Laws* IX 860d; cf. *Timaeus* 86e ff.: "The unjust man is surely bad, but the bad man is bad unwillingly"). The *Laws* make clear that if action done in ignorance is involuntary, so also is action done when one is overcome by pleasure or mastered by fear.

If it is not true that virtue is an art, it is also not true that virtue is knowledge. Art, since it implies knowledge, is relational: it is always of or about something. Each art is defined and distinguished from others by the objects toward which it is directed, and it must follow that there is an

---

76. Compare Philippa Foot, *Virtues and Vices,* Berkeley, Calif., 1978, pp. 7–8: "Aristotle has sometimes been accused, for instance by von Wright, of failing to see how different virtues are from arts or skills; but in fact one finds, among the many things that Aristotle and Aquinas say about this difference, the observation that seems to go to the heart of the matter. In the matter of arts and skills, they say, voluntary error is preferable to involuntary error, while in the matter of virtues (what we call virtues) it is the reverse. The last part of the thesis is actually rather hard to interpret, because it is not clear what is meant by the idea of involuntary viciousness. But we can leave this aside and still have all we need in order to distinguish arts or skills from virtues. If we think, for instance, of someone who deliberately makes a spelling mistake (perhaps when writing on the blackboard to explain this particular point) we see that this does not in any way count against his skill as a speller: 'I did it deliberately' rebuts an accusation of this kind. And what we can say without running into any difficulties is that there is no comparable rebuttal in the case of an accusation relating to a lack of virtue. If a man acts unjustly or uncharitably, or in a cowardly or intemperate manner, 'I did it deliberately' cannot on any interpretation lead to exculpation. So, we may say, a virtue is not, like a skill or an art, a mere capacity: it must actually engage the will."

For Plato, of course, involuntary viciousness has a precise meaning: it is doing what seems good, or what one desires, but not what one wishes. Since all men wish for the good, all viciousness is involuntary.

object peculiar to virtue, if virtue is an art. Virtue, judged by this criterion, seems useless, for it has neither object nor product.[77] The *Euthydemus* (279d–282d; cf. 288d ff.; *Charmides* 174c), indeed, suggests that virtue is an art of the second order, an art of using arts; but this founders on the fact that art involves the capacity to produce opposites. In the *Lysis* (218d–220b), wisdom or virtue implies knowledge of a criterion, τό πρῶτον φίλον, in terms of which the value of everything else may be judged: virtue implies knowledge of good and evil. But knowledge of good and evil cannot be virtue, precisely because knowledge is relational, and the suggestion is therefore circular and empty. The good cannot be knowledge because the knowledge required can only be knowledge of the good (*Republic* VI 506b–c). So it is not true that virtue is knowledge, which again implies that virtue is not an art.

The "Naturalistic Fallacy"

Hedonism and utilitarianism unite in refusing to treat the virtues as of primary moral concern: virtues are mere dispositions to action, and the goodness of such dispositions must be defined by what actions are good. So actions are primary, virtues derivative. Kant, indeed, went further, and thought that virtues could be vices: the coolness of the villain deepens the dye of his villainy—temperance and courage being detachable from wisdom and justice.

The modern history of utilitarianism begins with Locke's *Essay on Human Understanding* (I iii) and his attack on innate ideas and thereby on intuitionist ethics of the sort maintained by Cudworth and the Cambridge Platonists: if empiricism is true, if nothing is in the mind that was not first in the senses, there are no self-evident moral axioms whose truth will be recognized if only the axioms are distinctly stated. Locke concluded that he could find no innate practical principles except "a desire of happiness and an aversion to misery," which are appetites, not intellectual intuitions. Since the one universal motive among mankind is the desire for happiness, moral claims must be analyzed in terms of that motive: issues of virtue reduce to issues of happiness.[78] Bentham defined the principle of utility as "that principle which approves or disapproves of every action whatsoever, according to the tendency which it appears to have to augment or diminish the happiness of the party whose interest is in question"; of principles averse to utility, he chiefly looked to what he called the principle of sympathy and antipathy, which approves of actions merely as

77. *Charmides* 165e, 162e; *Euthyphro* 13d–14a; *Gorgias* 452e; *Republic* I 346a.
78. For a survey of utilitarianism from Locke and Hume to Bentham, see Leslie Stephen, *English Thought in the Eighteenth Century,* vol. 2, London, 1902, i 84–139.

one is disposed to do and for no other reason; he condemned moral intuitions as leading to social anarchy for want of principle.

Bentham's own theory was distinguished by its uncompromising naturalism, his belief that goodness is reducible to pleasure. John Stuart Mill, in similar spirit, undertook a proof that the general happiness is desirable (*Utilitarianism*, chap. IV):

> The only proof capable of being given that an object is visible, is that people actually see it. The only proof that a sound is audible, is that people hear it: and so of the other sources of our experience. In like manner, I apprehend, the sole evidence it is possible to produce that anything is desirable, is that people do actually desire it. . . . No reason can be given why the general happiness is desirable, except that each person, so far as he believes it to be attainable, desires his own happiness. This, however, being a fact, we have not only all the proof which the case admits of, but all which it is possible to require, that happiness is a good: that each person's happiness is a good to that person, and the general happiness, therefore, a good to the aggregate of all persons.

No doubt Mill confuses two different meanings of "desirable," what can be desired and what ought to be desired. But Henry Sidgwick focused on the fact that the reasoning involves a fallacy of composition (*Methods of Ethics*, p. 388):

> Now, as we have seen, it is as a "standard of right and wrong," or "directive rule of conduct," that the utilitarian principle is put forward by Mill: hence, in giving as a statement of this principle that "the general happiness is desirable," he must be understood to mean (and his whole treatise shows that he does mean) that it is what each individual ought to desire, or at least—in the stricter sense of ought—to aim at realising in action. But this proposition is not established by Mill's reasoning, even if we grant that what is actually desired may be legitimately inferred to be in this sense desirable. For an aggregate of actual desires, each directed towards a different part of the general happiness, does not constitute an actual desire for the general happiness, existing in any individual; and Mill would certainly not contend that a desire which does not exist in any individual can possibly exist in an aggregate of individuals. There being therefore no actual desire—so far as this reasoning goes—for the general happiness, the proposition that the general happiness is desirable cannot be in this way established: so there is a gap in the expressed argument.

Hedonism, *pace* Mill, does not imply utilitarianism, nor utilitarianism hedonism: one may suppose that pleasure is the good without supposing there is a duty to act for the greatest good of the greatest number; this is surely so in the *Protagoras*. One may also suppose that there is a duty to act for the greatest good of the greatest number without supposing that pleasure is the good. Sidgwick, indeed, thought that utilitarianism requires the Kantian universalization principle: so act that the maxim of thy action may become a universal law. One can certainly will it to be a universal law that men should act to promote general happiness, and perhaps, Sidgwick thought, it is the only law one can so will. But if this is so, utilitarianism cannot replace moral intuition as a standard for judgment, since it rests on moral intuition. As a corollary, no set of inclinations can define a duty, and no description of facts, including feelings and psychological states, can define an ought. Between moral and psychological judgments there is a gulf fixed.

G. E. Moore in *Principia Ethica* carried the point further: any definition of goodness in terms of pleasure involves the "naturalistic fallacy." Goodness is a unique, nonnatural quality, whose presence or absence is directly and immediately intuited: "x is good" represents a judgment which is true or false but for which no reasons can be given. The rightness of action must be judged by the goodness of its total consequences; one ought always act so as to make the world as much better as possible, or produce the greatest amount of good; but goodness is indefinable, and in particular not definable in terms of pleasure. Moore is a utilitarian, but an "ideal" utilitarian. Yet Moore had a concept of intrinsic value, things which are worth having purely for their own sake; virtue has no intrinsic value whatever, since it is a mere disposition, a means to an end. But certain states of consciousness, the pleasures of human intercourse and the enjoyment of beautiful objects, are intrinsically valuable:[79]

> No one, probably, who has asked himself the question, has ever doubted that personal affection and the appreciation of what is beautiful in Art or Nature, are good in themselves; nor, if we consider strictly what things are worth having purely for their own sakes, does

79. *Principia Ethica* 188–89. Moore takes for granted as obvious what Plato would have questioned. Is personal affection good if it is affection for a bad man? Is the enjoyment of beautiful objects good if it is a cause of bad character? Moore's examples of intrinsic good are qualified by opposites, sometimes good and sometimes not. *Principia Ethica* had great influence on Bloomsbury both before and after the First World War. E. M. Forster, a member of that group, said, "I certainly can proclaim that I believe in personal relationships" and went on, "If I had to choose between betraying my country and betraying my friend, I hope I should have the guts to betray my country." The year was 1938.

it appear probable that any one will think that anything else has nearly so great a value as the things which are included under these two heads.

Discounting the Naturalistic Fallacy, we have not, it seems, traveled so very far from Mill's version of hedonism after all.

From Moore's intuitionism, and from the associated deontological intuitionism of Pritchard and Ross,[80] there came by no very mysterious alchemy of ideas the moral subjectivism of Charles Stevenson in *Ethics and Language:* "*x* is good" is neither true nor false; it means, and means only, "I approve of *x*. Do so as well." "Good" has emotive meaning, in that the word has a tendency to produce affective responses and to express rather than report a feeling; it is this emotive meaning which accounts for the normative element in ethical sentences. The distinctively moral element in moral discourse reduces to a cheer or a boo, along with a command that others cheer and boo with us. Moral judgments are similar in nature to advertising slogans or propaganda, a result of which Protagoras and his modern followers can only approve, for it replaces the art of measurement with the power of appearance, so that image becomes the only reality. A theory meant by Bentham, Grote, and Mill to give an objective foundation for moral judgments has ended, without, surely, losing a particle of its hedonism, in the vagaries of spin control.

The curious dialectic of nineteenth- and twentieth-century moral philosophy may perhaps call into question its underlying assumption: that actions are either in themselves or in their consequences in some primary sense good or bad, and that the virtues and vices are mere dispositions to action and only instrumentally good or bad. This was also the sophists' assumption, according to the *Protagoras,* and the plain man's too. The Socratic view was otherwise: virtue or justice is good in itself. It is to us as health is to our bodies, which must mean that we are more than our bodies: justice is the health of the soul, and actions are to be judged good, derivatively, insofar as they tend to promote or preserve goodness of soul. Socrates, who believed that justice and virtue are good in themselves, supposed they are, as Kant supposed the good will to be, a supreme principle of morality, and of primary value apart from any consequences.

80. Who maintained that moral philosophy, including Platonic philosophy insofar as it supposes that justice is a good to the just man and equivalent to happiness, rests on a mistake in that it undertakes to prove our obligations: since those obligations are self-evident, the attempt is illegitimate. What is right cannot be determined by what is good because what is right is a matter not of consequences but of moral intuitions. The affinity of this treatment of "right" with Moore's treatment of "good" is manifest. They differ not in their intuitionism but in their estimate of the moral relevance of rules as opposed to consequences.

In the *Republic,* Glaucon's suggestion that Socrates undertake to show that justice is a good to the just man, and that justice should therefore be considered apart from consequences of reward and punishment, fore-shadows historical fact, for the primacy of justice is the basis on which Socrates went to his death. The *Crito* is of utmost importance to any account of Socratic ethics and shows the ethical necessity of the Socratic doctrine of the soul, for voluntary acceptance of execution was of no benefit whatever to his body. Goodness of soul is the ultimate moral crite-rion of all action, and Goodness itself, *summum bonum,* τό πρῶτον φίλον, is the foundation of goodness of soul.

Psychiatric Hedonism: Freud

The link between Socratic ethics and Freudian psychoanalysis and psy-choanalytically oriented psychotherapy may seem tenuous. There is a connection, however, based on psychological hedonism.[81]

Psychological hedonism, with its attendant egoism, has had little or no place in ethical theory since Bentham and Mill. But Freud made it central to his economic theory of psychical functioning,[82] economic because it involves the investment of scarce resources: to get something you have to give up something. The primary aim of mental activity is directed toward achieving pleasure and avoiding pain or unpleasure: it is automatically regulated by the pleasure principle. The pleasure principle, however, requires modification by the reality principle, which itself seeks to obtain pleasure but renounces immediate satisfaction in order to obtain greater pleasure in the long run. Freud here replicates the contrast in the *Pro-tagoras* between immediate pleasures and the long-run balance of plea-sure of pain—the reality principle corresponds to ἡ μετρικὴ τέχνη, the art of measurement as opposed to the power of appearance: where id was, there let ego be. The reality principle is important to the development of

81. It may be observed in passing that the sophist Antiphon, a hedonist, appears to have taken up the practice of psychiatry very much as now understood: "He invented an art of painlessness [τέχνη ἀλυπίας] comparable to the medical therapy of the diseased. In Corinth he fitted up a room near the agora and advised that he could cure the distressed by words. What he did was to bring consolation to those in trouble by questioning them as to the causes" (Pseudo-Plutarch, *D.K.* A6, trans. Guthrie).

82. *Introductory Lectures on Psycho-Analysis,* Standard Edition, vol. 16, pp. 356–57. These lectures were delivered in 1916–17 and represent Freud's mature work. A few years later, in 1920, Freud published *Beyond the Pleasure Principle* (Standard Edition, vol. 18, pp. 7–64) where he put forward, as an inference from a compulsion to repeat unpleasant experiences, a death instinct alongside the life instinct defined by the aim of pleasure. There is consider-able conceptual unclarity in this. If there is an instinct toward death and destruction, one's own or another's, this implies the pressure or tension attaching to a drive, the release of which is (by definition) pleasant.

the ego, for it involves the ability to defer and alter satisfactions; when this ability is diminished, one may speak of ego regression.

Freud takes a further step. The human ego, required to forgo immediate pleasures because of the pressures of reality, finds pleasure in fantasy freed from the claims of reality-testing.[83] But retreat to fantasy is a stage on the path to the formation of symptoms, actions which are detrimental or at least useless, and productive of suffering. Fantasy is in the nature of a wish, and wishes which cannot be fulfilled can be pathogenic, a source of mental illness. A case in point is hysteria, which, through Charcot and Breuer, served as the clinical base for the development of psychoanalysis.

Hysteria derives from the Greek *hustera,* womb, and the ancients thought it a disease characteristic of women. Here is Plato in the *Timaeus* (91c, trans. Cornford): "In women again . . . what is called the matrix or womb, a living creature within them with a desire for child-bearing, if it be left long unfruitful beyond the due season, is vexed and aggrieved, and wandering throughout the body and blocking the channels of breath, by forbidding respiration brings the sufferer to extreme distress and causes all manner of disorders."

There is an interesting pun in this passage: the womb is treated as itself a living thing, and there is a play on *hustera*—not only a womb, but a second woman. Psychically, one of the marks of hysteria is *double conscience,* that is, dissociation, a splitting of the mind, for which the womb as a second woman may be taken to stand as a physical analogue. The blocking of the channels of breath suggests a characteristic hysterical symptom, constriction in the throat which makes it difficult to speak or swallow. And the *Timaeus* suggests that hysteria is directly connected with sexuality, or more precisely the lack thereof: physical symptoms are caused by malposition of the uterus, which, when aggrieved through lack of sexual intercourse and childbirth, wanders through the body and can put pressure on the channels of breathing. The Hippocratic doctors treated the disease by fumigating the vagina, the intent being to draw the uterus back to its normal position. Uterine fumigation was pre-Hippocratic and indeed pre-Greek, for it was used in Egypt. No doubt it often worked, in that it removed symptoms for a time or at least changed them, allowing the patient to speak and swallow, and relieving anxiety: these patients are highly suggestible.

There is a difficulty in understanding hysteria. It is attended by falsehood, and it is a great imitator. Its falsehood and imitation are by no means confined solely to women; despite its etymology, men suffer from it

83. *Introductory Lectures,* pp. 271–73.

too. So the ancients were wrong in thinking it had to do with the womb. Hysterical symptoms may simulate almost any disease—though often with a difference, for hysteria is ignorant of anatomy, a fact often important to differential diagnosis from genuine physical ailments. Hysterical physical symptoms can also often be identified, as Charcot proved, because they can be produced under hypnosis and removed under hypnosis, though this treatment may be contraindicated, because it may result in severe emotional turmoil and anxiety. Freud held that hysterical symptoms may be supposed to have a sense or purpose in the economy of the soul, and that it is dangerous to remove them without dealing with the emotions which those symptoms both mask and express.

Hysterical symptoms fall into two broad groups, as involving conversion or dissociation—the "or" is inclusive.[84] In conversion, the symptom may mimic almost any physical disability, but throat constriction, sometimes accompanied by vomiting, skin anaesthesias, disturbances of vision or hearing, functional paralyses of limbs, and wandering backaches are characteristic. Dissociation may involve amnesia or fugue, or it may involve dual or multiple personalities with different behavior and values, which may or may not be aware of each other. At the extreme, it tends toward schizophrenia.

Early in his career, shortly after his cooperation with Breuer on *Studies in Hysteria*,[85] Freud came to the conclusion in *The Aetiology of Hysteria*[86] that hysteria was caused in every case by childhood sexual abuse, including infant sexual abuse, usually of girls but sometimes of boys, frequently by the father or other near relative. This is the so-called Seduction Hypothesis, though it is not seduction which is in question but rape, since consent is impossible. But the fantasy theory of symptom formation led him to reject this claim and to regard the memories of his hysterical patients as fantasies produced by a wish—the wish to be seduced by and to have intercourse with the father and the fantasy that this had indeed happened, even if to Freud's definite knowledge those memories some-

84. To be distinguished from what is sometimes called hysterical personality disorder, characterized by shallow, labile emotions, manipulative behavior, a tendency toward self-dramatization, lack of self-criticism, and fickle flirtatiousness with little capacity for sustained sexual relationships—in male or female, a kind of caricature of femininity. This is compatible with conversion or dissociation, but does not imply it.

85. Standard Edition, vol. 2. Much of this work was concerned with that exemplary patient Anna O., Bertha Pappenheim, who suffered from headaches, disturbance of vision, partial paralyses, and anesthesias. Hysteria as a psychiatric diagnosis is no longer in fashion, having been broken down into a variety of more narrowly defined disorders; for this reason Anna O. would not now be diagnosed as a hysteric, as the editors of the *DSM-III-R Casebook* (pp. 465–66) explain.

86. Standard Edition, vol. 3, pp. 191–221.

times rested on fact. This is a main pillar of his theory of infantile sexuality and the Oedipus complex. One wonders whether Freud, the erstwhile philosophy student, had not applied the Kantian principle that since existence is evidently not a real or determining predicate of things, there is no more content in a hundred actual dollars than in a hundred possible dollars.[87]

Psychoanalysis might then ignore externalities, what actually occurred, and take as its own peculiar province what, subjectively, the patient thought had occurred: it is the content of ideation, not the putative fact, that matters—or rather, for psychoanalysis, the mental content is the fact, thus clouding the distinction between a memory and a fantasy, but providing psychoanalysis with a subject matter of its own. Absent the fallacy of composition involved in Cartesian doubt, this notion of "content" ignores causation in its relation to existence; one thinks of the downright wisdom of William James and his remark that imaginary fire is the kind of fire that won't burn real sticks.

The pleasure principle, by way of fantasy, becomes the basis of symptoms—often very strange and debilitating symptoms. The psychological hedonism of the *Protagoras* is a foundational principle of Freudian analysis in abnormal psychology. And if abnormality implies a theory of normality, psychological hedonism provides a basis for defining what normality is. Symptoms are self-defeating because they are unpleasant, either in actual experience or in their tendency. The aim of psychoanalysis is to remove symptoms, thereby, as Freud wrote, transforming hysterical misery into ordinary unhappiness. This is the world-weariness characteristic of hedonism, which arises because there is never enough, and it issues in a love of death characteristic of romanticism: we are creatures of a longing which can never be satisfied. However often we gain release from the pressure or tension of an instinct or drive, the want keeps recurring, not to be stilled this side of the grave. Late in life, Freud put it directly: "The aim of all life is death."[88] His death instinct is so deeply imbedded in his life instinct, his hedonism, that they cannot constitute two distinct principles as he supposed.

The psychological hedonist will deny, as Freud in fact did deny, that he is concerned with ethics. Psychological hedonism analytically precludes

87. Jeffrey Masson, *The Assault on Truth*, New York, 1992, argues that Freud abandoned the seducation hypothesis and introduced the theory of infantile sexuality for personal reasons—a failure of moral courage in face of the disapproval of his Viennese colleagues: Freud as a young doctor with a family needed referrals. As a biographical fact, this may be true, but it does not take account of the suggestion that it was the Kantian analysis of existence which was at work.

88. "Beyond the Pleasure Principle," Standard Edition, vol. 18, p. 38.

ethical hedonism, since the obligation to pursue pleasure reduces without remainder to the pleasantness of pursuing pleasure: the "ought" of the psychological hedonist is purely instrumental. But psychological hedonism is the foundation of a theory of conduct, for it implies that the aim of life is pleasure for the individual. Psychological hedonism thus implies egoistic hedonism,[89] and this carries over into the didactic of therapy, teaching patients how to think and behave as egoistic hedonists, their end being their own good, and that good not merely pleasure but their greatest pleasure. Except by negation, this is not a moral theory.

Is it a curative theory? If it were, it might be justified clinically, by its results. There is reason, however, to think it is not curative. Here is the psychoanalyst Heinz Kohut's comment on the clinical results of Freud's work:[90]

> Almost all the great cases are now known; their identities have been established. Some have been investigated throughout their whole lifetime and are being reinvestigated. What happened is that most of these patients lost their symptoms; instead, most began to act out. They began to have what is nowadays called *fate neuroses,* to reenact their former pathology in their real lives, whereas formerly their pathology was expressed in hysterical symptoms. So their mode of pathology at that time changed because of all-too-quick symptom relief. Even though an insight was gained into their pathology, not enough working-through occurred, so that the pressure of the essentially unconscious conflict was still active. What followed was that these people involved themselves in all kinds of deleterious activities.

Kohut holds that Freud was too quick, that his treatment was harmful to his patients, that nowadays psychoanalysis can do better. This is unclear. It is human to remember cases that turn out well, and to forget cases that don't—or to find after the fact that those cases were unanalyzable. Outcome studies are not dispositive and do not take account of the effect of psychoanalysis on others besides the analysand: the family devastation which often results from turning a patient into a convinced psychological hedonist. Beyond this, the placebo effect, the medical fact that expectation of cure is itself curative, given the positive expectations with which patients enter therapy, would dictate dramatic improvement—improvement far beyond what in fact obtains, if Kohut is right. One is led to wonder whether, if psychoanalysis were a drug, it would be licensed by the Food

89. One may in this connection consider the argument of Donald C. Abel, *Freud: On Instinct and Morality,* New York, 1989, esp. chap. 5.
90. *The Kohut Seminars on Self Psychology,* ed. Miriam Elson, New York, 1987, p. 76.

and Drug Administration. Given that psychoanalysis assumes egoism and psychological hedonism, given further that egoism and psychological hedonism are false, this suggests that psychoanalysis is perhaps relatively ineffective or may be deleterious. In Platonic terms, it is a form of sophistry based on rhetoric, random falsehood appearing to be knowledge to those who do not know. It may be that Socratic psychotherapy or psychagogy, with its concern for the virtues, is better founded on truth and on cure.

Hippias and Prodicus Agree (358a–b)

At this point Socrates asks Hippias and Prodicus whether they agree. They do. Specifically, they agree that being overcome by pleasure is ignorance, and that the pleasant is good and the painful bad—but then, they have just been told that the Many refuse to spend money on sophists because of their doubt that this is so. Prodicus even consents to abandon his practice of distinguishing the meaning of terms in order to indicate his agreement.

This bit of byplay suggests that sophistry is based on hedonism, and that Protagoras's cavils indicate a misunderstanding of his own position. That point is made explicitly in the *Gorgias*, which describes what the *Protagoras* exhibits: sophistry and rhetoric are classed together as εἴδωλα, insubstantial imitations of genuine arts; they are species of κολακεία, servile flattery, aiming not at what is good but at what is pleasant. As pastry cooking pretends to be medicine, and claims to know what foods are good as doctors do, so sophistry and rhetoric pretend to be statesmanship and jurisprudence. But they aim at pleasure and are indifferent to truth or the good of the soul. If this is so, the whole profession of sophistry, the profession not only of Hippias and Prodicus but of Protagoras himself, presupposes that pleasure is the good, an ultimate end. Their rhetoric is flattery, aimed at gratification and pleasure and indifferent to truth or the good of the soul; it stands in contrast to philosophical rhetoric, exhibited by Socrates' speech in the *Apology* and the speech of the Laws of Athens in the *Crito*, aimed at truth and the good of the soul, whether it gives pleasure or pain to the hearers. But Protagoras is unaware of this distinction.

In its hedonism, sophistry agreed with popular morality, even though popular morality and sophistry, as evidenced by Protagoras, also inconsistently supposed it possible to be overcome by pleasure.

This concludes two dialectical analyses. The hedonic equation has been analyzed by *reductio ad absurdum*, showing that the Many in denying it assume it. To this Hippias and Prodicus, but not Protagoras, have agreed; Protagoras, however, will soon be reduced to silence, as the Many were silent when asked to suggest an alternative to the hedonic equation. The claim that knowledge is a sufficient condition for continence has also been analyzed by *reductio ad absurdum,* using the hedonic equation as a lemma, and showing once again that the Many by denying it assume it. Hippias and Prodicus agree; Protagoras, the teacher of virtue, had agreed to begin with.

The proposition that knowledge is a sufficient condition for continence will be followed by a dialectical synthesis, that is, a proof. Significantly, the hedonic equation will not be provided a synthesis.

No One Voluntarily Chooses Evils (358b–d)

Socrates now sums up, offering a synthesis of the proposition that knowledge is a sufficient condition for continence. All actions which aim at living pleasantly and without pain are χαλαί, noble or beautiful or excellent, and what is noble is good and beneficial. So if the pleasant is good, no one who believes there is a course of action better than the one he is following will fail to choose it. No one voluntarily (ἑχών) pursues what he believes to be evil, for it is not in human nature to pursue evil instead of good—that is, given the hedonic equation, pain instead of pleasure—and if compelled to choose between evils, no one will choose the greater when he can take the less. To this the company all agree.

And rightly, for it follows from the hedonic equation. If the aim of life is pleasure, no one can be overcome by pleasure or lack self-control, and the salvation of life consists in acquiring an art by which pleasure and pain can be measured. Wrongdoing is the pursuit of things which are painful rather than pleasant, and it is therefore involuntary.

The argument has proved that incontinence, ἀχράτεια, implies ignorance. This is equivalent to proving, on the basis of the hedonic equation, that knowledge implies continence, even as Socrates had said at the beginning of the argument. Synthesis has been achieved.

Socratic Intellectualism

The principle that no one willingly does wrong, or voluntarily chooses evils, began as a sophistic paradox: Gorgias is known to have propounded it in a set speech, the *Palamedes.*[91] The claim is also made by Socrates himself, who erects it on a new foundation in dialogues other than the *Protagoras,*[92] without reference to the hedonic equation. In the *Symposium*

91. See Guido Calogero, "Gorgias and the Socratic Principle *Nemo Sua Sponte Peccat,*" in *Essays in Ancient Greek Philosophy,* ed. John P. Anton and George L. Kustas, New York, 1971, pp. 179–81.

92. See, e.g., *Apology* 25d–26a; *Hippias Minor* 376b; *Gorgias* 488a, 509b–e; *Republic* I 336e, IX 589e; *Timaeus* 86d–e; *Laws* V 731c–732b, 733e–734d, IX 860d–864c.

(204c–205a), Diotima defines the object of Eros, desire, as the possession of good things and thereby of happiness. In the *Meno* (77b–78b), when Meno claims that some men desire evil knowing it to be evil, he is met with the claim that to desire evil is to desire what is harmful, and to be harmed is to be made unhappy: no one wishes that. It has been suggested that this account confuses harm to another with harm to oneself; but assuming premises made explicit in the *Crito* and *Republic*, to do harm to another is to act unjustly, and to act unjustly is to harm one's own self, that is to say, one's own soul. The good is what every soul pursues in all its actions (*Republic* VI 505d).

If this is so, wrongdoing is involuntary: no one willingly and wittingly does evil, or chooses it in preference to what is good. In the *Gorgias* 466b ff.), Polus praises rhetoric because it is powerful: orators are like tyrants, who can kill or exile whom they wish. To which Socrates replies that one can do what seems good without doing what one wishes, and those who lack wisdom to understand what is good for them are to that extent not powerful. The tyrant, who does what seems best to him but not what he wishes, is least of all men free. One may choose to do evil and intend it but cannot wish it—cannot, that is, choose it willingly and wittingly. What is apparently good is distinguishable and often distinct from what is really good: there is then a contradiction between wish and desire, and the self is inwardly divided in conflict of motives, a conflict which is in some sense knowing, in that to wish and to desire is in some sense to be aware of what it is one wishes and desires.

So the doctrine that wrongdoing is involuntary is compatible with the fact of self-division, and indeed implies it. To mistake apparent good for real good is ignorance, but it is not ignorance as the bare not knowing of something; it is the not knowing of something one knows, ignorance as a kind of false consciousness of self-deceit. Virtue is knowledge if and only if knowledge is wisdom; to know the good is to do it if and only if one is wise. No such distinction between wisdom and knowledge is drawn in the *Protagoras*.

The notion that if wrongdoing is involuntary, then virtue is knowledge or knowledge implies virtue, is, absent the hedonic equation, merely mistaken. In the *Republic*, which maintains that no one voluntarily does injustice, the analysis of the soul into different elements or parts is founded on the self divided in conflict of motives; ἀκράτεια has an opposite, namely ἐγκράτεια, self-control (V 461b). In the *Laws* (V 734b; cf. X 886a–b), men are involuntarily (ἄκων) licentious or intemperate through either ignorance (ἀμαθία) or incontinence (ἀκράτεια). And in *Laws* VI, in a passage important for understanding Plato's theory of tort and criminal liability and the distinction between punishment and compensable damages, injustice or wrongdoing is involuntary (860d), and injustice consists in the tyranny in the soul of anger and fear, pleasure and pain, envy and desire (863e). In short, the claim that wrongdoing is involuntary is, absent the hedonic equation, compatible with being overcome by anger and fear, pleasure and pain; the soul can indeed be dragged about like a slave, and the point of living is to live well and thereby become free. That wrongdoing is involuntary does not imply that virtue is knowledge, or that to know the good is to do it, and the "Socratic Paradox" is undoubtedly a paradox, but not Socratic.[93] The early and early-middle dialogues nowhere state that knowledge implies virtue: in the *Meno* the implication is assumed as a hypothesis, and in the *Protagoras* it is required by the hedonic equation. In the *Republic* (VI 505a–b) it is neatly refuted. The claim that Socrates thought that virtue is knowledge is mistaken; he did not think that if you have knowledge, you are virtuous; he thought that if you do not have knowledge, you are not virtuous; so that if you are virtuous, you have knowledge. This perhaps is paradox enough: we shall not, it seems, in this world be saved by faith. The interpretation which derives from Aristotle, that virtue and knowledge are logically equivalent or perhaps identical, rests on the fallacy of affirming the consequent.

Yet the *Protagoras* maintains not that virtue implies knowledge but (in effect) that knowledge implies virtue. The horseshoe runs the wrong way. Once again, an element of parody, something like the truth and yet untrue. Compare Socrates' parody of the principle that no one voluntarily does wrong in commenting on Simonides (345d–e, 346a).

The Unity of Courage and Wisdom (358d–360e)

Dread and fear (δέος τε καὶ φόβον) are expectation of evil. No one pursues what he fears if he can pursue what he does not fear, for what he fears he believes to be evil, and no one pursues or voluntarily accepts what he believes evil. Put in terms of the hedonic equation, if pain = evil, then no one voluntarily pursues evil because no one voluntarily pursues pain.

Fear is an expectation of evil; therefore, no one willingly or wittingly pursues what he fears. Return then to Protagoras's claim that courage is detachable from the other virtues, that men may be unholy, unjust, intemperate, and ignorant, but courageous. Protagoras has also agreed that the courageous are confident. Now, people generally say that cowards pursue only what they are confident about, while courageous men pursue what they fear. But Protagoras himself must suppose this is impossible, since he

93. See also Xenophon, *Memorabilia* IV v 6–7.

agrees that no one pursues what he believes fearful. On the contrary, everyone pursues things they are confident about, cowards and courageous men alike, so in this respect cowards and courageous men pursue the same things.

Protagoras offers the appropriate counterargument: cowards pursue different things from courageous men. For example, courageous men are willing to go to war, cowards refuse. The elenchus follows immediately. Going to war is agreed to be excellent or noble or honorable or beautiful (καλόν); what is beautiful is good; what is noble and good is also pleasant.[94] Can we then say that cowards knowingly (γιγνώσκοντες, 360a 4) refuse to pursue what is more noble and better and more pleasant? If we do, Protagoras admits, we'll destroy our former agreements.

It follows that cowards must unknowingly refuse to pursue what is more noble and better and more pleasant. If cowards fear with shameful fear and are confident with shameful confidence, the cause of this can only be folly and ignorance. Ignorance of what is to be feared makes them cowards, and if what makes them cowards is cowardice, then cowardice must be ignorance of what is and is not to be feared. And if courage is the opposite of cowardice, and wisdom about what is and is not to be feared is opposite to ignorance of what is and is not to be feared, which is cowardice, then wisdom about what is and is not to be feared is courage. In short, wisdom and courage are not detachable: the claim that men can be courageous and unwise is not only false but impossible. Grote put the argument as follows:[95]

> No man affronts evil, or the alternative of greater pain, knowing it to be such: no man therefore adventures himself in any terrible enterprise, knowing it to be so: neither the brave nor the timid do this. Both the brave and the timid affront that which they think not terrible, or the least terrible of two alternatives: but they estimate differently what is such. The former go readily to war when required, the latter evade it. Now to go to war when required, is honourable: being honourable, it is good: being honourable and good, it is pleasurable. The brave know this, and enter upon it willingly: the timid not only do not know it, but entertain the contrary opinion, looking upon war as painful and terrible, and therefore keeping aloof. The brave men fear what it is honourable to fear, the cowards what it is dishonour-

94. This consequence—that since going to war is noble and good it is also pleasant—is a practical *reductio ad absurdum* of the hypothesis that goodness and pleasure are equivalent, and by itself refutes the claim that Socrates is a hedonist in the *Protagoras*.

95. Plato, vol. 2, p. 80.

able to fear: the former act upon the knowledge of what is really terrible, the latter are misled by their ignorance of it. Courage is thus, like the other virtues, a case of accurate knowledge of comparative pleasures and pains, or of good and evil.

Reduced to lowest terms, Protagoras has assumed that it is not the case that courage implies knowledge or wisdom (339b). But he is led by Socrates to agree, using a substitution argument based on the hedonic equation, that cowardice implies ignorance of what is and is not to be feared, from which it follows that courage implies knowledge of what is and is not to be feared.[96]

Nowhere else in any early or early-middle dialogues is virtue, or any of the virtues, successfully defined, but it has been suggested that the *Protagoras* here offers an adequate definition of courage: courage is by definition knowledge of what is and is not to be feared. But the perplexity which can attach to such a formula is shown by the *Laches,* and its inadequacy is shown by the *Republic* (429b–430b, 442b–c), where courage is defined as preservation of right opinion about what is and is not to be feared, independently of pleasure, pain, desire, and fear. This definition is incompatible with the hedonic equation: pleasure is not the good, because there are bad pleasures (505c–d).[97] Indeed, knowledge (φρόνησις) is not the good either, for if we ask what kind of knowledge, we are compelled in the end to say it is knowledge of the good (505b–c). This reasoning is surely Socratic, and sufficient to explain why the sophistic claim that virtue is knowledge is false.

"Plato's Moral Theory"

This may be contrasted with Terence Irwin's account in the book he called *Plato's Moral Theory.*[98] His account of the *Protagoras* is directed to its last argument, involving hedonism; that argument, he claims, presents the

96. One may compare the *Laches* (197e–199e). Nicias claims that courage is knowledge of what to fear and what to be confident about. But fear is expectation of future evils, and this leads Nicias to agree that knowledge of future goods and evils is courage. But this, Socrates argues, is equivalent to knowledge of good and evil generally, which is equivalent to virtue, and Nicias had agreed that courage is not virtue but a part of virtue; so he has identified part and whole and has not succeeded in saying what courage is. It cannot be that courage is a part of virtue, that courage is knowledge of good and evil, and that knowledge of good and evil is virtue—unless, of course, part is logically equivalent to whole and the virtues are one as being coimplicatory. This question is addressed in the *Protagoras* but not in the *Laches,* and Nicias, on the basis of his own admissions, accepts that he has been refuted.

97. See also 561c. At *Gorgias* 499b–c, Callicles admits that some pleasures are better, others worse. Socrates takes this to mean that some pleasures are useful, others harmful (cf. *Lysis* 221a). We seek the former kind for the sake of the good, and will submit to beneficial pain. Inferred: that we do what is pleasant for the sake of the good, and not vice versa (500a).

98. Irwin, *Plato's Moral Theory,* chap. 4. Vlastos thought this book one of the main contributions to Socratic moral theory in this century, and said that to read it was one of the outstanding learning experiences of his life.

fundamental premises of Socratic ethics, "Plato's first systematic defense of Socratic ethics," for Socrates there undertakes to show "that virtue can be taught as a craft" (p. 102). "Craft" is offered as a translation of τέχνη; it is perhaps an unfortunate translation, if the *Oxford English Dictionary* is right in identifying the chief modern sense of the word as "skill or art applied to deceive or overreach; guile, fraud, cunning"—or, as Hobbes put it in *Leviathan,* "that crooked wisdom, which is called craft." Again, though Irwin speaks of the Craft Analogy, the assumption that virtue is analogous to a craft, it is clear by his discussion that he does not mean that virtue is merely analogous to a craft, but that it is a craft.

To rephrase, then, Irwin thinks that Socratic ethics requires that virtue is an art, and that virtue can be taught. This implies the unity of the virtues, he claims, in the sense not of reciprocal implication but of identity, because if knowledge is a sufficient condition for virtue, "then each of the virtues includes the same knowledge of good and evil, and nothing more—they are all the same virtue" (p. 104).

Knowledge is a sufficient condition for virtue because of Socrates' hedonism: pleasure is the final good, that for the sake of which everything is done. Because this is so, virtue is an art with a definite subject matter and procedure, the measurement of pleasure and pain; because it is an art, it is teachable; because it is an art, it is also merely instrumental, a means to happiness. Socrates does not suppose that virtue is good in itself.

Now, this is not in fact a moral theory. Irwin suggests, borrowing Sidgwick's distinction, that the hedonism of the *Protagoras* is both psychological and ethical (p. 104). Psychological hedonism is the doctrine that volition is always determined by pleasures or pains actual or prospective —the doctrine of the *Protagoras*—whereas ethical hedonism is the doctrine that volition ought to be so determined, that the pursuit of pleasure is a precept or moral principle. But that one ought to pursue pleasure can only mean, to a psychological hedonist, that it is good to pursue pleasure, and that it is good to pursue pleasure can only mean that it is pleasant to pursue pleasure. This is clearly not an ethical claim.[99] The hedonism of the *Protagoras* is sophistry: it looks like a moral theory but isn't.

---

99. Cf. Sidgwick, *Methods,* p. 41: "If, as Bentham affirms, 'on the occasion of every act he exercises, every human being is' inevitably 'led to pursue that line of conduct which, according to his view of the case, taken by him at the moment, will be in the highest degree contributory to his own greatest happiness,' then, to any one who knows this, it must be inconceivable that Reason dictates to him any other line of conduct. But at the same time, as it seems to me, the proposition that he 'ought' to pursue that line of conduct becomes no less incapable of being affirmed with any significance. For a psychological law invariably realised in my conduct does not admit of being conceived as 'a precept' or 'dictate' of reason; this latter must be a rule from which I am conscious that it is possible to deviate."

If it is not a moral theory, neither is it Plato's. Elsewhere, in other early dialogues, Socrates is made to offer powerful reasons for denying that virtue is teachable and that virtue is an art. It is the sophists, or some of them, who claimed this, and Socrates who challenged them—as he challenges Protagoras. Nor does Socrates, except in the *Protagoras*, assert that knowledge is a sufficient condition for virtue; once again, it is the sophists, or some of them, who claimed this; Protagoras can't deny it, because he claims to teach virtue. Socrates, it is true, affirms that virtue is knowledge and that it is teachable at the conclusion of the *Protagoras*—but he does so assuming the hedonism of the Many, while urging that the inquiry continue because he and Protagoras have not discovered what virtue is: as in the *Meno*, he supposes that virtue is teachable while explicitly denying that he knows what virtue is. In both dialogues, the dialectic ends in a tangle.

One need only look to the *Crito* to realize that Socrates did not suppose that virtue or justice is a means to pleasure, and that he did suppose that virtue and more specifically justice—a virtue not mentioned in the concluding argument of the *Protagoras*, since from the point of view of egoistic hedonism it is "another's good"—is good in itself. But if virtue or justice is good in itself, then virtue is not an art, since arts are concerned with choice of means, not ends. Irwin, assuming in effect that justice is "another's good," criticizes the *Crito*'s argument on the ground that "either justice is a virtue and not all virtues benefit the agent, or virtues do benefit the agent, and justice is not a virtue" (p. 59). He criticizes Socrates' argument that since it is wrong to do injustice it is wrong to do harm, a variant of the claim that it is better to suffer injustice than to do injustice, by suggesting that "the argument will be plausible only if Socrates explains what the psychic benefit will be, and how intentional infliction of harm on someone else damages my soul. His defence is as weak as his overall defense of justice" (pp. 59–60). Morally, of course, the proposition that it is better to suffer injustice than to do it, which Irwin thinks tendentious, is necessarily true. Since Socrates, as a historical matter, almost certainly went to his death on the basis of the argument put in the *Crito*, whose foundation is that that in us which is benefited by justice and harmed by injustice is of greater worth than the body, it must follow either that Socrates was fatally confused about justice in its relation to the human soul, or that Irwin is confused about Socrates.[100]

100. Irwin says of Socrates in the *Crito:* "His comments on happiness, the good of the soul, and justice are not supported by a clear account of happiness or the soul's good; until a clear argument is found, the large claims about justice cannot reasonably be accepted or finally rejected." As it happens, happiness is not mentioned in the *Crito*, nor the soul except by the periphrasis, "that in us to which justice and injustice pertain." And justice is not mentioned in the concluding argument of the *Protagoras*.

If not a moral theory, and not Plato's, it remains to inquire whether it is a theory. Irwin is an unabashed proponent of The More Fool Plato style of exegesis: "Much of what he [Plato] says is false, and much more is confused, vague, inconclusive and badly defended" (p. 4). Plainly, this involves a heuristic assumption: the exegete, faced with a Platonic text he does not understand, can assume either that he does not understand Plato, or that Plato is confused. It is much easier and quicker to assume the latter. Irwin supposes it is not he but Plato who is confused, and this assumption cannot be refuted, for to adduce Platonic texts which contradict Irwin's assertions may always be taken as evidence of further confusion. Irwin's exegesis is not only self-congratulatory but self-justifying, in that in principle it admits of no denial. That is to say, it is unfalsifiable, which is a reason to suppose that it is also unverifiable, and therefore not a theory. It is to the interpretation of texts as astrology is to astronomy.

Plato's Moral Theory? Holy Roman Empire.

Conclusion (360e–362a)

At this point the argument itself accuses Socrates and Protagoras of foolishness. Socrates began by doubting that virtue can be taught, but now suggests that justice, temperance, and courage are knowledge, from which it would surely appear that virtue can be taught. Protagoras claimed that virtue is other than knowledge, which suggests that it cannot be taught, yet puts himself forward as a teacher of it. Socrates would therefore like to go on to inquire what virtue itself is, and afterward return to the question of whether it can be taught. Otherwise, Epimetheus may cheat us in our inquiry. Socrates prefers Prometheus to Epimetheus, for in being concerned with such questions as these he is taking forethought for his own life. If Protagoras will consent, Socrates would like to take up the inquiry again.

Protagoras will not consent. He approves of Socrates' earnestness and his skill in discussion; Socrates is likely one day to win high repute for wisdom. But Protagoras will pursue the question of what virtue is another time.

Socrates and Protagoras have not discovered whether virtue can be taught, because they have not discovered what virtue is. The question Socrates repeatedly puts in the *Meno* is central to the *Protagoras*. If we are to know what attributes are connected with virtue—teachability, for example—we must first know what virtue is. Failure to answer that question is an inevitable source of perplexity, dogged by inconsistency.

Both the *Protagoras* and the *Meno* fail to define virtue, and both end in a dialectical perplexity over the issue of teachability. At the conclusion of the *Protagoras,* Socrates and Protagoras have become so tangled that the argument itself intervenes to mock them. Socrates began by asserting that virtue is knowledge, which suggests that it therefore can be taught; Protagoras, as a sophist who teaches virtue and thus maintains that virtue can be taught, ends by affirming that courage is a virtue yet denying that it can be taught. The moral is explicitly drawn: Socrates and Protagoras must first find out what virtue is, and then go back to inquire whether or not it is teachable. The "What is it?" question, the question of essence, is prior to all other questions about virtue. The *Protagoras,* which began with concern for the good of the soul, ends with a demand for essence, an account of the nature of demand for essence, an account of the nature of something which is.

There is in all this a contrast between appearance and reality, and that contrast accounts for the complex humor which lights the *Protagoras* and provides much of its surface charm. The *Protagoras* is a very funny dialogue. Here is Hippocrates, coming at dawn before first light in great excitement to tell Socrates that Protagoras—a sophist of whose teachings he knows nothing—is in town, and to beg an introduction. There is the scene when they reach Callias's house where Protagoras is staying, and the butler who grunts, "Sohpists!" and slams the door in their face—evidently holding an opinion on the subject of sophists somewhat at variance with that of Hippocrates. There is the wonderful description of Protagoras talking as he walks back and forth in the portico of the house, with his audience hanging on the words of the great man and wheeling and turning in perfect order behind him. And the touch of epic dignity used to describe Prodicus lying abed. Then there is the wonderful speech of Protagoras, a sales-talk for his own rhetorical wares which invokes Zeus and other gods, though the audience for whom the *Protagoras* was originally written knew that Protagoras was agnostic and believed in no gods. Appearance and reality.

Socrates himself catches the spirit. After almost breaking up the meeting by his insistence on short answers to questions, not speeches, he proceeds to imitate the sophists by giving a speech himself on a poem by Simonides, and parodies not only sophistical method but his own doctrine that wrongdoing is involuntary. The speech goes on and on, to the point of tedium which we are clearly meant to feel, and when at last it is done, Socrates politely remarks that it's useless to try to interpret poets anyway. Appearance and reality again. Humor having become parody turns to satire.

But the search for essence continues. Are the virtues equivalent? Protagoras, who is in fact dealing with a genus/species relation, thinks the parts of virtue are parts like the parts of the face, a material analysis of a logical relation. Are the parts of virtue detachable? Protagoras thinks they are, or that courage at least is detachable in that it is possible to be courageous and yet unjust, unholy, intemperate, and unwise.

In response, Socrates offers a theory which would make the virtues not only equivalent but identical—though it is hard to find a place for justice in the list. He provides an eminently sophisticated (in both senses of that word) statement of hedonism, and one which moves on several different levels at once. It is a brilliant exposition of hedonism, which greatly influenced the ancient schools. It provides an account of popular or demotic morality, the morality of common sense, which reduces it to hedonism, and further suggests that sophistry reduces to popular morality and thereby to hedonism too. Finally, it suggests but does not state that the hedonism of popular and sophistic morality is an εἴδωλον, a deficient likeness, of living well, that is, of living justly, by reason of which Socrates himself died. The humor of the *Protagoras* culminates in an argument whose essence is incongruity. The humor of incongruity is not always funny; sometimes it would be funny if it weren't so sad.

It is not that Protagoras is refuted; the truth-value of the claim that virtue is knowledge is left undetermined, as it must be, if one does not know what virtue is. But as Callicles' mouth is stopped in the *Gorgias,* as Thrasymachus's mouth is stopped in the *Republic,* Protagoras's mouth has been stopped in argument. He is left with nothing to say.

TRANSLATION

SOCRATES / UNNAMED COMPANION

Dramatic Introduction (309–310a)

309a COMP. Where from, Socrates? Hunting the vernal beauty of Alcibiades, no doubt? Well, I saw him just the other day, and he's looking still beautiful as a man, Socrates, but a man nonetheless, to speak among ourselves, and at this point getting quite a beard.

SOC. Well, what of it? You don't mean you disapprove of Homer,
b who said, "With beard new grown, the most graceful time for a youth"[1]—as Alcibiades is now.

COMP. How are things? Were you just with him? How's the lad disposed toward you?

SOC. Well disposed, I thought, especially today. Actually, he said many things in my behalf and helped me, and in fact I only just left him. But I'll tell you something surprising: though he was present, I paid no attention and often forgot he was there.

c COMP. Something serious has happened between you and him? For you surely haven't met anyone else handsomer, at least not in this city.

SOC. Yes, much handsomer.

COMP. What? Citizen or foreigner?

SOC. Foreigner.

COMP. Where from?

SOC. Abdera.

1. *Iliad* xxiv 348. Cf. *Odyssey* X 279.

169

COMP. And you thought a foreigner so handsome that he appeared
handsomer to you than the son of Cleinias?

SOC. Won't the wisest appear most handsome, my friend?

COMP. You've just left someone wise?

d SOC. Surely the wisest of our generation, if you think Protagoras is
wisest.

COMP. You mean Protagoras is in town?

SOC. For three days now.

COMP. So you've just come from being with him?

310a SOC. Yes, and said and heard many things.

COMP. Then unless something prevents, why not relate the conversation to us, Socrates? Sit down here, and let this slave get up.

SOC. Very well. Indeed, I'll be glad if you listen.

COMP. And I'll be glad if you speak.

SOC. Double delight, then. Please listen:

Narrative Introduction (310a–312b)

During this past night, just before dawn, Hippocrates son of Apollodorus, brother of Phason, knocked hard on my door with his
b   staff, and when somebody opened it for him, he immediately
came rushing in shouting, Socrates! Are you awake or asleep?

I recognized his voice and said, Here's Hippocrates! No bad
news, I hope.

Nothing but good news, said he.

Excellent, I said. But what brings you here at this hour?

Protagoras has come, he said, standing beside me.

Yes, the day before yesterday, I said. You've only just found out?

By heavens, only last night, he said. And at that he groped for
the bed and sat down by my foot and said: It was just last night. I
c   got back quite late from Oenoe: my slave Satyrus ran off, you see,
and of course I meant to tell you I was going after him, but for
some reason it slipped my mind. When I got back and had supper
and was about to go to bed, that's when my brother tells me Protagoras had come. And late as it was, I tried to come straight to
you, but then I thought it was much too late; but as soon as sleep
d   relieved my weariness, I got up immediately and came straight
here.

And I said, discerning his manly agitation. What do you care?
Protagoras hasn't done you a wrong, has he?

And he laughed. Heavens no, Socrates, he said. Except maybe that only he is wise and doesn't make me so.

Why of course he will, I said. If you give him money and persuade him, he'll make you wise too.

e
Zeus and gods! If it only depends on that! he said. Because I'd spare nothing that belongs to me or my friends. But that's just why I've come to you now, so you can speak to him in my behalf. I'm too young, and I've never even seen Protagoras or heard him; I was still a child when he last came to town. But everybody praises the

311a
man, Socrates, and says he's extraordinarily wise in speaking. Why don't we walk to where he's at, so we can catch him at home? I heard he's staying with Callias, son of Hipponicus. Let's go.

And I said, Not yet, my friend—it's early. Instead, let's get up and walk around here in the courtyard to pass the time until it's light. Then we can go. As a matter of fact, Protagoras passes most of his time there, so cheer up, we'll very likely catch him at home.

After that, we got up and walked about in the courtyard, and I examined Hippocrates, questioning him to test his mettle. Tell

b
me, Hippocrates, I said. You're now undertaking to go to Protagoras and pay him money for your tuition. Who are you going to, and what will you become? For example, suppose you intended to go to your namesake, Hippocrates of Cos, one of the Asclepiads,[2] and pay him money for your tuition, and someone

c
asked, Tell me, Hippocrates, since you intended to pay a fee to Hippocrates, what is he? How would you answer?

I'd say he's a doctor, he replied.

And what will you become?

A doctor too, he said.

Suppose you intended to go to Polyclitus the Argive or Phidias the Athenian[3] and pay them tuition, and somebody asked you, What are Polyclitus and Phidias, that you intend to pay them money? How would you answer?

Sculptors, I'd reply.

And what will you become yourself?

A sculptor, clearly.

2. The "sons of Asclepius," a school of doctors in Cos and Cnidus. Hippocrates was born about 460 B.C. at Cos. His fame as a doctor was such that the surviving body of Greek medical works is ascribed to him, though none are known to have been written by him and many appear to date from a later time; this accords with the Greek practice of ascribing all discoveries of a school to its founder. See also *Phaedrus* 270c, where Hippocrates is offered as a paradigm of inquiry about the body.

3. Cf. *Meno* 91d.

Very well, said I. But now we're going to Protagoras, you and I,
d ready to pay him money in your behalf—our own money, if it
suffices to persuade him, but if not we'll spend that of our friends.
Suppose then someone should ask, since we're so intent on this,
Tell me, Socrates and Hippocrates, what is Protagoras, that you
intend to pay him money? How would we reply? What other name
e do we hear applied to Protagoras? We hear of Phidias that he's a
sculptor and of Homer that he's a poet; what name of that kind do
we hear of Protagoras?

Why, they call the man a sophist, Socrates, he said.

So we're going to pay money to him as a sophist?

Certainly.

312a Then suppose someone asked you in addition, What do you
yourself intend to become by going to Protagoras?

He blushed even as he spoke—there was just enough daylight
by then to see it: Clearly a sophist, he said, if it's at all like the
previous examples.

Good heavens, I said. Wouldn't you be ashamed to hold yourself out among Greeks as a sophist?

Of course I would, Socrates, if I'm to say what I really think.

But perhaps after all, Hippocrates, you assume your instruc-
b tion from Protagoras won't be of this sort, but the kind you got
from your writing master and music teacher and trainer. You
learned each of those subjects not with a view to becoming a public
practitioner of an art but for education, as befits a private citizen
and a free man.

Of course, he said, I think that's more the kind of instruction
one gets from Protagoras.

Sophistry and the Soul (312b–314c)

Then do you know what you're now intending to do, or does it
escape you? I said.

About what?

You intend to put your own soul in the care of a man who is, as
c you say, a sophist. But I'd be surprised if you know just what a
sophist is. And yet if you're ignorant of this, you don't know to
whom you're entrusting your soul, or whether the thing is good
or bad.

I at least think I know, he said.

Then say what you believe the sophist is.

I believe that as the name implies, he has knowledge of wise things, he replied.

d   Well, I replied, it's also possible to say of painters and builders that they have knowledge of wise things. But if someone asked us what wise things painters know, we'd surely reply that they know about the production of likenesses, and so in other cases. But if someone were to ask what wise things the sophist knows, what would we answer? Of what sort of work is he master?

What would we say he is, Socrates, except a master at making people speak cleverly?

Perhaps we'd be telling the truth, said I, but it's hardly enough, for our answer still requires a question: About what does the sophist make people speak cleverly? The musician surely makes

e   people speak cleverly about what he also makes them know, namely, music. Not so?

Yes.

Very well. Then about what does the sophist make people speak cleverly?

Clearly, about that which he also makes them know?

Yes, very likely. But what is it about which the sophist has knowledge himself, and makes his pupil know?

Good lord, Socrates, I no longer can tell you.

313a   And I said next, Really? Then do you know to what sort of danger you're going to subject your soul? If you had to entrust your body to someone and run the risk of it becoming better or worse, you'd consider very carefully whether or not you should do it; you'd summon your friends to counsel and inquire of your relatives for days on end. But about something you believe more important than the body, namely the soul, on which all that is yours depends for faring well or ill according as it becomes good or bad—about this you consult neither your father nor brother

b   nor any of us who are your friends as to whether or not you should entrust your soul to this foreigner who has just arrived. On the contrary: you heard only last night, you say, yet you come before dawn, not to discuss the matter or seek advice about whether you should entrust yourself to him or not, but ready to spend your own money and that of your friends because you've already decided that you must at all costs study with Protagoras, whom you admit c   you don't know, and with whom you've never once talked. You call him a sophist, but you appear ignorant of what the sophist is to whom you are about to entrust yourself.

He heard this and said, It does seem so, Socrates, from what you say.

Well, Hippocrates, isn't the sophist a kind of merchant or huckster of wares by which the soul is fed?[4] He seems that way to me.

But what does a soul feed on, Socrates?

On learning, surely, I said. And we must beware, my friend, that the sophist not deceive us in praising what he sells, as mer-

d   chants and hucksters do with food for the body. In fact, they don't know which among their wares are good or bad for the body, but they praise everything they sell; nor do those who buy of them know either, unless they happen to be physicians or trainers. It's the same way with these folk who tour our cities peddling knowledge to whomever desires it; they praise everything they sell, but perhaps some of them, dear friend, are ignorant whether the

e   things they sell are good or bad for the soul. So too for those who buy from them, unless they also happen to be physicians of soul. So if you know what is good and bad, you can safely buy your knowledge from Protagoras and anyone else; but if you don't, look

314a   to it, dear friend, lest you risk and hazard things of utmost value. In fact, the risk is actually much greater when you purchase knowledge than when you purchase food. For it's possible to buy food and drink from a huckster or merchant and carry it away in another container, and before talking it into your body by eating or drinking, it's possible to set it aside in your house and summon an expert to consult about what should be eaten and drunk and

b   what should not, and how much, and when. So there's no great risk in the purchase. But learning cannot be carried away in another container. On the contrary, having paid the price, you necessarily take what is learned into your very soul, and depart either benefited or harmed. Let us then consider these things in company with our elders; for we are still too young to decide for ourselves a thing of such importance. Now, however, let's go and hear the man as we started out to do, and after we've heard him we'll also consult others. Actually, it's not only Protagoras who is

c   here but Hippias of Elis and, I think, also Prodicus of Ceos, and many other wise men too.

4. Cf. *Sophist* 223c–224e, 231d.

A Foregathering of Sophists (314c–316b)

This seemed good to us and we set forth. When we arrived at the front door, we stood and discussed an argument which occurred to us on the way; so in order that it might not be unfinished but settled, we stood in front of the door before we went in discussing

d   until we reached agreement. Well, I suppose the doorkeeper, a eunuch, overheard us, and very likely he was irritated at those who kept coming to the house because of the multitude of sophists. At any rate, when we knocked at the door, he opened it and saw us and said, Ho! Sophists! He's busy! And with that, he very spiritedly slammed the door shut with both hands as hard as he could.

We knocked again and he answered us through the closed door: Gentlemen, didn't you hear? He's busy.

e   I replied, My good fellow, we haven't come to see Callias, and we're not sophists. So cheer up. We came because we need to see Protagoras. Please announce us.

Well, after some hesitation, the fellow opened the door for us.

When we entered, we found Protagoras walking up and down in the portico. Walking with him in a line there was, on one side,

315a   Callias, son of Hipponicus, and his stepbrother Parolus, son of Pericles, and Charmides, son of Glaucon; on the other side, there was Pericles' other son, Xanthippus, and Philippides, son of Philomelus, and Antimoerus of Mende, the most highly regarded of Protagoras's pupils, who is learning the art with the purpose of becoming a sophist himself. Others followed along behind to hear what was being said; for the most part they appeared to be foreigners whom Protagoras had drawn from every city through

b   which he'd passed, enchanting them with his voice like Orpheus while they, enchanted, follow wherever the voice may lead. But there were some of our own countrymen also in the chorus. It was a pleasure to see how careful that chorus was never to get in front of Protagoras or block him; on the contrary, when he and those with him turned, their followers somehow split their ranks in perfect order, this way and that, and wheeling in a circle, fell in behind him very beautifully every time.

"After him I was aware," as Homer says,[5] of Hippias of Elis,

c   sitting on a kind of throne in the portico opposite; around him, seated on benches, were Eriximachus, son of Acumenus, and

5. *Odyssey* XII 601.

Phaedrus the Myrrhinousian, and Andron, son of Androtion, and some foreigners, his own fellow citizens and others. It appeared they were asking Hippias something about nature and things in the heavens having to do with astronomy,[6] while he, seated on his throne, distinguished their several questions and discussed them.

"And I saw Tantalus too"[7]—Prodicus was also in town, you

d   know. He was in a room which Hipponicus used to use as a store-room, but now, due to the multitude of guests, Callias had emptied it and made it into a guest room for visitors. Well, Prodicus was still in bed wrapped up in fleeces and blankets, quite a few of them, it appeared, and seated next to him on the neighboring beds was Pausanias of Cerameis, and with Pausanias was a young fellow, still a lad, noble and well born, I believe, and certainly very fair of form. I think I heard his name is Agathon, and I shouldn't

e   be surprised if he's Pausanias's favorite. Well, this young fellow was there along with both Adeimantuses, the sons of Cepis and of Leucolophidas, and there appeared to be certain others too. From

316a the outside I couldn't tell what they were talking about, even though I was greedy to hear Prodicus—for I think the man is all-wise and divine—but because of the depth of his voice, there was a kind of droning murmur in the room which made what was said indistinct.

And we'd just come in when Alcibiades entered close behind us—the fair Alcibiades, as you say and I believe—along with Critias, son of Callaeschrus. So we went in, and after whiling away a little time looking at the scene, we went up to Protagoras, and I said, Protagoras, Hippocrates here and I have come to you.

b   Do you wish to discuss with me alone, he said, or in the company of others?

It makes no difference to us, I said. You can decide for yourself when you hear why we've come.

Very well then, he said. Why did you come?

Can Virtue Be Taught? (316b–320c)

Hippocrates here is my fellow countryman, son of Apollodorus, of a great and happy house, and he himself seems a match for

---

6. Cf. *Hippias Minor* 367e.

7. *Odyssey* XI 582. Cf. *Cratylus* 395e. The comparison of Prodicus to Tantalus has been taken to imply physical suffering, but it may also have suggested greed, thirst and hunger. It is at the very least a double-edged compliment.

c anyone his age in natural ability. I think he wants to become distinguished in his city and supposes the best way to do it is to become your pupil; at this point, then, please consider whether you think you should discuss this matter with us privately or with others present.

Your thoughtfulness in my behalf is proper, Socrates. For when a man goes as a stranger to great cities, and in them persuades the best of the young men to leave their other associations, relatives and acquaintances old and young, and associate with him, so that they will be as good as possible through their associa-

d tion with himself, he must beware. For no small jealousy arises over it, and other ill will, and plots. I claim that the sophistic art is ancient, but those who had a hand in it among the ancients were afraid of the opprobrium attaching to it, and disguised and concealed themselves—some as poets, like Homer and Hesiod and Simonides, others again as prophets and soothsayers, like Or-

e pheus and Musaeus and their followers. Some even as trainers, I've observed, like Iccus of Tarentum and Herodicus of Selymbria, formerly of Megara, still living and a sophist inferior to none. Music was the disguise of your own Agathocles, a great sophist, and of Pythocles of Ceos and many others. All of them, as I say, used these arts as a screen for fear of jealousy. But I don't

317a agree with any of them in this: I believe they didn't accomplish what they wished. The reason for these disguises didn't escape the notice of people powerful in the affairs of their cities, even though the Many of course are aware of almost nothing but merely sing

b the praises of anything the others announce. Well, running away without being able to run away except to be discovered is great folly even in the attempt, and necessarily brings men much greater ill will, for people believe a man like that is unscrupulous in other things too. No, I've traveled quite the opposite road: I agree that I'm a sophist and that I educate men, and I think this agreement a better precaution than denial. I've taken other pre-

c cautions in this too, so that, please god, I suffer nothing terrible from agreeing I'm a sophist. And yet I am now many years in the art; in fact, the sum is so great that in respect to age, there's not one of you whose father I might not be. So it's much more pleasant for me, if you're willing, to give an account of all this in front of those within.

And I—for I suspected he wanted to make a display in front of Prodicus and Hippias and show off because we'd come as his d   admirers—I said, Why not then call Prodicus and Hippias and those with them, so they can hear us?

Why, of course, said Protagoras.

Then do you want us to arrange a seated session, said Callias, so that you can sit and talk?

It seemed we should do so. We were all delighted at the prospect of hearing wise men, and we picked up the benches and

e   couches ourselves and arranged them beside Hippias—for some benches were already there—and in the meantime, Callias and Alcibiades came bringing Prodicus, risen from his bed, and the people with Prodicus too.

When we all were seated, Protagoras said, Now that these people are also here, Socrates, you might say something about the subject you mentioned to me a moment ago in the young man's behalf.

318a   And I said, I'll begin the same way I did just now, Protagoras, about why I've come. Hippocrates here desires your tutelage; he says he'd like to learn what will result for him if he studies with you. That's the extent of our tale.

Young man, said Protagoras in reply, this is what you'll get if you study with me. On the day you come to me, you'll return home better, and the next day the same; and each day you'll always improve.

b   I heard this and said, Protagoras, this isn't at all surprising but probable, since even at your age and wise as you are, you'd improve, if somebody taught you what you didn't know. But take a different case. Suppose Hippocrates here suddenly changed his desire and wanted to be a pupil of this young fellow who's just recently come to town, Zeuxippus of Heraclea. And suppose he went to him as he's now come to you, and heard exactly the same things you've said, how each day he's with him he'll get better and

c   improve. Suppose he asked him, In what do you claim I'll be better? How will I improve? Zeuxippus would tell him, In painting. Or suppose he met Orthagoras the Theban and heard him say the same things you do, and asked him in what, through his association with him, he'd daily become better. He'd reply, In flute

d   playing. In just the same way, tell the young man, and me as I question you in his behalf: Suppose Hippocrates here associates with Protagoras and departs a better man on the same day he becomes his pupil and so on each subsequent day. How will he improve, Protagoras, and in what?

Protagoras, on hearing this from me, replied, You ask an excellent question, Socrates, and I delight in answering questions excellently asked. For if he comes to me, Hippocrates will not experience what those who associate with some other sophists do. For they maltreat the young who have fled the arts: they lead them back against their will and throw them into the arts, teaching them

e   calculation and astronomy and geometry and music—and at this he glanced at Hippias—but if he comes to me, he won't learn anything except what he came for. The subject of study is good judgment about his own affairs and how he may best order his own house, and about the affairs of the city and how he may be most powerful in those affairs both in action and speech.

319a   Do I follow you? I said. I think you speak of the political art and undertake to make men good citizens.

That's exactly my promise, Socrates, he said.

What a fine product of art you possess then, I said—if indeed you possess it; for I won't say anything to you except what I think. I didn't suppose this could be taught, Protagoras, though if you say

b   so, I can hardly doubt it. Still, it's right for me to say why I believe it can't be taught or provided by men for men. Like other Greeks, I claim the Athenians are wise. Well, I observe that when we gather in the Assembly and the city needs to deal with something having to do with building, builders are summoned to advise, and shipfit-

c   ters to advise about shipbuilding, and so in everything else they believe can be learned and taught; if somebody else undertakes to advise them whom they don't think is a craftsman, even if he's quite handsome and rich and well born, they don't at all accept it, but jeer and make a disturbance until the person undertaking to speak is shouted down and withdraws, or the officers remove or expel him by order of the magistrates. That's what they do about matters they think involve art. But when something about the

d   administration of the city must be taken under advisement, a carpenter or smith, a shoemaker, merchant or shipowner, rich or poor, well born or common, may equally rise to advise them about it, and no one criticizes him, as before, for never having studied anywhere or for not having a teacher but still undertaking to offer advice; for it's clear they don't believe it can be taught. Why, it's so

e   not only of the common constitution of the city but also in private affairs: the wisest and best of our politicians are unable to hand on this virtue they possess to others. Look at Pericles, the father of these young men here; he educated them excellently and well in

320a   subjects which can be got from teachers, but in those in which he is
himself wise he neither taught them himself nor handed them
over to anyone else; no, they were allowed to wander at large and
graze like untended cattle, on the chance they might somehow
happen on virtue spontaneously. If you wish, take Cleinias, the
younger brother of Alcibiades here; this same gentleman, Pericles, acting as his guardian and afraid lest he be corrupted by
Alcibiades, removed him and placed him in Ariphron's house to
b   be educated; and before six months passed, Ariphron gave him
back, because he didn't know what to do with him. And I can
mention a host of others who were themselves good but never
made anyone else, of their own or another's, better. So when I look
to this, Protagoras, I doubt that virtue can be taught. But when I
hear you say it can, I must defer; I think you're saying something
important, due to my belief that you've had wide experience and
learned many things and discovered some yourself. If you can
exhibit to us more clearly that virtue can be taught, then, please
don't at all begrudge us, but do so.

c   Why Socrates, he said, I'll not begrudge you. Shall I exhibit to
you as older to younger by telling a story, or by going through an
argument?

Well, many of those sitting by him replied that he should proceed in whichever way he wished.

Then I think it's more graceful to tell you a story, he said.

The Speech of Protagoras (320c–328d)

The Myth of Prometheus and Zeus (320c–324c)

Once upon a time, there were gods but no mortal kinds. When the
d   time destined for birth came, the gods shaped them within the
earth from earth mixed with fire and everything compounded of
fire and earth. And when they were about to lead them upward to
the light, the gods ordered Prometheus and Epimetheus to arrange and distribute to each such powers as were proper. Epimetheus himself asked Prometheus to let him to perform the
distribution: I'll distribute, he said, and you'll oversee. Thus persuading him, he distributed.

In distributing, he attached strength to some without speed,
e   but the weaker he adorned with speed. Some he armed, others he
left unarmed but gave another nature and devised power of pre-

servation for them. Some he surrounded with smallness, and distributed winged escape or subterranean dwelling places; others he increased in size and by this very thing preserved them. And he distributed the rest of the powers this way, balancing them equally.

321a   These things he devised, taking care lest any kind should be destroyed. When he supplied them with means of escape from mutual destruction, he also devised protection against the seasons sent from Zeus, clothing them in thick hair and tough hides sufficient to ward off winter cold but able also to resist summer heat, and so that each would have the same for his very own personal and self-grown mattress when he went to bed; and some he shod
b   with hooves, some with tough and bloodless hides. Next he provided different foods for different kinds, grasses from earth for some, fruits from trees for others, for others roots; but to some he gave as food the flesh of other animals, and these he made less prolific, but their prey he made very prolific, providing preservation for their race.

Well, because Epimetheus was not very wise, he heedlessly
c   lavished powers on the brute beats, but the human race was still left unprovided by him, and he was at a loss what to do. He was in perplexity when Prometheus came to oversee the distribution, and saw that while the other animals were well provided in everything, man was naked and unshod and unbedded and unarmed.

And the destined day was now at hand in which man also must go forth from earth into the light. So Prometheus, in perplexity about what he might discover for the preservation of man, stole
d   form Hephaestus and Athena wisdom in the arts, along with fire—for without fire there was no means for anyone to possess or use art itself—and so gave them to man. In this way man got wisdom for the needs of life, but he did not have the political art, for that was in the keeping of Zeus. Prometheus was no longer permitted to enter the Acropolis which is the dwelling place of
e   Zeus—and in addition the guards of Zeus were terrible—but he secretly entered the building shared by Athena and Hephaestus, in which the two liked to practice their arts, and stole the fiery art of Hephaestus and the other art belonging to Athena[8] and gave

8. The reference is unclear, the result of sophistical vagueness. Athena was a war goddess, expert in battle, female but fully armed. She was also goddess of spinning and weaving, pottery, and of arts in general. In Athens the Chalceia, the Festival of Smiths, was held in her honor, so she plainly overlapped Hephaestus in function. As patroness of multiple arts, she was a personification of wisdom generally.

them to man; from this man got easy provision for the needs of life. But afterward Prometheus, it is told, thanks to Epimetheus, was put on trial for theft.

322a   Since man had a share of divine apportionment, he was, first, the only animal that acknowledged gods because of his kinship to the god,[9] and he undertook to set up altars and images of gods; next he quickly invented speech and names by his art, and discovered houses and clothes and shoes and beds, and food from the earth. But men, thus provided, dwelt in the beginning scattered

b   and apart, and there were no cities; so they were destroyed by wild beasts because they were everywhere weaker. The craftsman's art was sufficient to help them relative to food, but lacking relative to war with wild beasts: for they did not yet have the art of politics, of which the art of war is a part.

So they sought to collect themselves together and preserve themselves by founding cities. Well, when they were collected together they did injustice to each other because they did not have the art of politics, so they were scattered again and destroyed.

c   Zeus, then, fearing that our race would be completely destroyed, sent Hermes to bring reverence and right to men, so that there might be good order for cities and binding ties of friendship. Well, Hermes asked Zeus in what manner he should give right and reverence to men: Do I distribute them as the arts have been distributed? They've been distributed thus: one man with medical art suffices for many laymen, and so with the other craftsmen. Am I to put right and reverence among men in this way too, or distrib-

d   ute to all? And Zeus said, To all. Let all have a share. For there would be no cities if only a few, as with other arts, partook of these. Yes, and put it as my law that he who is incapable of partaking of reverence and right is to die as a civic disease.

Thus then, Socrates, and for these reasons, when there is speech about virtue in the art of building or any other art, Athenians as well as others think they should consult only a few, and if

e   someone besides those few offers advice, they do not allow it, as you say—reasonably, as I claim. But when they come to consult about political virtue, which must all come through justice and

---

9. Protagoras claims that men have kinship to the gods. The basis of that kinship has just been explained: it is not that men are made in the image of God, but that they possess fire and the arts. Note that Protagoras passes from singular to plural, from god to gods, without any clear sense of transition: if "the god" were Athena, we should expect the feminine article. This is characteristic of Greek usage, and common in Plato.

temperance, they quite reasonably accept advice from all men,
323a   because all must have a share of this virtue lest there be no city.
That, Socrates, is the cause of this.

But so that you may not think yourself misled, accept this
further proof that all men really believe that every man partakes
b   of justice and the rest of political virtue. For in the other virtues, as
you say, if someone claims to be a good flute player or good at any
other art when he's not, people either scoff or become angry, and
his relatives will come and admonish him as if he were mad. But in
justice and the rest of political virtue, even if they know that someone is unjust, yet still, if he himself tells the truth about himself in
front of many people, honesty which they elsewhere count as
temperance they here count as madness; they say that everyone
ought to claim to be just whether they are or not, or that anyone
who doesn't pretend to justice is mad. Because they think everyone without exception must necessarily partake of it somehow or
other, or not exist among men.

c   I claim then that they reasonably accept advice from all men
about this virtue in the belief that all share it.

That they don't believe it exists by nature or arises spontaneously, but can be taught and comes to be present, in those in
whom it comes to be present, by study, this I shall try to demonstrate for you with this. For no one is angry over such evils as men
believe each other to possess by nature or by chance, or admon-
d   ishes or instructs or punishes those who have them in order that
they not be that way, but they pity them. Who, for example, is so
irrational as to undertake to do any of this to those who are ugly or
small or weak? Because, I suppose, they know that things beautiful and the opposite come to people by nature and by chance. But
e   as to the good things they think people get from study and practice and teaching, if someone possesses not them but the evils
opposite to them, anger rises against them, and punishments and
admonishment.

One among these evils is injustice and impiety and, in sum,
324a   everything completely opposite to political virtue. But where all
are angry at all and admonish them, it is clearly because possession
derives from study and learning. For if you will consider punishment, Socrates, and what it effects on those who do wrong, it will
teach you that men believe virtue can be produced. No one punishes those who do wrong attending to and because of the fact that
they did wrong, unless he exacts irrational vengeance like a wild

b   beast. Whoever undertakes to punish in accord with reason does not exact requital for the crime which has been committed—what has been done cannot be undone—but for the future, in order that neither the fellow himself nor anyone else who sees him being punished shall again do wrong. And having such an intention as

c   this, he conceives virtue to be taught; at any rate he punishes for the sake of deterrence. Now, everyone holds this opinion who exacts requital in public and private. But other people, and not least the Athenians, your fellow citizens, exact requital and punish those they think do wrong; so by this account, Athenians too are of the belief that virtue can be produced and taught.

In this way it is sufficiently demonstrated to you, Socrates, at least as it appears to me, that your fellow citizens reasonably accept the advice of smiths and cobblers in political matters, and that they believe virtue can be produced and taught.

Argument: Everyone Teaches Virtue (324d–328c)

d   There remains still the perplexity which perplexes you about good men: Why do good men teach their own sons other things which have teachers and make them wise, but make them no better than anyone else in the virtue in which their own goodness consists? About this, then, Socrates, I'll no longer offer you a story but an argument. Consider the following:

Is there or is there not some one thing of which all citizens

e   must necessarily have a shore if there is to be a city? For the perplexity which perplexes you is resolved here or nowhere. If there is, and if this one thing is not the art of the builder or smith

325a or potter, but justice and temperance and the holy, and in sum one thing by itself I call virtue in a man—if it is of this that all must partake, and with this that every man must thus act if he wishes to learn or do anything else, and not without it; if we must teach or punish him who does not partake of it, man, woman and child, until by being punished he becomes better, if we must cast out of the city or put to death as incurable whoever does not comply after

b   being punished and taught—if this is so, then given that it is so, if good men teach their sons other things but not this, consider how strange good men become. For that they believe that it can be taught in public and private, we proved. But since it can be taught and cultivated, do they perhaps then teach their sons other things for which the penalty is not death if they are ignorant, but where the penalty for their children, if they do not learn and are uncultic vated in respect of virtue, is death and exile—and in addition to death, confiscation of property and, in short, the total overturn of their houses—these things, then, they do not teach nor care for with all care? So we are to suppose, Socrates.

They teach and admonish them, beginning in early childhood, for as long as they live. As soon as a child understands what is being said, nurse and mother and tutor and the father himself

d compete to make him as good as possible, teaching and showing in every word and deed that this is just, that unjust, this beautiful, that ugly, this holy, that unholy, do this, don't do that. And if he willingly obeys—good. But if not, they correct and straighten him out like a warped piece of wood, with threats and blows. After that,

e they send him to teachers charged to care much more about the deportment of the children than their letters and lyre. Their teachers do care, and when they've learned their letters and are beginning to understand what is written as before they under-

326a stood the spoken word, they set before them at their benches the poems of good poets to read and make them learn them by heart; these contain many admonitions and narratives and songs praising good men of old, in order that the child may zealously imitate and desire to become like them. The lyre teachers, again, are similarly concerned for temperance, and that the young should

b do no ill; in addition to learning to play the lyre, they also teach them poems of other good lyric poets, accompanying the poems on the lyre, and compel the rhythms and modes to dwell in the souls of the children so that they may be more gentle, and by becoming better attuned and more rhythmical may be useful in speech and action; for the whole life of man needs rhythm and attunement. Still again they send them to the trainer, so that by having better bodies they may minister to their excellence of mind, and not be compelled to cowardice in warfare and other

c actions through the badness of their bodies. Those who are especially powerful do this; the richest are especially powerful; and their sons begin school earliest and are released latest. But when they're released from teachers, the city also compels them to learn its laws and live by them as by a pattern or example, in order that they may not act at random on their own. It is as when writing

d masters trace the outline of letters with a stylus for children not yet skilled at writing, and so give them the copybook and compel them to write following the lines; in the same way the city traces the outline of its laws, discoveries of good and ancient lawgivers,

and compels them to rule and be ruled according to them. Whoever steps beyond them she punishes, and a name for this punish-
e   ment among you and in many other places is correction, because
the just penalty corrects.

Since, then, there is so much concern about virtue in public
and private, are you surprised and perplexed, Socrates, if virtue
can be taught? You should not be surprised, but much rather if it
were not taught.

Why then are many worthless sons born to good fathers?
Learn this too. For it is hardly surprising, if indeed I told the truth
327a   in what I said before, namely, that no one must be unpracticed in
this thing, virtue, if there is to be a city. For if what I say is so—and
it is most certainly so—then consider any other pursuit or study
you choose. Suppose it were impossible for a city to exist unless we
were all flute players, as far as each of us was able; and further
suppose that everyone taught everyone in public and private, and
reproved those who did not play well and did not begrudge him,
b   as at present no one is grudging in matters of justice and lawful-
ness, or conceals it like the devices of other arts. For I suppose the
justice and virtue of each is profitable to the others: that's why all
speak eagerly to all and teach what things are just and lawful. Well,
suppose we were that eager and ungrudging in teaching each
other flute playing. Do you think, Socrates, he said, that the sons
of good flute players would become good flute players any
the more than the sons of worthless ones? I think not. Rather, the
c   son who happened to be born with most natural ability for the
flute would grow up to be distinguished, the son who lacked
natural ability would be left in the shade; often the son of a good
flute player would turn out worthless, and often the son of a
worthless flute player good, yet all would then at any rate[10] be
adequate flute players compared to laymen who know nothing of
fluting.

In the same way now, you should suppose that whoever ap-
d   pears to you most unjust, among those raised among laws and
men, is himself just and indeed a very artist at the thing compared
to men who have neither education nor courts nor laws nor any
necessity compelling them constantly to be concerned for virtue;

10. Reading γοῦν with BTW. Modern editors do not like the clash with οὖ in the same line;
it is here attested that Protagoras did, and surely not impossible: compare for example the
jingle in τις ὅστις in 328a 8.

on the contrary, they'd be wild beasts of the sort the poet Pherecrates produced last year at the Lenaea.[11] No doubt if you found
yourself among such men as the misanthropes in his chorus, you'd
be delighted to meet even Eurybates and Phrynondas,[12] and
e   you'd cry out in longing for the wickedness of people here. But as
it is, Socrates, you're spoiled. Because all teach virtue so far as each
328a is able, it appears to you that no one does. Why, it's as if you were to
ask who teaches Greek; no one person would appear, nor would
any appear, I think, if you were to inquire who teaches the sons of
our artisans the same art they've learned from their father, insofar
as the father was competent and his friends were fellow craftsmen.
As to who else would teach them, Socrates, I doubt it would be easy
to show a teacher for them, but easy for those completely without
experience; so too for virtue and everything else.

But even if someone surpasses us by only a little in promoting
b   virtue, it is to be welcomed. Of whom indeed I think I am one: that
I surpass the rest of mankind in assisting a person to become noble
and good, and that I'm worthy of the fee I charge and still more, as
seems true even to the pupil himself. That's why I've devised the
following manner of setting my fee: when someone learns from
c   me, he may if he wishes pay what I charge; but if not, he can go to a
temple, swear on oath how much he claims my instruction is
worth, and deposit that amount.

Conclusion (328c–d)

There, Socrates, he said. I've told you in both story and argument
that virtue can be taught and Athenians believe so, and that it is
not at all surprising that worthless sons are born of good fathers
and good sons of worthless fathers, since even the sons of Poly-
cleitus, who are the same age as Paralus and Xanthippus here, are
nothing compared to their father, and other sons of other crafts-
d   men too. But they don't yet deserve this charge; there's still hope
for them, because they're young.

11. A winter festival held in January/February of the Athenian luni-solar year. "Last
year," given the dramatic date of the *Protagoras*, would be perhaps 435/4. So if this passage
refers to Pherecrates' play *The Savages*, which was produced in 421/20, it is a pointless
anachronism. But it need not so refer: Pherecrates won his first dramatic competition in 438
and may well have returned to such an obvious theme several times. Besides, the title of the
play here mentioned appears to have been *The Misanthropes*. Plato uses anachronism, but
generally with a dramatic purpose in view.
12. Two real-life scoundrels.

The Unity of Virtue (328d–334d)

After such and so great a display, Protagoras ceased speaking. Spellbound, I for some time still kept looking at him, all eagerness to hear, as if he would go on; but when at last I realized he had really stopped, I somehow with difficulty collected myself, as it were, and glanced toward Hippocrates and said: Son of Apollodorus, how grateful I am to you for urging me to come here, for

e   I count it important to have heard what I've heard from Protagoras. I formerly believed it is by no human care that good men become good; but now I'm persuaded. Except for a certain small

329a   difficulty, which it's clear Protagoras will easily explain, since he's already explained so many. Actually, if one went to any of the orators about these same matters, one might perhaps hear just such speeches as this from Pericles or any other able speaker. But if they're asked a question, they're like books which can neither answer nor put questions themselves; on the contrary, if someone asks some little question about what's been said, it's like a gong that continues—unless one takes hold of it—to sound long after it's struck; in the same way these orators, asked a short question,

b   stretch out a lengthy speech. Protagoras here is capable of giving long and beautiful speeches, as he's shown, but he's also capable of answering briefly when questioned, and after putting a question, to wait and accept the answer—a thing few are prepared to do.

Now then, Protagoras, I'd lack little of having everything if you'd just answer me this. You say that virtue can be taught,[13] and if indeed I could be persuaded of it by any other man, I'd be

c   persuaded by you. But please satisfy my soul about something which surprised me in what you said. For you said that Zeus sent justice and reverence to men, and again in several places in your speech that justice and temperance and holiness and all that are in sum one thing, namely, virtue.[14] Give me then a precise account of just this: is virtue one single thing, but justice and temperance and holiness parts of it, or are these things I just now mentioned all names for one and the same thing? That's what I still want to know.

d   Why, that's easy, Socrates, he said. Virtue is one, and what you ask about are parts of it.

13. διδακτόν. The first verbal adjective denotes possibility, *teachable*, as the second verbal adjective denotes necessity; but the first verbal adjective also sometimes has the force of a perfect passive participle, *taught*.
14. See 324e–325a, 323a, e.

Are they parts like the parts of the face, I said, mouth and nose and eyes and ears, or like the parts of gold, which don't differ at all one from another and from the whole except in largeness and smallness?

e   The former, it appears to me, Socrates: as the parts of the face are to the whole face.

Then when people come to partake of these parts of virtue, I said, do some partake of one, others of another, or is it necessary if someone receives one to have all?

Not at all, he said, since many are courageous but unjust, and just again, but not wise.

330a   These then are also parts of virtue, I said, namely, wisdom and courage?

Most certainly so, he said. And the most important among them, surely, is wisdom.

Each of them, I said, is different from any other?

Yes.

Does each of them also have its own peculiar power? As with the parts of the face, the eye is not such as the ears, nor is its power the same, nor is one such as any of the others in respect to either power or anything else. Is it then so also that one part of virtue is

b   not such as another, either in itself or in its power? Or isn't it clearly so, if indeed it's like the example?

Why, it's so, Socrates, he said.

And I said, So no other part of virtue is such as knowledge, nor such as justice, nor such as courage, nor such as temperance, nor such as holiness?

No, he said.

Come then, I said, let's jointly inquire what sort each of them is. First this: Is justice a kind of thing, or not a thing at all? For it seems to me it is. Does it to you?

c   And to me, he said.

Well then, suppose someone should ask you and me, "Protagoras and Socrates, will you two please tell me, is this thing which you just now named, justice, itself a just thing or an unjust thing?" I'd answer him that it's a just thing. How would you vote? The same as me, or different?

The same, he said.

So justice is of such sort as to be a just thing, I'd answer the questioner. And you would too?

d   Yes, he said.

Suppose then he next asked us, "Then you also say that holiness is something?" We'd agree, I suppose.

Yes, said he.

"Then you say this too is a kind of thing?" We'd agree, wouldn't we?

He also concurred in this.

"Do you say this thing itself is by nature of such sort as to be an unholy thing, or of such sort as to be a holy thing?" I'd be annoyed at the question, I said, and I'd reply, Don't blaspheme, fellow! It could scarcely be that anything else would be holy, if holiness itself is not to be a holy thing. What about you? Wouldn't you reply the same way?

e   Of course, he said.

Then suppose next he were to ask us: "Then what were you saying a moment ago? Didn't I hear you correctly? I thought you said that the parts of virtue are so related to each other that one of them is not such as any other." I'd myself reply, You heard the rest correctly, but in thinking I said this, you misheard. Protagoras

331a   here said it in answer to my question. Suppose then he said, "Is he telling the truth, Protagoras? Do you say one part of virtue is not such as any of the others? Is that your account?" What would you answer him?

I must necessarily agree, Socrates, he said.

Then what answer shall we give him, Protagoras, once we agree to this, if he should go on to ask us, "So holiness is not such as to be a just thing, nor justice such as to be a holy thing, but such as

b   not to be a holy thing? And holiness such as not to be a just thing, but perhaps then an unjust thing, what is unholy?"[15] What shall we answer him? For my part, I'd say that justice is a holy thing and holiness a just thing, and if you allow me, I'd give the same answer for you: that more probably justice is either the same as holiness or a thing most like it, but it is beyond question that justice is such as holiness and holiness such as justice. But see if you forbid this answer, or whether you accept it too.

I don't think it's quite so simple, Socrates, he said, as to agree

c   that justice is a holy thing and holiness a just thing; I think there's some difference in it. But what difference does it make? he said. If you wish, let justice be a holy thing and holiness a just thing for us.

15. Unjust, or not just; unholy, or not holy. ἄρα, translated "perhaps then," as weakly inferential. For the inference, cf. *Charmides* 161a: "Temperance is good, since it makes those things to which it is present good, but not bad."

No, I said, it's not "if you wish" and "if you think so" I need to examine, but you and me: I say "you and me," because I suppose the account would thus best be examined if one subtracted the "if" from it.

d   But of course, he said, justice does have a certain resemblance to holiness; in fact, everything in some way or other resembles everything else. For white in a way resembles black, and hard resembles soft, and other things which seem most opposite to each other. And the parts of the face, which we just claimed to have a different power, and one not such as any other, in some way or
e   other resemble each other, and one is such as the other; so in this way you could even prove, if you wished, that they're all like each other. But it's not right to call things alike which have only some likeness, even if the likeness is very small, nor things unlike which have only some unlikeness.

I was surprised, and said to him, Then you think the just and the holy are so related that they have only some small likeness to each other?

332a   Not quite that, he said, but on the other hand not as you seem to think either.

Very well, I said, since you seem annoyed with this, let's dismiss it and consider the other thing you were saying. There is something you call folly?

He assented.

Is not wisdom the utter opposite of this thing?

I think so, he said.

when people act rightly and beneficially, do you think they're then temperate in so acting or the opposite?

Temperate, he said.

Now, they are temperate by temperance?[16]

b   Necessarily.

Now, those who do not act rightly act foolishly, and they are not temperate in so acting?

I concur, he said.

So acting foolishly is opposed to acting temperately?

He assented.

Now, what is done foolishly is done by folly, but what is done temperately by temperance?

16. The dative is instrumental, to be blossed by ὑπό and the genitive of agent (332c 1–2), as well as μετά and the genitive of accompaniment which implies causation.

He agreed.

Now, if something is done by strength, it is done strongly, and if by weakness, weakly?

He thought so.

And if with quickness, quickly, and if with slowness, slowly?

He assented.

c And if anything then is done in the same way, it is done by the same thing, and if in the opposite way by the opposite?

He concurred.

Come then, I said, is there something beautiful?

He conceded it.

Is there anything opposite to it except the ugly?

There is not.

Then is there something good?

There is.

Is there anything opposite to it except the bad?

There is not.

Then is there something high in pitch?

He assented.

Is there anything opposite to it except the low?

He said not.

Now, there is only one opposite, I said, for each one of the opposites, and not many?

He concurred.

d Come then, I said, let's reckon up what we've agreed. We've agreed that for one thing there is only one opposite, and not many?

We have.

And that what is oppositely done is done by opposites?

He assented.

But we've agreed that what's done foolishly is done oppositely to what's done temperately?

He assented.

but what's done temperately is done by temperance, and what's done foolishly by folly?

e He conceded it.

Then since done oppositely, it would be done by an opposite?

Yes.

The one is done by temperance, the other by folly?

Yes.

Oppositely?

Of course.

Then done by opposite things?

Yes.

So folly is opposite to temperance.

It appears so.

Do you recall then that we earlier agreed that folly is opposite to wisdom?

He concurred.

But for one opposite there is only one opposite?

333a   I agree.

Then which account should we let go, Protagoras? That one thing has only one opposite, or the account in which it was said that wisdom is different from temperance but each of the two is part of virtue, and that in addition to being different they're also unlike both in themselves and in their powers, as with the parts of the face? Which then should we let go? For these accounts, taken together, are not very musical:[17] they are neither in concord nor in attunement with each other. How indeed could they accord,

b   since for one thing there is necessarily only one opposite and no more, but wisdom appears opposite to folly, which is one, and temperance does too? Isn't that so, Protagoras? I said. Or is it otherwise?

He agreed, much against his will.

Then temperance and wisdom would be one? But on the other hand, it appeared to us before that justice and holiness are pretty nearly the same thing. Come then, Protagoras, I said, let's not falter but complete the remainder of the inquiry. Does a person doing injustice seem to you temperate in respect to what he unjustly does?[18]

c   I'd be ashamed to agree to this, Socrates, though the majority of men at least say so.

Then shall I direct the argument to them, I said, or to you?

If you will, he said, please examine the account of the Many first.

Why it makes no difference to me, if only you answer, whether then you think it true or not. For I primarily examine the argument, though it perhaps also results that both I as the questioner and the respondent as well are examined.

17. Cf. 326b.
18. Construed following Adam and Adam, Cf. 333d 6.

d   Well, at first Protagoras was mock-modest with us—he alleged the argument was hard to deal with—but finally, he agreed to answer.

Come then, I said, answer me from the beginning: Do you think some people are temperate in doing injustice?

Let it be so, he said.

But you say that to be temperate is to be reasonable?

He assented.

But to be reasonable is to be well advised in respect to what they unjustly do?

Let it be so, he said.

If they fare well by doing injustice, I said, or if they fare badly?

If they fare well.

Now, you say some things are good?

I do.

Now, I said, those things are good which are beneficial to men?

e   Yes, by Zeus, he said, and even if they're not beneficial to men, I call them good.

I thought Protagoras at this point was ruffled and contentious and prepared to struggle against answering. So when I saw he was that way, I took care to question gently.

334a   Do you mean, Protagoras, said I, what is not beneficial to any man, or what is not beneficial to anything at all? Do you call even such things as that good?

Not at all, he said. But I know many things which are useless to men—food and drink and drugs and countless others—but some are beneficial; and some things are neither the one nor the other to men, but to horses; some only to cattle, others to dogs; yes, and some to none of these, but to trees; and some good for the roots of the tree but bad for the branches, as for example dung is good

b   when thrown around the roots of all plants, but if you throw it on shoots and young branches it destroys everything. Then again, olive oil is quite bad for all plants and most inimical to the hair of other animals except man, but serviceable to the hair of man and the rest of the body. So various a thing is the good, and varied in kind, that in this case it is good for the man on the outside of his

c   body, but the same thing is extremely bad on the inside, and for this reason, all doctors forbid sick people to use olive oil in what they're going to eat, except in the smallest possible amount, just enough to quell disgust at the smell in their nostrils arising from food and drink.

Interlude: Questions and Speeches (334c–338e)

Well, when he said this, the company loudly applauded how well he spoke, and I said: I'm a forgetful sort of fellow, Protagoras, and if someone speaks at length, I forget what the discussion was

d   about. Just as if I were hard of hearing, you'd suppose you had to speak louder to me than to others if you intended to carry on a discussion with me, so now, since you've met someone forgetful, you must chop up your answers for me and make them briefer if I'm to follow you.

How then do you bid me answer briefly? Am I to answer you more briefly than is required? he said.

Not at all, said I.

The length required? he said.

e   Yes, said I.

Then are my answers to be as long as I think required, or as you do?

I've heard, at any rate, said I, that you're able to speak about the same things yourself and teach others, if you wish, both at such

335a   length that the speech leaves nothing out, and again, so briefly that no one could be briefer.[19] Now, if you intend to discuss with me, please use the other way toward me, the short-speech style.

Socrates, he said, I've at this point entered on verbal contests with many a man, and if I did what you bid and discussed as my opponent bid me discuss, I'd have appeared no better than anybody else, nor would the name of Protagoras have become famous among the Greeks.

And I—for I realized he was dissatisfied with himself for his

b   previous answers and wouldn't willingly answer in discussion—I believed it was no longer my job to be present at the meeting.

Why really, Protagoras, I said, I'm not at all desirous of continuing our meeting against your better judgment, but when you're willing to discuss so that I'm able to follow, I'll discuss with you then. For you, as is said of you and indeed as you claim yourself, are able to conduct meetings in either long-speech style or short-

c   speech style—for you're wise—but I'm not capable of these long ones, though I might wish I were. Surely it's for you who are capable of both to give way to us, so the meeting may go on. But as it is, since you refuse, I have other business and can't stay while you

19. Cf. *Gorgias* 449c, 461d–462b; *Phaedrus* 267b.

stretch out long speeches—I must go somewhere—I'll go. Though it would perhaps not be unpleasant to have heard you.

At that I rose to leave. And as I stood up, Callias took my hand
d in his right hand and took hold of this cloak here with his left, and said, We won't let you go, Socrates, for if you leave, our discussion won't be the same. So I beg you to stay with us, because there's nothing I'd more gladly hear than a discussion between you and Protagoras. Please oblige us all.

And I said—I'd already risen to go—I always admire your love
e of wisdom, son of Hipponicus, and certainly I praise and value it now, so I'd wish to gratify you if you requested something I could do. But as it is, it's as if you asked me to keep up with Crison, the runner of Himera, in his prime, or to compete and keep up with
336a some long distance or cross-country runner; I'd tell you I wish far more than you that I could keep pace with them, but of course I can't, so if you want to see Crison and me running in the same place, you must ask him to moderate his pace, because I can't run fast and he can run slowly. If then you want to hear me and Protagoras, you must ask him also to answer me now as he did at
b first, with short replies to the exact questions asked. Otherwise, what will be the character of the discussion? I thought meeting for mutual discussion and public speaking were separate things.

But Socrates, he said—Don't you see?—Protagoras seems justified in asking to be allowed to discuss as he wishes, and you also as you wish.

Then Alcibiades broke in. Wrong, Callias, he said. Socrates here agrees that he lacks the long-speech style and yields to Pro-
c tagoras, but I'd be surprised if he yields to any man in being able to discuss, and in knowing how to render and receive an account. Now, if Protagoras in fact agrees he's inferior to Socrates in discussion, it's enough for Socrates; but if he disputes it, let him discuss by asking and answering questions, without stretching out a long speech on each question, evading the arguments and refusing to
d render an account, but drawing things out at length until most of his hearers forget what the question was—though I promise Socrates at least won't forget, even if he jokes and says he's forgetful. So I think what Socrates says is more fair; after all, each of us must declare his own judgment.

After Alcibiades, I think, Critias spoke: Prodicus and Hippias, Callias seems to me to be very much in favor of Protagoras, and
e Alcibiades is always ambitious for whichever side he's cheering on.

But it's not for us to take sides with either Socrates or Protagoras, but to ask them jointly not to break up our meeting in the middle of things.

337a   When he said this, Prodicus replied, I think you're right, Critias. For those present at discussions such as this should give joint but not equal ear to both of two discussants. For it's not the same: one should hear both jointly, not assigning equal importance to each of the two, but instead more to the wiser, less to the unwise. For my part, Protagoras and Socrates, I think you should accede, and disagree with each other over arguments but not dispute—for friends disagree with friends through good will, but

b   those who quarrel and are enemies dispute with each other—and in this way the meeting would be best for us. For you who speak in this way would be especially esteemed, not praised, among us who hear—for esteem is present in the souls of those who hear without deception, but praise often in the speech of those who speak falsely contrary their opinion. Again, we who hear would in this way be especially gladdened, not pleased—for gladness is learn-

c   ing something and having a share of wisdom in the mind by itself, but being pleased is eating something or otherwise experiencing pleasure in the body by itself.

Well, when Prodicus said this, quite a few of the company approved. After Prodicus, next spoke Hippias the wise: Gentlemen here present, he said, I believe you are all kinsmen and

d   relatives and fellow citizens by nature, not by law; for by nature like is akin to like, but law is a tyrant of mankind and forces many things contrary to nature. Now, it would be shameful in us to know the nature of things and yet, though the wisest of Greeks, and now met for that very reason here at the very hearth of the wisdom of

e   Greece, and in this, the greatest and most magnificent house of this city—to yet show ourselves unworthy of this dignity, but to quarrel among ourselves like the most inferior of men. So I re-quest and advise you, Protagoras and Socrates, to come to terms in

338a   the middle as though brought together by us as arbitrators. You, Socrates, are not to seek this precise form of discussion with too much brevity, if it does not please Protagoras; you must give way and slacken the reins of your arguments so that they may appear more imposing and elegant to us. Nor again is Protagoras to stretch out all sail and run before the wind, fleeing into the ocean of arguments beyond sight of land. Both are to steer a middle course. So do this, then, and be persuaded by me to choose an

umpire and overseer and president who will watch the measure of
length of the speeches of you both.

b This was agreeable to the company and everyone applauded,
and Callias refused to let me go, and they begged me to choose an
overseer. So I said, It would be shameful to choose a judge of the
speeches. For either the person chosen will be inferior to us, and it
would not be right for the worse to oversee the better; or he will be

c like us, and also act like us, so that choosing him will be superfluous. Perhaps then you'll choose someone better than us? In
truth, I think it's impossible for you to choose anyone wiser than
Protagoras here, and if you choose no better but you claim it is, it's
an insult, as though you were choosing an overseer for an inferior
man. As for myself, it makes no difference. But here's what I am

d willing to do in order that the meeting and discussion you're eager
for may take place. If Protagoras doesn't wish to answer questions,
let him ask, and I'll answer, and at the same time I'll try to show
him how I claim the answerer should answer. But when I answer
as many questions as he wishes to ask, let him again in like manner
render an account to me. Now, if he doesn't seem eager to answer
the exact question put, you and I will beg him jointly, as you beg
me, not to wreck the meeting. And for this there is no need of one
single overseer; all will oversee jointly.

e It seemed to everyone that this should be done. Protagoras
wasn't very willing; nevertheless, he was compelled to agree to ask
questions, and when he'd asked enough, to render an account
again by offering short answers.

The Poem of Simonides (338e–347a)

Well, he began his questioning something like this:

I believe, Socrates, he said, that the most important part of
339a education for a man is to be skilled in poetry. But this is to be able
to understand what things said by the poets have been rightly
composed and what have not, and to know how to distinguish
them and render an account when questioned. Specifically, the
present question will concern the same subject you and I are now
discussing, virtue, but carried over into poetry; that will be the
only difference. Simonides somewhere says to Scopas, son of
Creon of Thessaly,

b   Hard is it on the one hand truly to become a good man,
    In hands and feet and mind foursquare,
    Well wrought without flaw.

Do you know the lyric, or shall I recite it all to you?

And I said, No need, for I know it; it happens I've studied the
lyric quite carefully.

Good, he said. Then do you think it beautifully and correctly
composed, or not?

Yes, I said, very correctly.

But do you think it beautifully composed if the poet contradicts himself?

I do not, said I.

Then take a better look, he said.

c   Why, I've sufficiently examined it, my friend.

Then you know, he replied, that, as the lyric goes on, he says,

    Nor do I suppose it said suitably by Pittacus,
    and yet he was surpassing wise:
    Hard is it, he said, to be good.[20]

Do you conceive that the same person said this and the foregoing?

I know it, I said.

Then, he said, do you think this agrees with that?

It appears so to me (yet at the same time I was afraid there was
something in what he was saying). Doesn't it appear so to you? I
said.

d   How could anyone who says both these things appear to agree
with himself? First he assumed that it's hard to become a good
man in truth, but a little further on in the poem he forgot and
criticized Pittacus for saying the same thing he said himself, that
"it is hard to be good"; he refuses to accept from him the same
thing he says himself. And yet, when he criticizes him for saying
the same thing as himself, clearly he criticizes himself, so either
the earlier or the later claim is wrong.

Well, his saying this provoked loud applause from many of the
e   hearers. At first I was blinded and made dizzy by what he said and
by the applause of the others, as though I'd been punched by a
good boxer. Then—to tell you the truth, it was to gain time to

20. Adam and Adam cite a scholium on *Hippias Major* 304e: Pittacus, when ruler of
Mitylene, after hearing that Periander had quickly become a tyrant, asked before an altar to
be relieved of his rule, on the ground that "it is hard to be good."

consider what the poet might mean—turned to Prodicus and
340a   called on him: Prodicus, I said, you're a fellow citizen of Simonides; you ought to come to his aid. So I think I'll summon you
as Homer claims Scamander summoned Simois when pressed
hard by Achilles:[21]

> Beloved brother, let us both join to hold back
> the strength of the man.

So do I also summon you, lest Protagoras wreck Simonides for us.
Clearly, correcting Simonides needs that special music of yours by
b   which you distinguish wishing and desiring as not the same, and
many other fine distinctions of the sort you just made. And now
consider whether you agree with me, for it doesn't appear that
Simonides contradicts himself. Please, Prodicus, declare your
opinion: do you think that to become and to be are the same or
different?

Emphatically different, said Prodicus.

Well, said I, in the first lines Simonides declared his own opinion, that it would be hard to become in truth a good man?

c   True, said Prodicus.

But surely he criticizes Pittacus, I said, not as Protagoras supposes, for saying the same thing as himself, but for something
different. For Pittacus didn't say it is hard to become good, as
Simonides did, but that it is hard to be good. But Protagoras, to be
and to become are not the same, so Prodicus here says. Yet unless
to be is the same as to become, Simonides did not contradict himself. Perhaps Prodicus here and many others would say with Hesiod that it's hard to become good:

d   For the gods have set toilsome obstacles on the path to
        virtue.[22]

But when somebody has reached its summit,

> Though hard before, it's easy then to keep.

Well, when Prodicus heard this he applauded me. But Protagoras said, Your correction contains a greater error, Socrates,
than what you're correcting.

21. *Iliad* xxi 308–09.
22. Somewhat misquoted from Hesiod, *Works and Days* 289 ff. Cf. *Republic* II 364c; *Laws*
IV 718e.

And I said, Then it seems I've done badly, Protagoras, and I'm
e   a ridiculous doctor; my treatment makes the disease worse.

Exactly so, he said.

But how? said I.

It would be very foolish of the poet, he said, to thus claim it's a
paltry thing to possess virtue. Which is of all things most difficult,
as all men suppose.

And I said: Why really, it's opportune that Prodicus here is
341a present for our discussion. For very likely the wisdom of Prodicus
is ancient and divine, Protagoras, and either derived from Simonides or even older still. Experienced as you are in many other
things, you appear inexperienced in this: you lack the experience
I gained from being the pupil of Prodicus here. As it is, I think you
haven't understood that Simonides perhaps didn't take "hard" in
the sense you do. It's like the word "terrible." Prodicus here always
corrects me when in praising you or anyone else, I say that Pro-
b   tagoras is a terribly wise man; he asks if I'm not embarrassed to call
good things terrible. For what is terrible, he says, is bad; at any
rate, no one ever says "terrible wealth," or "terrible peace," or
"terrible health," but rather "terrible disease" and "terrible war"
and "terrible poverty," because they think what is terrible is bad.
Perhaps then the Ceans and Simonides also took "hard" to mean
bad, or something else you don't understand. So let's ask Prodicus
—for it's right to question him about the dialect of Simonides—
What did Simonides mean by "hard," Prodicus?

c   Bad, he said.

Then that's why Prodicus, he also blames Pittacus for saying
that it's hard to be good, I said. It's as if he heard him say it's bad to
be good.

Why, what else do you think Simonides means, Socrates? he
said. He's reproaching Pittacus for not knowing how to distinguish
names correctly, because he's a Lesbian and raised in a barbarous
dialect.

Do you hear what Prodicus here is saying, Protagoras? I said.
Do you have anything to say against it?

d   And Protagoras said, It's far from being so, Prodicus. I know
well enough that Simonides meant by "hard" what the rest of us
do—not what's bad, but what's not easy but comes about through
many difficulties.

Why, I also think Simonides meant that, Protagoras, said I—
yes, and Prodicus here knows it too, but he's joking and means to

test whether you'll be able to support your own argument. Because there's ample proof right in the next line that Simonides didn't mean that the hard is bad. For he says that

e   God alone could have this honor.

He surely doesn't mean it's bad to be good: he says god alone can have this, and assigns this honor only to the god. Prodicus would be claiming that Simonides is some sort of scoundrel, and not by no means a Cean. But I'll tell you what I think Simonides intended
342a   in this lyric, if you wish to test my grasp of poetry, as you put it;[23] but I'll listen to you if you wish.

Well, when Protagoras heard me say this, he replied, If you wish, Socrates.

Prodicus and Hippias heartily urged me to go on, and so did the rest.

Then I'll try to explain to you what I think about this lyric, I said. Philosophy is most ancient and abundant among the Greeks
b   in Crete and Sparta, and sophists are abundant there too. But they deny it and act as if they're ignorant, so that it won't be evident that they surpass the rest of Greece in wisdom, like those whom Protagoras claimed are sophists; instead, they seem to excel in fighting and courage, since they believe that if it were known in what they actually excel, namely, their wisdom, everyone would prac-
c   tice it. But now they conceal it, and mislead the Spartanizers in our cities who bind their fists in imitation of them and get cauliflower ears, and go in for physical training and wear short cloaks, as though it were by these means that the Spartans maintain their power among Greeks. But the Spartans, when they wish to meet with the sophists among them freely and grow tired of meeting them in secret, cause an expulsion of foreigners, both these Spartanizers and any other foreign residents among them, and associate with their sophists without foreigners knowing about it. Nor
d   do they allow their young people to travel to other cities, any more than the Cretans do, so that the young people won't unlearn what they teach. There are in these cities not only men who pride themselves on their education, but women too. You can tell that what I say is true, and that Spartans are the best educated in philosophy and argument, by this: if one associates with the most inferior Spartan, one at first finds him somewhat inferior in

23. 339a, ἐπῶν. The word Protagoras uses specifically meant epic poetry.

speech; but then at some chance point in the discussion he throws
in a remark worth noticing, brief and terse, like a skilled marks-
man, so that the person he's talking to appears no better than a
child. Well, there are some, both at present and of old, who recognized

343a   that Spartanizing is much more a love of wisdom than a love of
physical exercise, knowing that the ability to utter such remarks
belongs to a perfectly educated man. Among these were Thales of
Miletus, and Pittacus of Mytilene, and Bias of Priene, and our own
Solon, and Cleobulus of Lindus, and Myson of Chen, and the
seventh of them was said to be Chilon of Sparta.[24] They all emu-
lated and admired and were students of Spartan education, and
one could tell their wisdom was of this sort by the brief but memo-
b   rable remarks they each uttered when they met and jointly dedi-
cated the first fruits of their wisdom to Apollo in his shrine at
Delphi, writing what is on every man's lips: Know thyself, and
Nothing too much.

Why do I say this? Because this was the manner of philosophy
among the ancients, a kind of laconic brevity. In particular, this
saying of Pittacus was circulated in private and highly approved by
the wise: It is hard to be good. Well, Simonides, because he was
ambitious to be accounted wise, knew that if he could overthrow
c   this saying it would be just as if he'd beaten a famous athlete, and
he'd become famous himself among the men of his day. So it was in
reference to this saying, and for this reason, that he composed the
whole lyric, planning to discredit it, as it appears to me.

But let us then all jointly consider it to see if I speak the truth.
Surely the very first part of the lyric would appear mad, if he
meant to say it is hard to become a good man but then threw in the
d   "on the one hand." For this would appear to have been inserted
without any reason at all, unless one understands that Simonides
is speaking as a controversialist against the saying of Pittacus.
When Pittacus says it's hard to be good, he disputes it and says, No,
but it's hard to become a good man, Pittacus, truly—not in truth
e   good, because he doesn't use the term truth for this purpose,
namely, to imply that some things are truly good, others good but
not truly so—this would appear simpleminded, and not Simonides
—but one must assume that "truly" in the lyric is transposed and
meant to introduce the words of Pittacus, as though we were to

24. The Seven Wise Men of Greece.

344a   assume that Pittacus himself is speaking and Simonides answering. Pittacus says, Gentlemen, it is hard to be good. Simonides answers, Pittacus, you're wrong: it's not being but becoming a good man, in hands and feet and mind four-square, well wrought and without flaw, that's truly hard.

Thus it appears that the insertion of "on the one hand" has a reason, and that "truly" is correctly placed at the end; and everything that follows testifies that this is what was meant. For there is much about each subject mentioned in the poem to show that it is

b   well composed—it's very gracefully and carefully done—but it would take too long to go through it that way. Let us rather explain its general outline and intent, which is more than anything to refute the saying of Pittacus throughout the whole lyric.

For he goes on a little after this to say, as if he were making a speech, that to become a good man is truly hard but possible for at least some period of time. But once having become good, to per-

c   sist in this state and be a good man is, as you say, Pittacus, impossible and not human; god alone can have this privilege,

> But it is not possible for a man not to be bad,
> Whom helpless fortune casts down.

Well, whom does helpless fortune cast down in governing a ship? Clearly not the layman, for he's always cast down. Now, just as one

d   can't throw somebody who's down, but one can sometimes throw somebody who's standing up so as to put him down, so too helpless fortune may on occasion cast down the man of resource, but not somebody who's always helpless anyway. The pilot might be rendered helpless by a big storm, the farmer by a bad season, and the same for a doctor. Because it's possible for the good man to become bad, as is witnessed by another poet, who says, "But a good man is sometimes bad, and sometimes good." But it's not possible

e   for the bad man to become bad; he necessarily always is so. So when helpless fortune overthrows a resourceful and wise and good man, it is not possible for him not to be bad. You claim, Pittacus, that it's hard to be good. Rather, it's hard to become good, though possible, but impossible to be good:

> For every man, when he does and fares well, is good,
> But bad if he does badly.

345a   Well, what does doing and faring in letters consist in, and what makes a man good at letters? Clearly, the study of them. What excellent practice makes a good doctor? Clearly, study of the care and cure of the sick. But, "bad if badly." Who then could become a bad doctor? Clearly, first he must be a doctor, and next, a good doctor; for he alone could also become bad. We laymen in medicine could never by practicing badly become either doctors or

b builders or anything else of the sort; but whoever cannot by practicing badly become a doctor clearly cannot become a bad doctor either. So too the good man could on occasion also become bad, due to time or toil or disease or some other accident—for the only bad practice is to be deprived of knowledge. But the bad man could never become bad, for he's always bad. On the contrary, if

c he's going to become bad, he must previously become good. So even this part of the lyric also tends to this, that it's not possible to be a good man and continue to be good, but it's possible to become good, yes, and for the same person to become bad too; and those best for the longest time are those whom the gods love.

Well, all this is directed against Pittacus, and it's even clearer in the lines which follow in the lyric. For he says,

> Therefore shall I never emptily cast away
> In vain hope my apportioned life,
> Seeking what cannot come to be:
> A man completely blameless
> Among us who reap the fruit of broad Earth.
> If I find him, I'll announce it to you,

d He says—in this way violently attacking through the whole lyric the saying of Pittacus—

> I praise and love all those willingly
> who do nothing shameful.
> Not even gods contend against necessity.

And this is directed to exactly the same point. For Simonides was not so uncultivated as to say he praised those who do not willingly do evil, as though he thought there were people who do evils voluntarily. For I hardly suppose any wise man believes that any

e human being errs voluntarily, or willingly does things shameful and evil; on the contrary, they know full well that everyone who does things which are shameful and evil does them involuntarily. Specifically, Simonides doesn't say he praises those who don't will-

ingly do evils, but applies the "willingly" to himself. For he believes
that a good and noble man often compels himself to become a
friend and praise someone such as a man estranged from his
mother or father or fatherland or something else of the sort. Well,
bad men, when this sort of thing happens to them, act as if they
were glad to see it, glad to point with blame and accuse the wickedness of their parents or fatherland, so that people may not criticize
and reproach them for their neglect because they're so neglectful;
they find fault with them all the more, and voluntarily add new
enmities to those they can't avoid.[25] But good men conceal it and
are compelled to offer praise, and if they become at all angry at
their parents or fatherland for acting unjustly, they soothe themselves and are reconciled, compelling themselves to love and
praise those who are their own.

I think Simonides must often have thought that he himself
praised and eulogized a tyrant or someone else of the sort, not
willingly but under compulsion. Indeed, he says it to Pittacus: I
don't find fault with you because I like to, Pittacus, since

> He who is not bad or too helpless suffices for me;
> Knowing justice, the benefit of cities, he is a sound man.
> With him shall I not find fault,—

for I'm no faultfinder,—

> For unlimited in multitude is the race of fools.

So if anyone delights in blaming, he'd have his fill in finding fault
with them.

> All things are beautiful in which ugly things are not mixed.

He doesn't mean this as though he were saying all things are white
in which black things are not mixed—that would be in many ways
absurd. Rather, he himself accepts things of the middle sort as free
of blame. I don't seek, he says, "a man completely blameless among
us who reap the fruit of broad Earth, if I find him, I'll announce
it to you"; So I'll praise no one for this reason; it's enough for me if
he's of a middling sort and does nothing evil, because,

---

25. Note that by this account bad men act voluntarily, whereas good men compel themselves to become friends to bad men and praise them: this is not the doctrine that wrongdoing is involuntary. Nor is the account of goodness, which amounts to flattery, Socrates' own.
He is not only "interpreting" Simonides' poem but offering a parody of sophistical reasoning.

> I love and praise all those—

e   and there he uses the Mytilenaean dialect, because he's speaking
     to Pittacus—

> I love and praise all those willingly—

     the pause should be there, in saying "willingly"—

> Who do nothing shameful,

     though there are some I love and praise unwillingly. So I'd never
347a blame you, Pittacus, if you'd speak what is middling true and
     fitting. But as it is, since you speak quite falsely about matters of
     utmost importance while seeming to tell the truth, I do blame you
     for that.
          I think Prodicus and Protagoras, said I, that this is what Si-
     monides had in mind in composing his lyric.

Interlude (347a–348c)

     And Hippias said, I really think you've given a fine explanation of
b   the lyric, Socrates. However, I've got an excellent discourse about
     it too, he said, which I'll display to you, if you[26] wish.
          And Alcibiades said, Yes, Hippias, some other time. Now Pro-
     tagoras and Socrates ought to do what they agreed, Protagoras to
     question if he still wishes and Socrates to answer; but if he wishes
     to answer Socrates, for the other to question.
          And I said, I leave it up to Protagoras which of the two pleases
     him. But if he's willing, let's dismiss lyrics and verses; I'd gladly
c   complete my inquiry, Protagoras, about the first subjects I asked
     you about. Actually, I think discussing poetry is much like attend-
     ing the drinking parties of worthless and vulgar people. They're
     unable to associate with each other through their own voice and
     words, due to their lack of education, so they run up the price of
d   flute girls and spend a great deal for the alien voice of the flute,[27]
     and associate with each other through such voices as that. But
     where the drinkers are gentlemen and properly educated, you'll
     see neither flute girls nor dancing girls nor harp girls; they're
     capable of associating with each other in their own voices without

26. Plural. Hippias is addressing the company.
27. Neither "flute" nor "pipe" happily translates *aulos*. The instrument was either single-reeded, like a clarinet, or double-reeded, like an oboe.

this childish nonsense, speaking and listening decorously each in
his turn even when they've drunk a great deal of wine. So too a
meeting like this, if it consists of men of the sort most of us claim to
be, has no need of an alien voice, nor of poets who cannot be
questioned about what they mean. The Many adduce them in
argument, some claiming the poet means this, others that, arguing about something they cannot test. But those met in familiar
intercourse among themselves dismiss this sort of meeting, and
test each other by receiving and rendering accounts in discussions
of their own. I think you and I should rather imitate people like
that. We should set aside the poets and fashion accounts with one
another, putting the truth and ourselves to the test. If you still
wish to ask questions, I'm prepared to answer. But if you wish, you
can answer me, and arrive at a conclusion about the subject we
stopped in the middle of discussing.

Well, when I said this and other things of the sort, Protagoras
gave no indication which of the two things he'd do. So Alcibiades
glanced at Callias and said, Callias, do you think Protagoras now
does well in refusing to make clear whether or not he'll render an
account? For I don't. Let him either discuss or say he refuses to
discuss, so that we may understand his position; Socrates can then
discuss with someone else, or another of us with whomever he wishes.

And Protagoras was shamed by Alcibiades saying this, I
thought, and by the request of Callias and pretty well everyone
present, so he reluctantly returned to the discussion and bid me
question him and he would answer.

The Unity of Virtue Revisited (348c–349d)

So I said, Protagoras, please don't suppose I wish anything else in
discussing with you except to inquire into what I am myself often
perplexed by. For I believe Homer is surely right in saying,

When two go, one observes before the other.[28]

For we're all somehow more resourceful in every deed and word
and thought when we're together. If "a man observes alone," he
forthwith goes about seeking someone to show it to, and with
whom he can confirm it. That's exactly why I'd rather discuss with

28. *Iliad* x 224.

you than anyone else, believing that you can best examine the
subjects a good man naturally considers, and especially virtue. For
e   who other than you? It's not only that you suppose yourself to be
noble and good; so do some others, who are themselves good but
unable to make others so. But you're both good yourself and able
to make others good, and so self-confident that whereas others
349a conceal this art, you openly call yourself a sophist and proclaim it
to the whole of Greece, declaring yourself a teacher of education
and virtue, the first to charge money for it. How then am I not to
summon you to inquiry about these things, to question and consult? It's impossible not to. And now, as to those thing I first asked
about, I want you to remind me again from the beginning of your
b   view about some of them, and to investigate others with your help.
The question, I think, was this: whether wisdom and temperance
and courage and justice and holiness are five names for one single
thing, or whether a certain peculiar nature and reality underly
each of these names, a thing in each case with its own power, one
not being of such sort as any other. Now, you were saying[29] that
they are not names for one thing; on the contrary, each of these
names is applied to a thing peculiar to it; but they are all parts of
c   virtue, not as the parts of gold are like each other and the whole of
which they are parts, but as the parts of the face are unlike each
other and the whole of which they are parts, each having a power
peculiar to itself. If this still seems true to you as it did then, please
say so. If it somehow seems otherwise, please distinguish it, because I won't blame you if you now say something else; I wouldn't
be surprised if you said it then to test me.

d   But Socrates, he said, I tell you they are all are parts of virtue,
and four of them are fairly like each other, but courage is much
different from them all. You'll know I tell the truth by this: you'll
find that many men are extremely unjust and unholy and intemperate and foolish, but surpassingly courageous.

The Unity of Wisdom and Courage (349e–351b)

e   Hold it right there, I said: surely it's worth examining what you
mean. Do you mean courageous men are bold,[30] or something else?

29. 329c ff.
30. θαρραλέους: bold, daring. At 359c, τά θαρραλέα = things to be confident, or bold, or
daring about, as opposed to τὰ δεινά, things to fear.

Yes, he said, and impetuous, going at what most people fear.

Come then, do you say that virtue is something excellent,[31] and because it's excellent you offer yourself as a teacher of it?

Why, it's most excellent, he said, at least if I'm not mad.

Then is some of it defective[32] and some excellent, said I, or is it excellent as a whole?

Excellent as a whole, surely, as excellent as can be.

350a   Now, you know that some people dive boldly into wells?

I do. They're divers.

Because they know how, or for some other reason?

Because they know how.

But some people are bold and confident in making war from horseback? Cavalrymen, or people ignorant of horsemanship?

Cavalrymen.

And some fight with light shields? Skirmishers, or not?

Skirmishers. Yes, and in all other cases, if here's what you're after, he said, those who know are more confident than those who don't, and themselves more confident once they learn than before they learn.

b   Have you ever seen someone who didn't know any of these things but was confident in each of them?

Yes, said he, and they're too confident.

These confident people are also courageous?

On the contrary, he said. Courage would then be a defect; because they're mad.

Then who do you say are courageous? I said. Not the confident?

Yes, I still say so, he said.

c   Well, these people who are confident in this way,[33] I said, appear to be not courageous but mad? And on the other hand, the wisest here are also most confident, and being most confident, most courageous? And according to this account, wisdom would be courage?

Socrates, you don't properly recollect my answer to you, he said. When you asked me if the courageous are bold, I agreed. But you didn't ask whether the bold are courageous, for if you had, I'd
d   have replied, Not all. And you've nowhere shown I was wrong in what I did agree to, that the courageous are bold. Next you show

31. Or beautiful, or noble, or good.
32. Or ugly, base, shameful, bad.
33. Sc., without knowledge.

that those who know are themselves more confident and bold than they were before, and more confident and bold than others who do not know, and in this way you think courage and wisdom are the same. But if you went on this way, you'd also think strength is wisdom. For first if you went on thus you'd ask me whether the

e   strong are powerful, and I'd say Yes. next, you'd ask whether those who know how to wrestle are more powerful than those who don't know how to wrestle, and more powerful after they learn than before. I'd say Yes. But once I agreed to this, you could use these same proofs to claim that, by my agreement, wisdom is strength. But neither there nor anywhere did I agree that the powerful are

351a strong, only that the strong are powerful. For power and strength are not the same; power derives from knowledge, and from madness and anger, but strength from nature and right nurture of the body. So too here, boldness and courage are not the same; so it follows that the courageous are confident and bold, but not surely

b   that the confident and bold are all courageous; for men become bold, as they become powerful, from art and anger and madness, but they become courageous from nature and the right nurture of the soul.

That Virtue Is Knowledge

The Hedonic Equation (351b–e)

Do you say, Protagoras, I said, that some men live well, others badly?

He assented.

Then do you think a man would live well if he lived in misery and pain?

He denied it.

But what if he lived out his life pleasantly to the end. Wouldn't you think he has thus lived well?

I would, he said.

c   So to live pleasantly is good, unpleasantly bad?

Yes, he said, if one lives being pleased by good things.

Really, Protagoras? Surely you don't, as the majority do, call some pleasant things bad and some painful things good? I mean just insofar as they are pleasant, aren't they in that respect good, unless something else will follow from them? And again, are not painful things in like manner bad insofar as they are painful?

Socrates, he said, I don't know whether I should answer so simply that all pleasant things are good and painful things bad, as you ask. On the contrary, I think it's safer for me to reply, looking not only to my present answer but to all the rest of my life, that some pleasant things are not good, and again, some painful things are not bad, but there are some which are, and a third kind which is neither good nor bad.

d

You call things which partake of pleasure or cause pleasure pleasant? I said.

Of course, he replied.

e

This, then, is what I mean: whether they're not good insofar as they're pleasant. I'm asking whether pleasure by itself is not good.

As you often say, Socrates, he said, let's examine it, and if the conjecture seems reasonable, and pleasant and good appear to be the same, we'll concede it. If not, we'll dispute it at that point.

Well, I said, do you wish to lead the inquiry, or shall I?

It's right for you to lead, he said. You began the argument.

The Authority of Knowledge (352a–353b)

352a

Well then, said I, would it become clear to us in some such way as this? It's as if one were estimating a man's health or any other bodily function from his appearance; one might inspect face and forearms and then say, "Come, uncover your chest and back and show them to me, so that I may examine you more thoroughly." I want something like that in our inquiry. Seeing that you're disposed toward the good and the pleasant as you claim, I need to say something like this: Come, Protagoras, uncover your thought for me on this: how do you stand on knowledge? Do you think of it as the majority of men do, or otherwise? The Many think that knowledge has neither strength nor authority nor power of command, that though knowledge may from time to time be present in a man, it does not govern him. Something else governs: sometimes anger, sometimes pleasure, sometimes pain, on occasion love, often fear—as though they conceived of knowledge as a mere slave to be dragged about by everything else. Does something like that also seem true to you? Or is knowledge authoritative, so that if one once knows what is good and evil, he cannot be prevailed upon to do other than knowledge commands—wisdom being sufficient to his aid?

b

c

I think it's as you say, Socrates, he replied. Then too, it would be shameful for me, if for anyone, to deny that wisdom and knowledge are of all things most powerful in human affairs.

d   Well and truly put, I said. Now, you know that the majority of
men don't believe us. They claim that many people know what's
best and refuse to do it though it's possible for them, but do
something else instead. And when I ask why this is, they reply that
people act this way because they're overcome[34] by pleasure or
pain, or mastered by other things I just mentioned.

After all, Socrates, he said, people say many other incorrect
things too.

e   Come then with me and try to persuade and teach people what
this experience of theirs is which they claim is being overcome by
353a   pleasure, and for that reason not doing what is best, though they
know it. Perhaps if we said, "Gentlemen, you don't speak correctly
but falsely," they'd reply to us, "Protagoras and Socrates, if this
experience isn't being overcome by pleasure, what is it? What do
you say it is? Will the two of you please reply?"

Really, Socrates, should we consider the opinion of the Many,
who say whatever happens to occur to them?

b   I think it's important, I said, for our finding out about courage
and how it stands relative to the other parts of virtue. So if you see
fit to abide by what we just decided, that I should lead in whatever
direction I think it will best become clear, please follow. But if you
prefer not, then if you like, I'll dismiss it.

Why you're quite right, he said. Go on as you began.

Reply to the Many (353c–354e)

c   Again then if they asked us, I said, "What then do you claim it is
which we described as being overcome by pleasures?" I'd reply in
this way: "Listen then, for Protagoras and I will try to tell you.
Don't you claim, gentlemen, that it frequently occurs, for example
when people are mastered by food and drink and sex, which are
pleasures, that they know they're bad but nevertheless do them?"

d   They'd agree. So you and I would ask them again: "In what way do
you claim they're bad? Is it because each of them is pleasant and
provides this pleasure immediately, on the spot? Or is it because at
a later time they produce disease and poverty, and many other
things of the sort? If some of them produce nothing afterward but
only cause delight, are they nonetheless evils because they cause us
in some way to experience delight?" Do we suppose they could
give any other answer, Protagoras, except that they're not evils in

34. ἡττωμένους: to be worsted, defeated.

respect to production of immediate pleasure by itself, but because of what comes later, diseases and the rest?

e   I suppose the Many would give that answer, said Protagoras.

Now, in causing diseases they cause pain, and in causing poverty they cause pain? They'd agree, I suppose.

Protagoras concurred.

"Then does it appear to you, gentlemen, that, as Protagoras and I claim, these things are evils for no other reason than because they terminate in suffering and take away other pleasures?" Would they agree?

354a   We both thought so.

Again, suppose we asked them the opposite: "Gentlemen, those of you who also say that good things are painful: don't you mean things like physical training and military service, for example, and medical treatment by cautery and surgery and drugs and starvation—these things are good, but painful?" They'd agree?

He concurred.

b   "Then do you call them good because they provide the extremity of immediate pain and suffering, or because healthy states derive from them at a later time, good condition of bodies and preservation of cities, and rule over others and wealth?" They'd agree, I suppose.

He concurred.

"Are these things good for any other reason than that they terminate in pleasures and relieve and avert pain? Can you men-

c   tion any other end except pleasure and pain to which you look in calling them good?" They'd say no, I suppose.

I think so too, said Protagoras.

"Then you pursue pleasure as being good and avoid pain as evil?"

He concurred.

"So you believe that pain is evil and pleasure is good, although you sometimes say that even delight itself is evil, when it takes away a greater amount of pleasure than it contains or produces pains

d   greater than the pleasures in it. Since if you call delight bad with respect to something else and looking to some other end, you could surely tell us what it is. But you can't."

I don't think they can either, said Protagoras.

"Then isn't it the same way again about being pained? Do you sometimes call being pained good, when it gets rid of pains greater than are in it, or produces pleasures greater than the pains? Since if you look to some end other than what I say when you call being pained good, then you can tell us what it is. But you can't."

e   True, said Protagoras.

The Hedonistic Calculus (354e–356c)

Then again, gentlemen, I said, if you were to ask me why I speak at such length about this, and in so many ways, I'd reply, Forgive me. First, it's not easy to explain what it is you call being overcome by pleasures. Second, all explanations depend on this. But it's still
355a   possible for you to take it back even now, if you can somehow say what is good is something other than pleasure, or what is evil something other than pain. Or does it suffice to live out your life pleasantly without pains? If it does, and if you can't claim anything else is good or evil that doesn't terminate in these, then hear what follows. For I tell you that if this is so, the argument becomes ridiculous when you say that a man frequently knows that evils are
b   evils and nonetheless does them when it's possible not to do them, because he's driven and distracted by pleasures. On the other hand, again, you say the man who knows what is good refuses to do it because he is overcome by immediate pleasures.

That this is ridiculous will be evident if we stop using many names at once—pleasant and painful, good and evil. On the contrary, since they've appeared to be two, let's call them by two names: first, good and evil; alternately, pleasant and painful. Assuming this then, let's say that a man who knows of evils that
c   they're evil nevertheless does them. If someone then asks us "Why?" we'll reply, "He's overcome." "By what?" he'll ask us. We can no longer reply, "By pleasure," because it's got another name instead of "pleasure," namely, "good." So let's answer him and say, "He's overcome." "By what?" he'll say. "By the good," we'll emphatically reply.

Well, if the questioner is an arrogant fellow, he'll laugh and
d   reply, "You're saying a ridiculous thing, if someone does evils knowing that they're evils without having to do them, because he's overcome by goods. Is this because the goods in you don't weigh enough[35] to conquer the evils, or because they do?" We'll clearly

---

35. οὐκ ἀξίων. Adam and Adam translate "less worthy," Croiset, "ne méritait pas"; but the sense of inequality in value or worth assumes too much to fit the argument. Though the term usually has moral import, in this context it must retain its root notion of not balancing, not weighing enough.

reply that they don't weigh enough to conquer; otherwise, the man we claim is overcome by pleasure would not have erred. "But how," he'll perhaps reply, "are goods outweighed by evils, or evils

e   by goods, except when one is greater, the other less, or one more numerous, the other fewer?" We can't deny this. "so it's clear," he'll say, "that this 'being overcome' you speak of is taking greater evils instead of fewer goods." Well, that's so.

Let's then change the names for these same things back again to pleasant and painful, and let's say a man does—before we said evil things, but now let's say painful things—knowing that they're painful, being overcome by pleasures, it being clear that they don't weigh enough to conquer.

356a   And what other inequality of weight is there in pleasure relative to pain except excess and defect one to another?[36] But this consists in becoming larger and smaller than each other, more numerous and fewer, more frequent and less.[37] For if someone should say, "But Socrates, what is immediately pleasant is very different from what is pleasant and painful at a later time," I'd reply to him, "Surely not in anything except pleasure and pain?

b   Not possibly in anything else. On the contrary: like a man good at weighing, add the pleasures, add the pains, balance also in the scale the near and the far, and state which is more. For if you weigh pleasures against pleasures, the greater and more numerous must always be taken; if pains against pains, the fewer and smaller; if pleasures against pains, then if the pains are exceeded by the pleasures, whether the near by the far or the far by the near, the action in which they're present must be done; if the pleasures are

c   exceeded by the pains, it's not to be done. Isn't it this way, gentlemen?" I'd say. I'm sure they couldn't deny it.

He concurred in this too.

The Art of Measurement (356c–357b)

"Then since this is so," I'll say, "answer me this: Does the same magnitude appear to sight larger when near, smaller when far?"[38]
They'll say Yes.

36. The language here, in which one quantity exceeds or falls short of another, matches that of application of areas in Greek geometrical algebra. The proportion involved is arithmetic.

37. Compare *Laws* V 734a, where pleasures are compared to pains in extent, number, and frequency.

38. Cf. *Republic* X 602d, VII 523c–524d; *Philebus* 42a.

"And so similarly for frequencies and multitudes? And equally, loud sounds are greater when close, smaller when far off?"

They'd assent.

d   Then if our doing and faring well consisted in so acting as to take large lengths but avoid small ones, what would appear as the salvation of our life? The art of measurement, or the power of appearances? Doesn't the latter frequently cause us to wander and change back and forth, to accept and reject the same things in actions and in choices of large and small? Whereas the art of measurement would render the appearance ineffective: by mak-
e   ing clear the truth, it would cause the soul to be at peace by abiding in the truth, and so save our life? Could people agree it's any other art except the art of measurement that would save us in this?

It's the art of measurement, he agreed.

"But what if the salvation of our life consisted in the choice of odd and even? Whenever it was necessary to choose correctly the more and the fewer, either absolutely or one relative to the
357a   other,[39] whether near or far, what would save our lives? Since the art required concerns excess and deficiency, wouldn't it be knowledge and an art of measurement? And since it's about odd and even, would it be anything except the art of arithmetic?" Would these gentlemen agree with us, or not?

Protagoras thought they would.

"Very well, gentlemen: since then the salvation of life has appeared to us to consist in the right choice of pleasure and pain—
b   more and fewer, greater and less, nearer and farther—doesn't it in the first place appear to be an art of measurement, an inquiry into excess and deficiency and equality relative one to another?"

Why, necessarily.

"But since of measurement, by necessity it is surely art and knowledge."

They'll agree.

"Now, just what art and knowledge this is we'll consider later; but that it's knowledge by so much suffices for the proof Pro-
c   tagoras and I must provide about what you asked us. You asked it, if you recall, when we agreed with each other that nothing is stronger than knowledge and that it always governs pleasure and all the rest wherever it is present. But you then replied that pleasure frequently masters even the man who knows, and when we

39. Cf. *Gorgias* 451b ff.

didn't agree with you, you next asked us this: "Protagoras and Socrates, if this experience isn't being overcome by pleasure, what is it? What do you say it is? Tell us."

d   "Well, if we'd told you right off that it's ignorance, you'd have laughed at us; but if you laugh at us now, you'll laugh at yourselves. For in fact you've agreed that those who err do you for lack of knowledge about the choice of pleasures and pains—that is, goods and evils—and not only for lack of knowledge but also for lack of what you've already further agreed is the art of measurement. But you yourselves also know, surely, that errant action without knowl-

e   edge is done in ignorance. So that's what being overcome by pleasure actually comes down to—the greatest ignorance. Of which Protagoras here claims to be a physician, and Prodicus and Hippias. But you, through supposing it something other than ignorance, neither go yourselves nor send your children to these teachers, these wise sophists here, because you think it can't be taught. Instead, you worry about money and don't pay it to them, and you do and fare badly in both public and private."

Hippias and Prodicus Agree (358a–b)

358a   This would be my answer to the Many. But along with Protagoras, I ask you, Hippias and Prodicus—for let the argument be shared —whether you think I speak truly or falsely.

They all thought what had been said was emphatically true.

So you agree, said I, that the pleasant is good, the painful bad. I beg to be excused from Prodicus's division of names, for whether you say "pleasant" or "delightful" or "enjoyable," dear Prodicus, or apply whatever name you like for such things, please answer with a view to what I mean.

b   So Prodicus laughed and concurred, as did the others.

No One Voluntarily Chooses Evils (358b–d)

Then what about the following point, gentlemen, I said: all actions directed toward a painless and pleasant life are excellent? And the excellent product is both good and beneficial?

He concurred.

So if the pleasant is good, I said, no one who knows or thinks that other things are better than what he's doing, and possible, will

c   do them if the better things can be done. Being overcome by oneself[40] is nothing but ignorance, mastering oneself nothing but wisdom.

---

40. τὸ ἥττω εἶναι αὐτοῦ: lack of self-control. Cf. 358c 2.

All concurred.

But don't you then mean by ignorance just this: having false opinion and being deceived about matters of great weight?

All concurred in this too.

Then surely, said I, no one voluntarily goes toward evils or what he thinks are evils, nor is it in human nature, it seems, to be willing to go toward what one thinks are evils instead of goods; and when compelled to choose one of two evils, no one will choose the greater if it is possible to choose the less.

All of us concurred in all this.

The Unity of Courage and Wisdom (358d–360e)

Well then, I said, is there something you call dread and fear? And is it what I claim?—I'm speaking to you, Prodicus. I claim it's an expectation of evil, whether you call it fear or dread.

Protagoras and Hippias thought this was dread and fear, Prodicus that it was dread but not fear.

It makes no difference, Prodicus, I said. But this does. If what was formerly said is true, will any man be willing to go toward what he fears, if it's possible to go toward what he doesn't? Or is it impossible, from what's been agreed? For we agreed that what he fears he believes evil; but what is believed evil one neither goes after nor voluntarily accepts.

Everyone thought so too.

Then this being so assumed, Prodicus and Hippias, said I, let Protagoras here defend for us the correctness of his first answer— not his very first, where[41] he said there are five parts of virtue, none of them such as any other but each with its own peculiar power. I don't mean that, but what he said afterward. For afterward[42] he said that four of them are fairly much like each other, but one is quite different from the others, namely courage, and he told me I could tell by the following proof: "For you'll find, Socrates, that there are people who are extremely unholy and unjust and intemperate and ignorant, but extremely courageous; by which you'll know that courage is very different from the other parts of virtue." I was much surprised at his answer at the time, and still more so since I've discussed it with you. So I asked him

41. 330a ff.
42. 349d ff.

whether he'd say that the courageous are bold. "Yes, and impetuous," he said. Do you recall giving this answer, Protagoras? I said.

c   He assented.

Come then, I said, and tell us: what do you say the courageous
are impetuous toward. Toward what cowards are?

No, he said.

Toward different things.

Yes, he said.

Do cowards go toward things to be bold and confident about,
the courageous toward things to be feared?

So people say, Socrates.

True, I said. But I didn't ask that, but rather what you say. Are

d   the courageous impetuous toward things to be feared believing
them fearful, or toward things not to be feared?

But it was just shown in the arguments you put that this is
impossible.

True again, said I. So if this was shown correctly, no one goes
toward what he believes fearful, since being overcome by oneself
was found to be ignorance.

He agreed.

On the contrary, everyone goes toward what they're also confident about, both cowards and the courageous, and in this respect
cowards and courageous men go toward the same things.

e   But surely, Socrates, he said, what cowards and the courageous
go toward is completely opposite. For example, the latter are willing to go to war, the former refuse.

Is it excellent or shameful to go?

Excellent, he said.

Then since excellent, then also good, as we agreed before; for
we agreed that excellent actions are all good.

True, and I always think so.

360a   And rightly, I said. But which sort do you say refuse to go to
war, if it is excellent and good to do so?

The cowards, said he.

Now, said I, since excellent and good, also pleasant?[43]

So it was agreed, at any rate, he said.

---

43. The consequence that since going to war is excellent and good, it is also pleasant,
would seem to be a practical *reductio ad absurdum* of the hypothesis that goodness and
pleasure are equivalent. If cowards are afraid with shameful fears (360b), there is a criterion
of good and evil other than pleasure and pain, and one needs still to answer the question of
the *Laches,* What is courage?

Then do cowards knowingly refuse to go toward what is more excellent and better and more pleasant?

Why, if we agree to that, he said, we'll destroy our former agreements.

What about the courageous man. Doesn't he go toward the more beautiful and better and more pleasant?

It's necessary to agree, he said.

b Now on the whole, courageous men don't fear shameful fears when they're afraid, nor are they confident with shameful confidence?

True, he said.

But if not shameful, are they not excellent?

He agreed.

But if excellent, also good?

Yes.

Then again the cowardly and the rash and the mad, oppositely, fear shameful fears and are confident and bold with shameful confidence?

He agreed.

Are they confident and bold about shameful and bad things through anything other than folly and ignorance?

No he said.

c Now, do you call that through which cowards are cowardly cowardice or courage?

Cowardice, he said.

They appeared to be cowards through ignorance of what things to fear?

Of course, he said.

So they're cowards through this ignorance?

He agreed.

It's agreed by you that it is cowardice through which they're cowards?

He concurred.

Then ignorance of what is and is not to be feared would be cowardice?

He nodded assent.

Moreover, said I, courage is opposite to cowardice.

d He agreed.

Now, wisdom about what is and is not to be feared is opposite to ignorance of these things?

And here he nodded again.

Ignorance of these things is cowardice?

Here he barely nodded.

So wisdom about what is and is not to be feared is courage, since it is opposite to ignorance of these things?

Here he was no longer even willing to nod agreement, and was silent.

And I said, why do you neither affirm nor deny what I ask, Protagoras?

Finish it by yourself, he said.

e   I have only one question for you still, said I: do you still think, as you did at first, that some people are extremely foolish but most courageous?

I think you're contentiously eager for me to answer, Socrates, he said. Well, I'll gratify you and say that from what's been agreed, it seems to me impossible.

Conclusion (360e–362a)

I ask all this, I said, for no other reason than my wish to inquire
361a   how it is with virtue, and what virtue itself is. For I know that if this once became evident, the issue you and I have each drawn out at such length—I claiming that virtue cannot be taught, you that it can—would be quite cleared up. It seems to me the present outcome of the argument mocks and accuses us as if it were a man; if it had voice it would say, "How absurd you both are, Socrates and Protagoras. You, Socrates, after previously saying that virtue cannot be taught, now for your own part urge just the opposite, un-
b   dertaking to show that all things are knowledge, both justice and temperance and courage, from which it would certainly appear that virtue can be taught. If virtue were something other than knowledge, as Protagoras undertook to say, clearly it could not be taught; but as it is, if it turns out to be wholly knowledge, as you urge, Socrates, it will be strange indeed if it cannot be taught. Protagoras, on the other hand, assumed before that it can be taught, but now seems to urge the opposite, making it appear to be
c   almost anything rather than knowledge; and thus it would be least of all teachable." Now Protagoras, when I see all this so fearfully agitated back and forth, my whole impulse is to get it cleared up. I would wish us to go on thoroughly to consider what virtue is, and then come back again to inquire whether it can or cannot be

taught—for fear that otherwise that Epimetheus of yours will
d   keep on tripping us up and misleading us in the inquiry as he also
neglected us in his distribution—so you claim. Well, I like Prometheus more than Epimetheus in the story: I make use of him by
exercising forethought for the whole of my own life and worrying
about all these things. As I said at the beginning, if you're willing
I'd be most pleased to inquire into them with you.

And Protagoras said, I admire your earnestness, Socrates, and
e   your way with arguments. Actually, I don't think I'm a bad man in
other ways, and I'm least of all men envious; indeed I've told many
people that among everyone I've met, I especially admire you far
beyond others of your age, and wouldn't be surprised if you became famous for your wisdom. As for these matters, we'll pursue
them later when you wish, but now it's time to turn to something
else.

362a   Why, we must do so, said I, if you think it best. Actually, it's long
since been time for me to go where I said, but I stayed to gratify
the noble Callias.

Saying and hearing these things, we departed.

INDEX